6.95

Bookkeeping: the basis of finance and accounting

2nd Edition   **Students' Text**

Bookkeeping: the basis of finance and accounting

2nd Edition

Students' Text

A W Brindley
J L Brindley
E D Agyeman

McGRAW-HILL Book Company (UK) Limited

London · New York · St Louis · San Francisco · Auckland · Bogotá
Guatemala · Hamburg · Johannesburg · Lisbon · Madrid · Mexico
Montreal · New Delhi · Panama · Paris · San Juan · São Paulo · Singapore
Sydney · Tokyo · Toronto

Published by
McGRAW-HILL Book Company (UK) Limited
MAIDENHEAD · BERKSHIRE · ENGLAND

British Library Cataloguing in Publication Data

Brindley, A. W.
 Bookkeeping : the basis of finance and
 accounting.——2nd ed.
 Students' text
 1. Bookkeeping
 I. Title   II. Brindley, J. L.   III. Agyeman,
 E. D.
 657'.2   HF5635

 ISBN 0–07–084966–8

1234   89876

Phototypeset by
Styleset Limited · Warminister · Wiltshire

Printed and bound in Finland by WSOY

Contents

Preface to the Second Edition

Aims

1 To teach bookkeeping and finance in a practical way by entering books, accounts, and records.
2 To deal thoroughly with the basic bookkeeping procedures and concepts, e.g., double entry.
3 To explain those closely related record keeping tasks, e.g., stock control and wages calculation.
4 To provide plenty of questions (and answers) which support the learning process.
5 To introduce computer-based bookkeeping through examples and the use of a disk provided with the *Teacher's Handbook*.

Approach

This book is suitable for those who wish to acquire the basic skills of bookkeeping and a knowledge of finance.

Anyone new to bookkeeping learns to keep records with Joe Wynn who has a small business selling carpets. Joe teaches his new bookkeeper why and how books are used, how to prepare the final accounts, and the procedures involved in, for example, stock control, job costing, and paying wages. He then shows how his computer is used in the business.

Questions and answers

Over 200 questions are set. Most questions have answers at the back of the book. Other questions have no answer (prefixed NA) in this book. It is hoped these will be useful for teachers as classwork and homework assignments (refer to the *Teacher's Handbook* for further information).

The suggested answers are entirely the responsibility of the authors and have neither been provided nor approved by any examining board.

Acknowledgements

We wish to acknowledge the permission to use examination papers given by the following:

The Royal Society of Arts Examination Board
The London Chamber of Commerce and Industry Examining Board
Pitman Examinations Institute
The Associated Examining Board
The University of London School Examining Board

We also thank the following for the use of documents as illustrations:

Barclays Bank PLC
The Vyner Group—manufacturers of the Simplex range of record books.
Kalamazoo PLC—simultaneous entry records.
Tollit & Harvey—manufacturers of the Guildhall range of record books.

Documents which are Crown copyright are reproduced with the permission of the Controller of Her Majesty's Stationery Office.

We are indebted to Geoffrey Arcus for his invaluable help in producing the prototypes for the computer programs. Without his help there would be no disk accompanying the *Teacher's Handbook*.

1. Introduction

Joe Wynn is starting a new business and he wants you to work for him. Part of your job will be to keep the records of the money he spends and the money he receives. Do not worry—Joe has been in business a long time and he knows what details he expects you to record. He is the owner and he naturally wants to know whether or not his business is becoming successful. One thing he needs to know is how much profit he is making—or how much of a loss, if the business does not go very well. Joe is going to teach you some rules about the records you will be keeping—and these are important.

Joe's new business is selling carpets. He is just starting, so there is not a lot of trade to begin with and all you have to do is to put down the money he spends on carpets and what he receives from the sales. To do this you need a *Cash Book*. Joe wants you to use a simple Cash Book; in fact, it could be a small note book. If you go into your local stationers and ask them to let you look at the Cash Books they stock, you will be surprised at the large number of different sizes, thicknesses, and colours. Also, the pages can be ruled in different columns. But you must remember one thing that Joe tells you: whatever book you use, remember that every sum of money spent you put down on the right-hand side of the book, and every sum of money received you put down on the left-hand side of the book. Open your Cash Book at the first double page. This is page 1.

Why do you think we have page 1 on both sides? Because both receipts *and* payments are recorded on the same page—receipts on one half of the page, payments on the other half. Note the headings. If you have not got a note book or a proper Cash Book, use a piece of paper with a line drawn down the middle—one side for receipts and the other for payments.

1	RECEIPTS		PAYMENTS	1

Joe's Rule No 1
Receipts are always on the left.
Payments are always on the right.

Now, if Joe asks you these questions what would you say?

1.01 Why would it be better to use a proper Cash Book rather than pieces of paper?

1.02 Who else is going to look at the Cash Book apart from you and me?

1.03 Why is it important to put the figures down neatly under each other?

1.04 At the end of each day I am going to check that the amount in the till is the same as the amount you show in the Cash Book. If the two amounts do not agree, what will happen?

Look at the back of the book to see what answers Joe would give.

Joe expects his bookkeeper to be neat and tidy, to be able to do arithmetic, and to write legibly (so that other people can read his figures and letters), and he asks you to do the following to see just how good you are.

1.05 Write down these amounts in a column on a piece of paper and add up the column.

> Forty-nine pounds 89 pence; seventy-six pounds 53 pence; one hundred and sixty-two pounds 40 pence; one thousand and nineteen pounds 75 pence; four hundred and fifty-three pounds 18 pence.

1.06 From your answer to **1.05** take away the following three amounts.

> Fifty-four pounds 68 pence; twelve pounds 35 pence; eighty-seven pounds 6 pence.

1.07 Add the columns down and rows across.

	Column 1	Column 2	Total
Row 1	10.07	11.30	
Row 2	4.03	74.56	
Row 3	6.91	68.95	
Row 4	3.28	25.74	
Total			

1.08 Now add the total column down and the two column totals across. They should be the same.

1.09 Do the same as for **1.07** and **1.08** with the following table:

	1	2	3	Total
1	91.83	17.89	65.73	
2	74.68	23.56	148.19	
3	28.51	34.67	172.45	
4	13.92	118.24	56.82	
Total				

The last question was difficult—particularly adding across. You should always practise your adding up. You should also check your totals, even when you are using a calculator.

If you want to pass an examination it is better for you to be able to do the arithmetic correctly. To help you to do this, the pages of any book used in bookkeeping are ruled with columns for pounds (£) and pence (p). If you ever have to use a book or paper without printed columns then rule some columns yourself—it makes your work so much neater. Look at the example below.

1	RECEIPTS					PAYMENTS			1
DATE	DETAILS	Folio	£	P	DATE	DETAILS	Folio	£	P

Many small shopkeepers use a simply ruled Cash Book such as this one. The words and signs are not usually printed—you can write them in yourself on your own paper. We can use this for Joe's business. Joe will tell you what the narrow column headed 'Folio' is for later on, when you have got used to entering the books.

2. The Cash Account

Take a quick look at page 3 again—you will see how a Cash Book is ruled. The Cash Book is the book in which the *Cash Account* is kept. 'An account', explains Joe, 'is a record of similar transactions'. You have to write down the cash receipts and payments side by side, in order to find out the amount of cash that still remains. By the way, account has an abbreviation: A/c. So you may write as a heading on the top of the book *Cash A/c*

The source of receipts and payments

Receipts

Most of the receipts that Joe will require you to record will come from sales of carpets and rugs. When the customer buys something in the shop, Joe (or you) will make out a receipt for the customer, as evidence that the customer has paid. The *Receipt Book* has a carbon copy so that you can make a note of the money received from the sale in the Cash Book, after the customer has left with his receipt.

Customer's Copy

	No. 33
Customer's Name A J Jones	Date 20/9/--
Goods	Price
1 Rug	12.50
2 metres Axminster @ £10 per metre	20.00
Total	32.50
Signature of Assistant	J Wynn

Receipt of Sale	No. 33
Customer's Name A J Jones	Date 20/9/--
Goods	Price
1 Rug	12.50
2 metres Axminster @ £10 per metre	20.00
Total	32.50
Signature of Assistant	J Wynn

2.01 You must often have received a similar receipt when you purchased goods yourself. In some large stores, and indeed smaller shops such as your local greengrocer, you do not receive a receipt—so how does the shop manager, or owner, know how much money has been taken during the day?

Payments

Very many payments are made by a business—wages, rent, rates, postage, petrol, repairs, advertising, purchases, and so on. Whatever amount of cash is paid out, it must be recorded in the Cash Book, together with details of what the cash has been spent on. Let Joe explain.

I have to visit suppliers to buy carpets and also have to pay your wages and all expenses connected with this shop and warehouse. Whatever is spent must have a bill or receipt to prove that it is genuine. So when I send you down to the local shops to buy stationery or groceries, make sure you get a receipt. Put all the receipts together in a file in date order and enter the Cash Book from these receipts. Here are today's customers' receipts and bills I have paid—so I will show you how to enter them in the Cash Book.

Customers' receipts copies

No 33—£32.50; No 34—£56.81; No 35—£24.25; No 36—£92.50; No 37—£86.42; No 38—£17.68.

Bills paid

Purchases £55; Petrol £13.85; Stationery £14.15; Purchases £40.00; Window cleaning £2.75; Carriage £2.75; Electric light bulbs £3.80; Purchases £80.00.

Cash Account

19-8	RECEIPTS			19-8	PAYMENTS		
Sept 20	Sales		32.50	Sept 20	Purchases		55.00
	Sales		56.81		Petrol		13.85
	Sales		24.25		Stationery		14.15
	Sales		92.50		Purchases		40.00
	Sales		86.42		Window cleaning		2.75
	Sales		17.68		Carriage		2.75
					Electric Light bulbs		3.80
					Purchases		80.00
					Balance	c/d	97.86
			310.16				310.16
Sept 20	Balance	b/d	97.86				

Note the following points.

1 Always enter the date.

2 On the receiving side, all receipts from customers during the day are recorded as sales.

3 Whatever has been spent has shown against it the details of what it was spent upon (*see* **Purchases of goods for resale** below).

4 The balance of £97.86 shows by how much the receipts exceed the payments and represents what should be left in the till.

5 The account is always balanced using the same layout as shown.

Joe's Rule No 2
The cash balance is the excess of the receipts over the payments.

Purchases of goods for resale

When Joe buys carpets and rugs to sell in his business, he records what he pays for them in the Cash Account and writes down 'Purchases'. You may think he ought to write 'Carpets' or 'Rugs', or whatever description is correct. Let Joe explain.

What I will need to find out, sooner or later, is the profit (or loss) that I have made. To do this I shall need to be able to compare what I have bought with what I have sold. Whatever I buy to resell, be it carpets, rugs, or any of the small items that go with carpets, they are all recorded as *purchases*. Remember that *purchases* are *goods purchased for resale*.

Assets

An asset is an item that is owned by the business.

If I buy something that I will *not* be reselling—for example, a carpet cutting machine, or some display rollers, or a motor van which I shall retain for use in the business—you must show in the Cash Book exactly what has been bought. Items such as these, which I shall use in the business, are called *assets*.

2.02 Which of the following are assets?

(a) Office desk and chair
(b) Cash in the till
(c) Postage expenses
(d) Petrol expenses
(e) Warehouse racking
(f) Warehouse heating expenses

Balancing the Cash Account

Cash itself is an asset. If you have any cash in your pocket, then it is one of your own assets. If you look at the Cash Account drawn up by Joe, you will see that all the cash received from sales is added together on the left-hand side of the account.

Payments of cash reduce that asset, and so all the payments added together will give the amount to be taken from the total of the receipts. The difference, or the cash that remains after making the payments, is called the *balance*. 'Balancing the account' is the term used when calculating the balance.

2.03 Try these questions.

	(a)	(b)	(c)	(d)
	11	14	27	49.15
	9	2	92	3.71
	8	19	16	8.42
	5	7	48	9.13
	4	23	5	6.18
Balance =		=	=	=
	49	94	203	116.10

Note You have probably realized by now that the following are essential to your bookkeeping work: pen, pencil, rubber, and ruler. Until you have gained confidence, always use a pencil for totalling and balancing. Always use a ruler to balance and underline account headings. Neatness is very important.

2.04 Using complementary arithmetic, or your calculator, calculate the balances on the following Cash Accounts:

(a) Cash Account		(b) Cash Account	
12.00	16.00	25.00	8.00
14.00	3.00	22.00	15.00
8.00		9.00	47.00
5.00		37.00	
	Bal c/d		Bal c/d
39.00	39.00	93.00	93.00
Bal b/d		Bal b/d	

	(c) Cash Account			(d) Cash Account	
47.00	36.00		32.00	13.00
31.00	4.00		76.00	7.00
19.00	28.00		9.50	22.00
7.00	1.00		17.00	35.00
63.00			3.00	1.00
			45.00	
	Bal c/d			Bal c/d
167.00	167.00			

Bal b/d   Bal b/d

	(e) Cash Account			(f) Cash Account	
17.25	3.50		11.48	33.93
86.40	8.40		32.91	11.47
93.30	17.30		173.86	3.84
11.10	6.20		49.74	6.55
16.45	9.60			7.93
	3.10			20.00
	Bal c/d			Bal c/d

Bal b/d   Bal b/d

If you use a calculator, add up the payments first and put the total into memory. Add up all the receipts and subtract from this total the payments total in memory. Always make an approximate check that the answer is right by adding the figures in your head. The answer gives you the Cash Account balance.

Ruling off an account

Turn back to page 5 and look at the Cash Account. Joe totalled the receipts to £310.16. This total was carried across on the same line to the payments side of the account. By complementary arithmetic Joe worked out the balance of £97. 86. Remember that, although the balance is first written on the *payments* side, it represents the amount by which the receipts *exceed* the payments—and the bookkeeping way of writing this is to show the calculated balance as *balance c/d* (carried down), and the amount of cash actually in the till—as the asset—is also shown, as *balance b/d* (brought down) on the left-hand side. This is the amount in the till to which will be added the next receipts from sales.

If the payments on the Cash Account had exactly equalled the receipts, there would be no balance—both sides would total the same amount and would be *ruled off* with no balance shown, as follows. There would be no balance b/d.

Cash Account

1 May	Sales		49.00	11 May	Purchases		98.00
9 May	Sales		82.00	14 May	Stationery		2.61
23 May	Sales		14.61	30 May	Wages		45.00
			145.61				145.61

This is most unlikely; you will almost always have a balance on the Cash Account. The balance will also always be on the left-hand side. Why? As Joe says: if you receive £10 and put it in your pocket—how much of it can you spend? You can spend any amount up to £10. If you do spend it all, you have got nothing left—*but you can't spend more than £10*. It is the same with the Cash Account you are keeping. I can always take out everything there is—but I can't take out of the till more than is in the till. If you ever balance the Cash Account and the result is a balance which shows you have spent more than you have received—you have made an error and you must check all your transactions and also your arithmetic. (This is not the case with other accounts.)

Drawings

When the owner of a business requires some money for his own use then he may take cash out of the till for himself. This is called *Drawings*. This is a payment and is recorded in the Cash Account in the same way as other payments. In the detail column is recorded 'Drawings'.

2.05 If you had to pay a bill by buying a postal order from the local post office, how would this be treated in the Cash Account?

Bookkeeping terminology

Debit
This term is used to denote an entry on the left-hand side of an account. Sales receipts are debited to the Cash Account. When written in a record book or account, the term debit is abbreviated to Dr.

Credit
This term is used to denote an entry on the right-hand side of an account. Cash purchases and expenses are credited to the Cash Account. This term has an abbreviation also: Cr.

Debit balance
A debit balance shows that the debit entries in an account exceed the credit entries. The balance brought down (or surplus of debits over credits) appears on the debit side.

Credit balance
If a credit balance arises on an account it will be shown on the right-hand side of the account as the balance brought down.

2.06   Look at the Cash Account on page 5. Is the balance of £97.86 a debit balance or a credit balance?

Debtor
A debtor is a person who owes money to the business. The balance on his account in our books will be a debit balance.

Creditor
A creditor is someone to whom we (i.e., the business) owe money. The balance on his account in our books will be a credit balance.

3. The Bank Account

Why a Bank Account?

So far you have only handled and recorded cash paid and received. Now I'm going to explain the Bank Accounts we are using. The majority of firms use a Bank Account for paying bills—apart from cash payments on small items such as bus fares, groceries, window cleaning, and so on. The advantage of a Bank Account is that actual cash is not handled in the business and there is no danger of cash being stolen or lost. Imagine the problem if Sainsbury's tried to pay cash to the delivery drivers of vehicles delivering goods to its premises. A great deal of money would have to be kept handy to pay them—and think of the dangers in this.

The Bank Account is kept in the Bank Book.

Types of Bank Account

Most businesses have two types of account and you are going to use both of them. The main one is the Current Account and the other one is the Deposit Account. These were opened after the bank had taken up references on the business and me, Joe, as the owner. As a client of the bank I was given a cheque book and a bank paying-in book for the Current Account, and a passbook for the Deposit Account.

Amounts paid in have to be recorded in the bank paying-in book, on both the slip and its counterfoil—so that when the bank removes the slip, I (the client) still have the counterfoil and this is the document from which the Bank Account in our books is entered. We must now keep a Bank Account similar to the Cash Account, recording amounts paid into and withdrawn from the bank. All withdrawals are made from the Bank Account by means of a cheque. A cheque is simply an order to our bank to pay a sum of money to the person we name on the cheque.

By putting 'cash' on the cheque we withdraw cash for the business.

If I want to draw an amount out of the bank for myself I can make the cheque payable to Joe Wynn. This would be recorded as 'Drawings'.

Current Account

A Current Account allows us to draw money out on demand—but the bank does not pay interest on the balance in the account. The bank will send us a statement of our account regularly, or upon request, and this is a copy of our account kept in the bank's records. It enables us to check that our Bank Account kept in our Bank Book corresponds to the one kept by the bank.

Let Joe explain how you will enter the Current Account.

Entries follow the same system as the Cash Account: amounts paid into the bank are debits and withdrawals are credits. Often transfers are made between the Bank Account and our Cash Account, since cash received is first recorded in the Cash Account. Cash taken out of the till or safe and banked will therefore have two entries:

Dr Bank Account (money is paid into bank)
Cr Cash Account (cash is paid out)

Of course, if we run out of ready cash and have to withdraw some money from the bank, the entries are reversed:

Dr Cash Account
Cr Bank Account

There is one important point concerning the Bank Account that differs from the Cash Account. With cash, we can only pay out the cash actually received, but with a Bank Account it is possible to withdraw more money than has been put into the account. This must be done with the permission of the bank manager, who may allow us to overdraw. An overdraft is really a loan—but instead of handing a specific sum of money to us, we are given permission to overdraw to the amount required. Look at this simple illustration.

			Bank Account				
Sept	Total receipts		1294	Sept	Total withdrawals		1594
	Balance	c/d	300				
			1594				1594
				Sept	Balance	b/d	300

How does it differ from, say, a Cash Account? The difference is that the balance is a *credit balance*. This means that the amount of £300 is owed to the bank. This is a *liability* of the business. You will recall that cash is an asset, whether in the Cash Account or the Bank Account. But if we take out more cash from the Bank Account than the amount paid in, not only have we *not* got the money but we owe the difference to the bank.

Liabilities

An amount owed by the business is a liability. An overdraft is a liability.

3.01 Give examples of other liabilities of the business.

Making the Bank Account entries

Joe explains further how you are to keep the Bank Account.

This account is ruled in the same way as the Cash Account, and the same details are recorded. There is one additional detail which may be entered: the cheque number of the payment made. Look at our cheque book: the first three counterfoils show:

Cheque no 5981234   20 Sept £13 for petrol
Cheque no 5981235   20 Sept £122 for carpets
Cheque no 5981236   21 Sept £52 for printing

We do not have the cheques—they have been given to the suppliers. The cheque counterfoils should have the details of the payments written upon them. The paying-in book counterfoils show:

19 Sept cheque from W Scanlon £243
22 Sept cheque from J Tanner £26

These details will be entered as follows:

		Bank Account					
19 Sept	W Scanlon		243. 00	20 Sept	Petrol 5981234		13. 00
22 Sept	J Tanner		26. 00		Purchases 35		122.00
				21 Sept	Printing 36		52.00

Balancing the Bank Account

Unlike The Cash Account, we do not know on which side of the Bank Account the balance will be. You may have difficulty where two sides look to be about the same amount. The key to balancing is to add, first, the side with the largest amount (which in the case of the Cash

Account is always on the left-hand side). You can always use a pencil to write in the total of each side as follows.

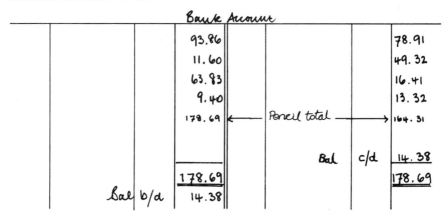

3.02 Work out the balance on the two Bank Accounts below:

(i) Bank Account		(ii) Bank Account	
92.00	18.00	87.00	277.50
163.00	162.00	254.00	32.00
349.00	75.00	196.50	312.50
	31.00		14.00

Joe's Rule No 3
A credit balance on the Bank Account means that we have overdrawn and this amount represents a liability of our business. Therefore a debit balance must represent an asset, since this is the money we have in the bank.

Drawings

You know from Chapter 2 that money taken out of the business for the owner's private use is called Drawings. Whether it is cash that is withdrawn or money taken out of the Bank Account, the detail to be shown is Drawings.

Receipts, payments, and withdrawals other than cheques

Receipts

The bank may add amounts to our account for interest or dividends received by it on our behalf—or payments made directly to the bank by someone who owes money to our business. These are by an instruction to the bank known as a *standing order* or by another method called *credit transfer*. These are payments *into* the bank and therefore the Bank Account is debited.

Payments

1 *Standing order*   If our business requires to pay a regular sum of money we can authorize our bank to pay this amount, whenever required, without making out a cheque. The payment is made direct to the bank account of the person to whom we are paying that sum.
2 *Direct debit*   This works in a similar way to a standing order. However, the payments can be made without writing out a cheque since the person requiring the payment is authorized to collect it from our bank.
3 *Credit transfer*   This enables us to pay several bills using only one cheque.
4 Our bank will deduct amounts from our account for *service charges* and any *interest on overdrafts*.
5 *Withdrawals*   All payments made by cheque will cause a 'withdrawal' of money from the Bank Account. Some withdrawals are not payments. For example, if cash is wanted for the business it is drawn out of the bank, but it is not leaving the business. It is being transferred from the bank to the office safe or till. Usually such withdrawals are made by cheque but when banks are closed they can be made by use of a Cash Point card.

In cases 1 to 4 above, the amount paid as withdrawals is entered as a credit in our Bank Account in our Bank Book. This is usually done when we receive our bank statement (see page 18).

Deposit Account

This is a savings account and will be used by a business to save its surplus cash because the bank will pay interest on balances kept in this account. Payments into it, like payments into a Current Account, are recorded in a paying-in book. Cheques are not used to withdraw amounts to pay bills because money is normally withdrawn only by presenting the passbook.

A specimen blank cheque

By completing a cheque and sending it to the person to whom we owe money, we save ourselves the risk of actually taking or sending cash to him. Attached to the left-hand side of the cheque and bound into the cheque book is the counterfoil which is completed at the same time, and from which we can enter our Bank Book. (Instead of counterfoils, some cheque books contain a separate sheet for recording the details of cheques paid.)

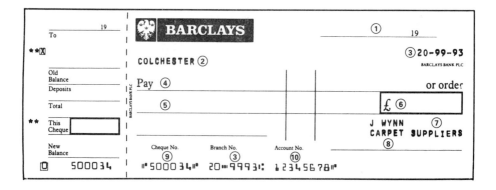

(1) Date; (2) Name of the account-holding branch; (3) The sorting code number of Colchester Branch; (4) Payee's name – the person to whom you are paying the cheque; (5) The amount in words; (6) The amount in figures; (7) The name of the account; (8) Signature; (9) The cheque number; (10) The account number.

A specimen completed cheque

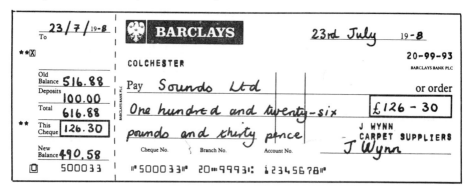

(1) Always write in ink or ball-pen – *never* pencil; (2) Write out the amount of cheque in both words and figures – this gives a double check on the amount you want to be paid, and prevents alteration of your cheques (particularly the figures); (3) Draw lines through any unused spaces (so that no one can add anything to the amount you want to pay out); (4) Sign your cheque with your usual signature; (5) Don't forget to complete the counterfoil – this is your record of what you've paid out, to whom and when; (6) Crossings – most cheque books are 'crossed' which gives you a lot of protection. If an 'open' cheque fell into the hands of a dishonest person, he might take it to a branch of the bank and obtain cash for it. If your cheque had been 'crossed' then it would have had to be paid into a bank account.

A specimen Current Account credit slip

This form is completed when putting money into our Current Account. We can either complete loose slips, which have a counterfoil attached in the same way as cheques and counterfoils, or we can have a book of credit slips which have duplicates made by the use of carbon paper.

(1) Date; (2) Name of account holding branch (as at (2) on specimen cheque); (3) Account name (as at (7) on specimen cheque); (4) Account number (as at (10) on specimen cheque); (5) Signature of person paying the money in; (6) Breakdown of cash paid in; (7) Amounts of cheques paid in; (8) Total of the credit to the account (cash and cheques).

A bank statement

There are several important points to note.

1 The account looks different from the account you have seen in the Bank Book being used by our business. The statement has three columns: Payments, Receipts, and a Balance column showing the amount in the account after the entries for a day have been made.
2 Amounts paid *into* our account are shown as a receipt by the bank with the particulars of the 'credit'. (In the bank's books we are a creditor for the amount paid into our account. The bank owes the money it holds to the clients for whom it is acting as a banker. Chapter 21 explains in detail.)

J WYNN CARPET SUPPLIERS

BARCLAYS

COLCHESTER, ESSEX

J WYNN ESQ
20 ANY STREET
COLCHESTER
Essex

CHEQUE
STATEMENT OF ACCOUNT

12345678

DIARY

18 NOV-5

POST   19-5/10

DETAILS		PAYMENTS	RECEIPTS	DATE	BALANCE
BALANCE FORWARD				1NOV	34.09
HAZRUM LIFE					
T206158910P	DDR	60.99		1NOV	26.90DR
TO DEP A/C	TFR	96.75		5NOV	69.85
COUNTER CREDIT			440.00	6NOV	509.85
HM CUSTOMS VAT					
123 4567 89	BGC		198.77	8NOV	708.62
	100 246	10.00		9NOV	
	100 248	233.49		9NOV	465.13
INTEREST CHARGES		4.92		12NOV	
COMMISSION		10.63		12NOV	449.58
DHSS INSURANCE A/C					
YE6 98765AWYNJ06	DDR	26.00		13NOV	432.58
ESTATE PUBL					
SDO/16/007/RP	STO	149.50		15NOV	274.08
	100 247	93.40		16NOV	
	100 249	10.00		16NOV	170.68

C204G 4/85   ABBREVIATIONS: DIV Dividend   STO Standing Order   BGC Bank Giro Credit   DDR Direct Debit   DR Overdrawn Balances

BARCLAYS BANK PLC. Registered in London, England. Reg. No. 1026167 Reg. Office 54 Lombard Street, London, EC3P 3AH

3 DDR   = Direct Debit
   TFR   = Transfer
   BGC   = Bank Giro Credit
   STO   = Standing Order
   Commission   = Bank Charges
   DR   = Overdrawn balance

4 Payments made by the bank on our behalf show the amount and the
   cheque number.

3.03 Enter the following in the Cash Account and Bank Account. Balance both accounts at the end of March and carry down the balances.

Mar 1 Received a loan of £500 from A Smith and paid it into the bank
2 Paid rent by cheque £25
3 Transferred £80 to the cash till
4 Paid office cleaner £15 in cash
5 Purchased goods by cheque £385
6 Cash sales £72
8 Paid cash for stationery £14
10 Cash sales £116
11 Paid cash for goods for resale £100
12 Transferred £129 to the bank from the cash till
13 The owner drew a cheque for £15 for his own use

3.04 Open a Bank Account and Cash Account and enter the balance on 1 April. Then enter the transactions and balance at the end of the month.

Apr 1 Balance at bank £455; cash balance £75
2 Paid wages in cash £48 and window cleaner £2
4 Received £16 for sales
5 Paid a cheque value £86 to J Walker
7 Withdrew £50 cash from bank (for office use)
8 Paid wages in cash £49, groceries £3
10 The owner withdrew £20 as Drawings from bank
14 Cash sales to date £163. Transferred £179 to bank
15 Received a cheque from F Taylor for £64
20 Paid the telephone bill by cheque £31
22 Cash sales to date £192
24 Drawings by the owner £25 in cash
28 Transferred £175 cash to the bank

NA 3.05 Complete the Cash Account and Bank Account for the month of January.

Jan 15 Balance at bank £562.00
Balance in cash £34.50
16 £85.00 withdrawn from bank
17 Wages paid in cash £57.50
17 Petrol paid in cash £24.85
18 Dividends received of £17.25 were paid direct to the Bank Account
19 Received a cheque from P Kaylor £49.70
20 The owner withdrew £30.00 cash
21 Cash sales to date £142.60
24 Shop fittings purchased by cheque £43.25
25 Cash sales to date £63.00

Jan 25   Paid cash of £112.75 into the bank
    28   The owner withdrew £50.00 by cheque
    29   Received a cheque value £25.00 from R Wood
    30   Payment by standing order for mailing machine rental £15.50
    30   The bank made a charge of £14.50 for services

NA 3.06 Complete the Cash Account and Bank Account for the month of February.

Feb 21   Balance at bank £98.50 (credit)
         Balance in cash £15.25 (debit)
    22   Cash sales £108.15
    22   Rent paid in cash £25.00
    23   The owner withdrew cash £15.00 for his own use
    24   £50.00 was paid into the bank, from cash
    25   A loan of £1000 was received from H P Finance Co Ltd and paid into the bank
    26   A secondhand motor van was purchased by cheque, £1250.00
    28   £35.00 was paid direct to the bank by standing order from P Spencer

NA 3.07 The drawer on a cheque is the

A person in the firm who writes out the cheques
B bank on which the cheque is drawn
C person who has signed it
D person who will get the money

(PEI Elem)

NA 3.08 A Bank Account which earns interest for a trader is called a/an

A Interest Account
B Loan Account
C Deposit Account
D Current Account

(PEI Elem)

4. Credit Sales

Recording credit sales

(This chapter requires you to be able to calculate percentages. If you are not sure of your ability to do this, look first at the section in this chapter headed **Percentages** and try the exercises.)

Joe's business—selling carpets to hotels, business firms, and similar organizations—requires him to sell on credit. This means for each sale an invoice is prepared. An invoice is simply the bill that the seller sends to the buyer, showing details of the goods supplied, the price, any discounts, and any extra costs (such as insurance, transport, and containers) that the buyer must pay. Printed on the invoice there will be the *terms of trade* which show the conditions under which the seller supplies the goods—for example, that the seller will allow the buyer a cash discount for prompt payment of the amount owing.

Joe hands a bundle of copy invoices to you— look at the top one and listen to what Joe says.

J Wynn (Carpet suppliers) Colchester	INVOICE TO: BELL HOTEL QUAYSIDE BOOLE	Inv no 2 Date Jan 1		
Goods		Qty	Unit Price	Total Price
Axminster A4		10 metres	£15.00	150.00
Wilton A1		5 "	£16.00	80.00
				230.00
Less Trade discount		at 25%		57.50
				172.50
Terms E & OE				

Copy invoice

Notes

1 The top copy of each invoice has been sent to the customer. These are our file copies.
2 E & OE means Errors and Omissions Excepted. We reserve the right to correct any errors, should there by any.

The customer's name and the invoice total need to be entered in the Sales Day Book. I call it the Sales Day Book, but other firms may call it the Sales Book or the Sales Journal. This book is needed to record credit sales and is described as a *book of original entry* (or *prime entry* or *memorandum book*). This is how it should be entered—I'll do the first one to show you.

SALES DAY BOOK

(Invoice Total column)

Date	Customer and Details	Folio	£ p	£ p
19-7 Jan 1	Bell Hotel Inv no 2			172.50

(Normal usage—note that only the date, name, invoice number and total are entered.)

I do it like this— but I'll show you how it is sometimes entered somewhat differently:

Date	Customer and Details	Folio	£ p	£ p
19-7 Jan 1	Bell Hotel Inv no 2			
	Axminster 10 metres		150.00	
	Wilton 5 "		80.00	
			230·00	
	Less Trade Discount at 25%		57.50	172.50

(Examination requirement)

Students should note that some examination questions set on this topic will require them to demonstrate the second method—which shows the details on the invoices copied into the Sales Day Book. *Please read all examination questions carefully.*

4.01 Now you have seen the first invoice entered, copy the entry into your own Sales Day Book and then enter the rest of the invoices.

Jan 4 Invoice no 3 sales to ABC Carpets Ltd
        15 metres of Wilton A3 @ £16 per metre
        10 metres of Wilton A2 @ £17 per metre
      6 Invoice no 4 sales to Poplar Treads Ltd
        5 metres of cord @ £14 per metre
        35 metres of underlay @ £1 per metre
        All less 50 per cent trade discount
     15 Invoice no 5 sales to Sounds Ltd
        14 metres Cordex @ £15 per metre less 20 per cent trade discount
        10 metres Cordex @ £14 per metre less 25 per cent trade discount

4.02 Add up the amounts you have entered in the Invoice Total column and write the sum underneath the last entry.

Percentages

You should be able to work out discounts which are expressed as percentages. The following calculation can be used.

(a) 25% (25 per cent) = 25 out of a hundred = $\frac{25}{100}$ (as a fraction)
in other words 25% = one-quarter (¼)
Therefore 25% of £80 = one-quarter of £80 = £20
To do the calculation you can write

$$\frac{25}{100} \times \frac{£80}{1} = \frac{2000}{100} = £20$$

Cancelling the fraction will help you to do the calculation more quickly, e.g.,

$$\frac{\cancel{25}^{1}}{\cancel{100}_{4}} \times 80 \, \frac{80}{4} = £20$$

(b) Convert the percentage into a decimal fraction and multiply the amount by the decimal fraction, e.g., 25% = $\frac{25}{100}$ = 0.25
Therefore 25% of £80 = £80 × 0.25
(using long multiplication or a calculator) = £20

4.03 Try the following exercises.
    (a) Calculate 50% of £180; £95; £143
    (b) Calculate 25% of £160; £125; £73
    (c) Calculate 12½% of £160; £125; £73
    (d) Calculate 15% of £200; £130; £85

    (e)   Calculate 2½% of £50; £20; £2
    (f)   Calculate 5% of £45; £12; £2.50

4.04   (a)   Calculate 10% of £11.00; £118.00
         (b)   Calculate 25% of £44; £120; £98.40
         (c)   Calculate 33⅓% of £66; £72; £18.90
         (d)   Calculate 45% of £70; £90; £130

NA 4.05   Open the Cash Book, Bank Book and enter these balances.

June 1   Cash £42.50 (Dr), bank £1240 (Dr)
          Enter the following transactions in the two books above and the Sales Day Book.
     2   Purchased goods by cheque £395.00
     4   Sold goods on credit to P P Berry for £125.00 net and T T Edwards £200.00 less 40 per cent trade discount
     5   Paid sundry expenses in cash: stationery 95p; fares 42p; office sundries £1.45
     8   Cash sales to date £342.00
     9   Paid £300.00 into bank
    12   Owner withdrew £50 from the bank
    15   Sold goods on credit to S S Jenkins £84 less 25 per cent trade discount; plus £10.00 for a returnable carton
    19   Made a loan to F Wood £100.00—giving a cheque
    24   Cash sales to date £450.00
    25   Paid all cash in hand into bank

Balance the Cash and Bank Accounts and total the Sales Day Book.

Trade discount

On Invoice no 2 a *trade discount* of 25 per cent was shown. It represents a reduction in the selling price or an allowance made by the seller to the buyer. It is usually allowed only on transactions between businesses 'in the trade'—i.e., the manufacturer will allow it to the wholesaler, the wholesaler will allow it to the retailer. The retailer will sell it at a *net price*— i.e., a price without any reduction. Between traders, the trade discount can represent the profit that the buyer will make on reselling the goods.

    When entering invoices in the Sales Day Book, you will see from the illustration on page 25 that only the net total of the invoice is shown in the final column. It is this net amount that is owed by the customer.

Quantity discount (or bulk discount)

This is a reduction in the selling price because the buyer has purchased a large quantity. The discount can increase as the quantity purchased increases. Suppliers will usually quote the rates of discount on the price lists they supply to customers. You are aware that the large stores and multiple shops often sell products at a price lower than the smaller shops. This is often because they can buy very large quantities from the manufacturer—and thus obtain substantial discounts. This lower buying price is then passed on to the customer in the form of lower selling prices.

SALES DAY BOOK

SDB 14

DATE	CUSTOMER AND DETAILS		FOLIO	£	p	£	p
Jun 1	Star Hotel (12)	Inv no 32				172	50
4	Eagle Ins Co (05)	33				89	75
4	Talyor Stores (16)	34				149	83
11	Woodman & Son (17)	35				61	90
11	Harper & Co Ltd (08)	36				187	60
12	Wilson Bros (18)	37				348	00
18	Boothroyd (03)	38				75	00
19	Cannon ~ Taylor (04)	39				143	00
Jun 30	Total Sales					1227	58

Note The figure in brackets is the customer's computer code.

Charges for containers

Companies that manufacture expensive or large products usually have to pack them very carefully. Liquids have to be kept in barrels or other containers, wire has to be coiled on to drums, and so on. Such containers can be very expensive, and it is usual to charge customers for the container as well as the product. This charge may be refundable on the return of the container. The charge is added to the net price of the goods on the invoice, so the net invoice charge entered in the Sales Day Book is for goods and containers. If the customer does return the container and is eligible for a refund, a separate record must be made of the returns, and this is explained later.

Documents

Invoice (Inv)

Prepared by the seller and sent to his customer, it shows the goods sold (or services rendered), with descriptions, quantities, prices, and trade discounts. It may include additional charges—for insurance, carriage, and containers. It then shows the total amount owed to the seller.

Debit note (D/N)

If the customer has been undercharged on the invoice (due to an error) the seller can send a debit note. It is used to debit the account of the customer in the same way as an invoice. It is recorded in the books and entered in exactly the same way as an invoice.

Joe's Rule No 4

The first record of any transaction must be made in a book of original entry. For credit sales, the first record is made in the Sales Day Book.

Charges for services rendered

Sometimes Joe arranges for a carpet layer to fit and lay the carpet in a customer's premises. The cost of this service has to be charged to the customer and this will be entered on the invoice. In this case we will be charging for a service rendered.

4.06 Enter the following transactions in the Sales Day Book, Cash Book, and Bank Book.

The cash balance on 1 November is £102.25 (Dr) and the bank balance is £2160.00 (Dr).

Nov 2 Sold goods on credit to Boothroyd for £652.50 net and Richards Flooring for £350.00 less 50 per cent trade discount

4 Cash sales to date £650. Paid £600 into the bank. Paid cash for stationery £26.52

8 Net credit sales to G Tyler £1025.16, Sounds Ltd £36.02, and Wilson Bros £152.95

12 Paid cheques for goods from wholesalers £928.00 and £521.75

15 Owner withdrew £150.00 from the bank

19 Sold goods on credit to Wilson Bros £26.00 net, Singer Ltd £200.00 less 25 per cent trade discount

24 Sold discount goods for cash—£722.58. Paid £700.00 into the bank
Owner withdrew £50 cash

Nov   25   Credit sales made to Franks & Son £92.20 net, S & R Supplies £94, and
            Boothroyd £426.81 net

Total the Sales Day Book.
Balance the Cash and Bank Accounts.

NA 4.07   Which of the following business documents is the source of information
              for sales made on credit?

    A   Invoice
    B   Copy of the invoice
    C   Credit note
    D   Bank statement

(PEI Elem)

NA 4.08   A document from a seller notifying the purchaser that an undercharge
              has been made is called a/an

    A   advice note
    B   credit note
    C   consignment note
    D   debit note

(PEI Elem)

5. Sales Ledger (or Debtors' Ledger)

The Sales Ledger records the amounts due to us from debtors—customers to whom we have sold goods on credit. You will probably say that the Sales Day Book that was discussed in the previous chapter records the same amounts. It does—but the invoices entered in that book are in strict date/number order. It does not show us how much a customer owes us for sales and chargeable containers, how much he has paid, and when he paid, what value of goods and containers he sent back to us (if any), or whether we gave him a discount for prompt payment of his bills. All these details are recorded in his account in the ledger. Let Joe explain.

Each customer has a separate page in the Sales Ledger to record the details of all the transactions between us. These details represent the *account* of the customer—so the Sales Ledger contains records of all customers who have bought goods on credit. Let me show you one of the accounts—which has a ledger reference number—S1.

Sounds Ltd Account   S1

Date	Details	Folio	£ p	Date	Details	Folio	£ p
19-7							
Mar 1	Sales	SDB33	49.00				
July 14	Sales	SDB48	171.00				

These are debit entries and show what is owed to us.

Look at these two items: Date and Folio. The date is that shown on the invoice; Sounds Ltd owes us money because we have sold goods to the company and the Folio column shows the page number in the Sales Day Book in which this invoice is recorded.

5.01 One part of the bookkeeper's job is to *post* the entries made in books of original entry to the ledger accounts. Can you remember the three books of original entry so far discussed?

Posting is the bookkeeping term for transferring the details of a transaction from the book of original entry (where the first book record is made) into the ledger account.

5.02 Two of the three books of original entry so far discussed are also accounts. Can you remember which ones?

You must remember that the Sales Ledger does *not* show the sales made by the business—it only records the accounts of debtors—that is why an alternative name for this ledger is the *Debtors' Ledger* (it contains the personal accounts of debtors). It may also be described as one of the *personal ledgers*—i.e., a ledger containing personal accounts. There are some things you must learn about debtors' accounts. First, a debtor owes us money and, since that money really belongs to us, it is an asset. So, *debtors* are *assets*. Second, an asset appears on the debit side of the account. (Debtors could be called 'debitors'—useful to remember that.) Third, the value of the asset is the debit balance on the account. You should be able to remember how to balance an account. Let us balance Sounds Ltd account.

Method 1 Proper balancing

Sounds Ltd Account

Mar 1	Sales		49.00	July 15	Bal	c/d	220.00
July 14	Sales		171.00				
			220.00				220.00
July 15	Bal	b/d	220.00				

Proper balancing does not need to be carried out every time a balance is required.

Method 2 (a) Pencil totals

Sounds Ltd Account

Mar 1	Sales	49.00	
July 14	Sales	171.00	
	Pencil total	220.00	

Method 2 (b)   Pencil totals when the account has both debit and credit entries. Sounds Ltd, for example, having paid £49.00, the account will be:

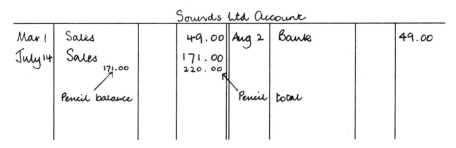

Procedure

This is the procedure for dealing with credit sales.

Step 1   Prepare invoices and send top copy to customer.

Step 2   From copy invoices enter the Sales Day Book.

Step 3   Post the entries in the Sales Day Book to the sales ledger accounts, entering the folio references in both books.

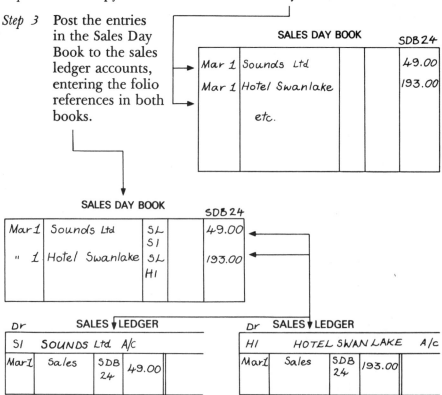

Books and accounts

The Sales Day Book is *not* an account. It does not show the balances owing by customers and it does not show the balance of sales made. It is a *memorandum book*—and from the weekly or monthly totals we can record the total credit sales in a *Sales Account*.

Joe's Rule No 5

Customers' accounts are debited with the value of credit sales made to them, by posting the entries from the Sales Day Book.

Books of original entry

There is another important rule that needs to be learned. In the previous chapter and in the illustrations in this chapter, you have seen that the very first record of credit sales is made in the Sales Day Book. The entry in the accounts is then made from the Sales Day Book. A similar procedure is adopted for *all* other transactions: that is, the *first* record of the transaction will be made in a book of original entry.

Let me give you an example that you know already. If cash sales are made, where do we record the receipt of cash? In the Cash Book. Therefore the Cash Book must be a book of original entry. If we pay a cheque for some petrol that we buy while delivering carpets, where does the first record of that expense appear? In the Bank Book. So the Bank Book is also a book of original entry. The other books of original entry that you will have to learn are:

The Bought Day Book
The Sales Returns Book
The Purchases Returns Book
The Journal
The Petty Cash Book

Now try the following exercises, remembering always to read the instructions carefully.

5.03 Enter the following transactions in your Sales Day Book, total the Sales Day Book, and post to the ledger accounts. (Use the same ledger accounts for **5.03, 5.04,** and **5.05.**)

Apr 1 Sold on credit to Sounds Ltd:
        5 metres Axminster A1 carpet @ £15 per metre
        7½ metres Wilton carpet @ £14 per metre
        14 metres underfelt @ £3 per metre

Apr   1   Sold on credit to Hotel Swanlake:
            2 doz rugs @ £11.50 each
            30 door mats @ £2.70 each
            50 metres stair carpet @ £6 per metre

5.04

Apr   10   Sold on credit to Bow Office Furnishers Ltd:
            25 metres Wilton carpet @ £14 per metre
            25 metres underfelt @ £3 per metre
            10 5-litre tins paint @ £8 per tin.

      10   Sold on credit to Hotel Swanlake:
            20 door mats @ £2.70 each
            8 tins paint @ £8 per tin
            3 tins emulsion paint @ £5.20 per tin

5.05

Apr   26   Sold to Metro Shopfitters & Furnishers Ltd on credit:
            16 tins gloss paint @ £6.25 per tin
            80 metres furnishing materials @ £8.10 per metre
            17 metres Axminster carpet @ £15 per metre
            Assorted end of range furnishing materials for £120.
            We allowed them 20 per cent trade discount.
            Returnable containers were charged at £15.00.

      27   Sold to Bow Office Furnishers Ltd:
            25 tins wood polish @ £1.60 per tin
            40 tins carpet shampoo @ £5.50 per tin
            120 metres furnishing material @ £8.10 per metre
            We allowed them 20 per cent trade discount.
            Returnable containers were charged at £12.50.

Save the ledger accounts you have entered for **5.03, 5.04,** and **5.05.** You will
need them for the next chapter.

6. Receipts from Debtors

Now we are going to use the Cash Book, the Bank Book, and also the Sales Ledger. Debtors owe us money and when they pay, either by cheque or cash, the receipt of that payment is recorded in the Cash Account or Bank Account, on the debit side (it *increases* our asset of cash). The asset of cash goes up, but the asset of debtors goes down; therefore we must reduce the debtor's account. Look at the account of Sounds Ltd in the Sales Ledger.

				Sounds Ltd account	
Mar 1	Sales	SDB 14	49.00	

When we receive payment of the debt of £49.00, where should the entry be made to show that Sounds Ltd has paid its debt? It can't be put on the debit side because that would make it appear that we were owed £98.00—therefore it *must* be entered on the credit side, as follows.

		Sounds Ltd account						
Mar 1	Sales	SDB 14	49.00	Aug 2	Bank	BB 3	49.00

There is now no balance on this account. Note that the credit entry shows the date that the payment was received and entered in the Bank Book, that it was a cheque paid into the bank, and the Folio column shows the Bank Book page on which it is recorded.

Remember The cheque was received and recorded in the *Bank Book*, which is the book of original entry, and only then was it posted to the ledger account. If we had received payment in cash, it would be debited to the Cash Account (and then credited to the ledger account of Sounds Ltd). You must learn the rule below.

Joe's Rule No 6
Receipts from debtors are entered in the Cash Account (or Bank Account) as a debit and in the debtor's personal account in the Sales Ledger as a credit.

Rule No 6 illustrates a principle which you have already learned regarding the Cash Book and Bank Book, that value received is debited and value given is credited. A quick look back at the Bank Book will show this. But the rule is now being extended to include value given by debtors; after all, when they pay, they give money to us. The receipt by us is recorded as a debit entry and their payment is recorded as a credit entry. These are the two aspects of each transaction—and each transaction must be both debited and credited. This is the principle of *double entry*, about which you will hear a lot more. One other point to look at and remember: each account has a Detail column. In this column is written the title of the account in which the second of the two entries appears. The following example should make it clear.

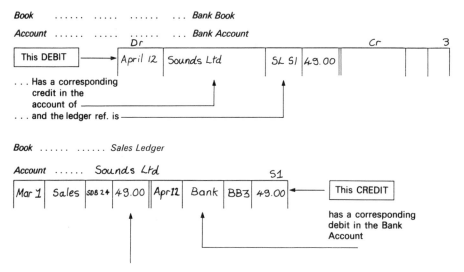

6.01 In which account is the corresponding credit entry for this debit?

When you have worked out the answer to **6.01** you will say that you haven't learned that account yet. And also, which ledger is that account kept in? Before explaining it in detail, try the following exercises.

6.02 Take out the ledger accounts you have prepared for exercises **5.03, 5.04,** and **5.05,** and the Cash Book and Bank Book. The following payments are received; enter the receipts in the appropriate book (Cash or Bank) and post to the debtors' accounts. Balance the debtors' accounts.

Apr 15   Received from Sounds Ltd a cheque for £222.00
     16   Received from Hotel Swanlake a cheque for £607.00
     19   Received from Hotel Swanlake cash £133.60
     27   Bow Office Furnishers Ltd paid us £505.00 by cheque

6.03 Enter the following transactions in the appropriate record books and post to the ledger.

May 1   Sold to James Garner on credit assorted rugs for £16.85
     2   Sold for cash 12 metres matting @ £4 per metre

May 2   Sold for cash 5 tins paint @ £5.60 each
      6   Received a cheque for £400.00 from Office Furnishers Ltd
   12   Sold the following on credit to Office Furnishers Ltd:
          25 door mats @ £1.40 each
          5 tins paint @ £12.50 each
          12 metres cleaning rug @ 45p per metre
          We allow them 20 per cent trade discount.
   16   Sold assorted furnishing materials for cash £16.50
   18   Shop Fitters Ltd paid us £473.00 by cheque
   21   Sold on credit to Shop Fitters Ltd:
          3 paint brushes @ £2.30 each
          5 metres Axminster A1 @ £12.30 per metre
          No discount was allowed
   23   Sold on credit to W Ing:
          10 metres Axminster A1 @ £12.70 per metre
          20 metres Axminster SA1 @ £15.60 per metre
          Trade discount of 25 per cent was allowed
          A charge of £20 was made for supporting containers.

The Sales Account

To keep an accurate record of sales, a separate account must be opened to record both cash sales and credit sales. Applying the principle of double entry to cash sales, we received cash because we sold (or gave) value of stock. (*Remember* We do not use a Stock Account for this purpose.)

The bookkeeping entries are:

    Debit Cash Account: Credit Sales Account

Applying the same principle to credit sales, the bookkeeping entries are:

    Debit Customer's Account: Credit Sales Account

Look at the following ledger entries:

Cash Account

| Oct 3 | Sales | PLS1 | 48.00 | | | |
| 10 | Sales | PLS1 | 31.00 | | | |

Customer A Account

| Oct 5 | Sales | SDB | 92.00 | | — | |

Customer B Account

Oct 15	Sales	S D B	137.50	

Customer C Account

Oct 8	Sales	S D B	73.50	

All of these accounts above are asset accounts. Cash is what actually exists; it has been received. Debtors' accounts record the amount owing to the business, which we will be receiving. The Sales Account is an income account—it shows the sales that the business has made. Cash sales and credit sales are both 'income'—after all, the customer will pay us in due course. The Sales Account records the selling price of stock sold.

Sales Account   S 1

		Oct 3	cash	C B 1	48.00
		5	customer A		92.00
		8	customer C		73.50
		10	cash	C B 1	31.00
		15	customer B		137.50

6.04   Can you remember *Joe's Rule No 4*? If so, how would it be applied to cash sales, credit sales, and payments received?

How smart are you? Two questions should have occurred to you. Firstly, what is the point of having a Sales Day Book if sales are entered in the Customer's Account and the Sales Account?

Secondly, why have the folio references in the Sales Account for customers A, B, and C been left out? The reason is because although the illustration above is correct as far as double entry is concerned, in practice the actual entries are different.

Posting credit sales to the Sales Account

Look at the folio references in the accounts of the customers above, what is their purpose?

Joe explains that every transaction is recorded twice—as a debit and as a credit. As I have shown in the illustration, the Detail column shows the title of the account in which the other entry has been made—the Folio column shows the source of that entry. In this case it is the Sales Day

Book. Once the Sales Day Book has ben totalled, the one total for sales can be entered in the Sales Account. The Sales Account will therefore be as follows:

Sales Account				S1
Oct 3	Cash	CB1	48.00
10	Cash	CB1	31.00
31	Total Sales	SDB	303.00

The total (credit) sales for October is the total of customers A, B, and C invoices, posted from the Sales Day Book. Posting one total to the Sales Account saves making individual entries for each customer.

Returned goods and returnable containers

If returnable containers have been charged to a customer, then the customer's account has been debited with the amount and the charge made added to the sales figure in the Sales Account. When the customer returns the containers, he needs to be refunded with the amount originally charged, if he has paid the original bill. If he has not paid, then his account is credited in order to reduce the amount owing to us.

Now, we *receive* the container, he *gives* it. So which account do we debit? The answer is: a *Sales Returns Account*. The Sales Returns Account shows the value of the sales previously made, now returned to us. Exactly the same treatment is given to goods that are returned which the customer may have found damaged or incorrect.

The book of original entry to record returns, of both goods and containers, is the *Sales Returns Book*, and this is explained in detail later; but look at the examples of the ledger entries below.

If we sell goods to S Hoe value £28.00:

Debit S Hoe's Account: Credit Sales Account

If S Hoe returns the goods as unsatisfactory and we allow full credit (i.e., full refund):

Credit S Hoe's Account: Debit Sales Returns Account

A simple rule to learn: if sales are credits (recorded in the Sales Account) then sales returns are debits (recorded in the Sales Returns Account). After all sales *returns* are the opposite to sales.

6.05 If a shop customer, who had paid cash for his goods, returned to the shop and he was refunded his money, what would the two ledger entries be?

Statement of account

If we look at a debtor's account in the Sales Ledger we should be able to see exactly what the latest position is regarding how much is owed to us. Like many firms, we send a copy of the account to the customer—thereby pointing out exactly what we believe the position is regarding his account. The copy we make is called a *statement*. It shows what transactions have taken place since the previous statement. The customer may not receive goods dispatched to him and we may not receive payments made by him. His accounts may show different figures to those on our statement—through the statement, these errors are quickly detected. A typical statement is shown below.

J Wynn (Carpet Suppliers)

STAR HOTEL
QUAYSIDE
BOOLE
      BR12 8QT

20, Any Street
Colchester
Essex CM2 7PR
Tel.Colchester(0206)8942

Statement

Date	Ref No	Details	VAT	Debit	Credit	Balance
Jan 2		A/c Rendered				7074 66
Jan 4		Goods	16 50	126 50		7201 16
Jan 5		Cash			7074 66	126 50
Jan 9		Goods	58 68	450 00		576 50
Jan 17		Carpet laying	7 02	53 80		630 30

Look at this example.

1 A statement is sent to the TV Centre on 30 September.

STATEMENT			
To TV Centre	dr	cr	Bal
Sept 10 Goods Inv no 97	45.00		
Sept 18 Goods Inv no 121	21.00		
			66.00
E & OE			

2 During October, sales are made to the TV Centre of £83.50 on 22 October and a cheque is received for £45.00 on 24 October. Invoice no 22 included a £5 charge for a returnable container. This was returned on 29 October and the full amount of £5 was allowed.

3 The account at the end of October will be as follows:

			TV Centre Account				T3
Sept 10	Sales		45.00	Sept 30	Bal	c/d	66.00
18	Sales		21.00				
			66.00				
Oct 1	Bal	b/d	66.00	Oct 24	Bank		45.00
22	Sales		83.50	29	Returns		5.00
				31	Bal	c/d	99.50
			149.50				149.50
Nov 1	Bal	b/d	99.50				

This is the usual method of handwritten accounts in ledgers, and is used in this textbook.

Three-column ledger accounts

Look at the illustration of a typical three-column statement and account on the next page.

It shows a different way of keeping a ledger account. Instead of two columns to record debits and credits, three columns are used. One is for debits, one is for credits, and the third one is to maintain a running balance of the account.

Three-column Ledger Account
The TV Centre Account

			Dr	Cr	Bal
Sept	10	Sales	45.00		45.00
	18	Sales	21.00		66.00
Oct	22	Sales	83.50		149.50
	24	Bank		45.00	104.50
	29	Returns		5.00	99.50

This type of account is found in systems using accounting machines and is also commonly used in handwritten business systems such as Kalamazoo.

The statement sent at the end of October will be exactly the same as the account—but printed on the statement form.

6.06   Draw up a statement to be sent to S Heep at the end of December from the following details.

Nov 30   Balance owing to us £144.00
Dec   5   Invoice no A/6142 for goods sold—net value £65.00
      8   Cheque received from S Heep value £5.00
   14   Invoice no A/6167 for goods sold—gross value £80, less 20 per cent trade discount. Containers charged at £7.50
   16   Debit note sent to correct Invoice no A/6167 which should have shown a gross value of £90
   29   Cheque received from S Heep in respect of Invoice no A/6142.

6.07   From the information prepare the account of G Oat as it would appear in the Sales Ledger of F Harmer and Co, balance the account, and bring down the balance on 1 June.

May   1   Balance due to F Harmer & Co £78.00
    6   Sales to Oat £48.00 net
    8   Harmer & Co charged Oat £14.00 for returnable containers
   15   Harmer & Co received the containers returned by Oat and full credit was allowed
   24   Oat sent a cheque for the balance due on 1 May
   28   Purchases by Oat of goods at a catalogue price of £80 less 15 per cent trade discount

NA 6.08   Prepare a three-column Sales Ledger Account for T Ree as it would appear in the books of A Wood after the following transactions.

Nov   1   Balance due to A Wood £42.00
          Wood sold goods to Ree at a catalogue price of £250.00 less 25 per cent trade discount. A charge of £22 was also made for containers
    5   Ree returned goods at a catalogue price of £50
   18   Ree returned the containers and was allowed a credit of £16.00
   24   Purchases by Ree of £86.75 net
   28   Ree paid the amount due on 1 November

7. Nominal (or General) Ledger

The Sales or Debtors' Ledger keeps debtors' accounts. The Creditors' or Bought Ledger keeps creditors' accounts (to be dealt with in Chapter 12). Therefore a Nominal (or General) Ledger keeps nominal accounts. But what are these? First, can you remember the definition of an account?

If you can you will know that the *Cash Account* keeps a record of *cash in hand*; and the *Bank Account* keeps a record of the *cash in the bank*. P E Smith's Account keeps a record of transactions with P E Smith.

7.01 Therefore, what name would we give to an account that keeps a record of:

(a) rent
(b) wages
(c) motor running expenses
(d) fixtures and fittings

(e) sales
(f) insurance
(g) discounts allowed
(h) rent received?

So far the only records you have of expenses paid are in the Cash Book and the Bank Book. If you wish to find out how much you have paid during the year for a particular expense, say motor running expenses (petrol, maintenance, repairs, licences, taxes), you would have to look through the whole of the Cash Book and Bank Book and add up all the individual entries. This would be a long and tedious job. The double entry principle, already explained, enables you to solve this problem.

The principle of double entry

Remember that the bookkeeper is working on behalf of a business, that is, his employer. All transactions are therefore considered from the view-point of the business in whose books the transactions are being recorded. The next important rule is that each and every transaction has two aspects—both a giving and a receiving one. Joe will have to explain.

We never pay money out unless we receive something in exchange. It may be stock, or it may be other assets, such as fixtures, cabinets, display stands, or motor vehicles. Even if we pay wages, we receive the services of

Double Entry Posting from the Cash Book

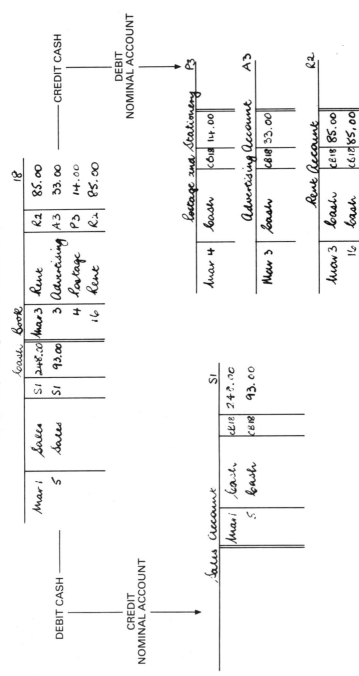

Step 1. Record details of the transaction in the Cash Book.
Step 2. Post details from the Cash Book to the appropriate nominal account.

the employee. If we pay rent, we receive the use of the premises; if we pay bank charges, we receive the use of the banking facilities.

What we must do is record both the giving and the receiving aspects of each transaction. You already know how to record the giving aspect.

7.02   Just to remind you: if we pay out £950 for a display cabinet and we pay by cheque, how is the payment recorded?

But that entry only records the giving aspect. In order to record the fact that we have *received* the *value* of a display cabinet, it must be entered also into a separate account, called the Fixtures and Fittings Account. (Chairs, desks, cabinets, and similar assets are usually entered into this one account rather than opening separate accounts). I have already told you that values given are credited (e.g., a payment of cash is credited in the Cash Account) and that values received are debited (for example, cash received is debited in the Cash Account). Now you must learn that this rule applies to *all* transactions; value received is debited and value given is credited. A simple rule, but one you must remember.

Joe's Rule No 7
For every debit entry there is a corresponding credit entry in another account.

Double entry from the Cash Book

Look at the illustration opposite. Imagine the accountant who is inspecting the books opening the Cash Book at page 18. He can see that certain entries in the book have been posted to the nominal accounts in the ledger because there is a folio reference in the Folio column of the Cash Book.

In posting details—copy the date, and the amount; enter Cash in the Detail column (this is the name of the account where the 'other' entry appears); enter the Cash Book folio reference page number; enter the nominal account folio reference number in the Folio column of the Cash Account.

Nominal accounts

Nominal accounts are those that record expenses and incomes. You are familiar with expenses, but are perhaps not aware that a business may receive income from sources other than sales. For example: rent received from subletting a part of its property; dividends on investments; interest on bank deposits; insurance claims; and sale of assets.

Double Entry Posting from the Sales Day Book

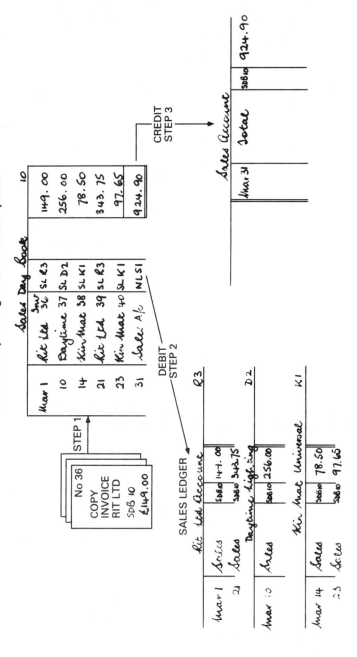

Step 1. Enter the Sales Day Book from copy invoices.

Step 2. Post the invoice total to the debtor's account in the Sales Ledger, weekly or daily.

Step 3. Total the Sales Day Book and post total to the Sales Account in the Nominal Ledger.

Real accounts

This name is given to those accounts that record real assets—machinery, buildings, vehicles, office equipment, and so on. These accounts are often kept in the Nominal Ledger although large businesses will keep them all in a separate Asset Ledger.

Personal accounts

These are accounts of people with whom our business deals—mainly customers and suppliers.

Double entry from the Sales Day Book

The illustration opposite shows the double entries required to record sales on credit. The person buying the goods—the debtor—must have his account debited, while the value of the sales made must be credited to the Sales Account. The first record, as you remember from Chapter 4, is made by entering the details of the sale from the copy invoice (Step 1). Remembering that the Sales Day Book is *not* an account, but only a memorandum book, the debtor's account will be debited (Step 2) and the Sales Account will be credited (Step 3) with the total of all the sales.

Do these exercises

7.03 Enter the name of the account to be debited and the account to be credited for these transactions.

Account to be
debited   credited

(a) Purchased a motor van, paying by cheque
(b) Purchased carpets for resale, paying cash
(c) Paid rent by cheque
(d) Sales for cash
(e) Sold goods on credit to A Smith
(f) Sold goods on credit to P Taylor
(g) Paid insurance by cheque
(h) Paid wages by cash
(i) Owner withdrew cash

7.04 Give the name of the ledger in which the following accounts will be kept.

(a) Sales
(b) Purchases
(c) A Smith—debtor
(d) Machinery and plant
(e) Wages

(f) Commissions received
(g) Losses on till takings
(h) Discounts
(i) D Jones—creditor

7.05 (a) Using the Cash Book, Bank Book, Sales Day Book, Sales Ledger, and General Ledger, enter the following transactions for May. As soon as you have recorded the transactions in a book of original entry, you should post the details to the ledger account.

     (b) At the end of the month, total the Sales Day Book and post to the nominal account. Balance the Cash Book, Bank Book, and Sales Ledger accounts.

Mar	1	Cash sales £148.00
	2	Paid cash into bank £100.00
		Paid wages in cash £22.00
	3	Paid printing expenses in cash £15.50
	4	Cash sales £95.00
		Sold goods on credit to P Brown £48.75
	5	Paid rent by cheque £48.00
		Sold goods on credit to A Shaw £65.25
	8	P Brown paid his account by cheque, paying £48.00 in full settlement
	10	Cash sales £173.60
		Paid wages in cash £22.00
		Paid cash into bank £110.00
	14	Sold goods on credit to M Miller £36.50
	18	Paid cash for shop display stand £18.90
	19	Sold goods on credit to A Shaw £42.30
	21	Paid for purchases by cheque £265.00
	23	Cash sales £162.00
		Paid wages in cash £44.00
	24	Miller returned goods valued £8.00 and was allowed full credit
	26	M Miller paid £20 on account by cheque
	28	The owner drew £10 cash for his own use

     (c) Make a list of the accounts with debit balances and a list of those with credit balances. Total each list. If your double entry has been correct, the two lists should agree.

7.06 In the illustration on page 44 Invoice no 36 has SDB 10 written on the front. What is this?

Purchase of assets on credit

So far we have purchased everything for cash. Many purchases are made on credit—that is, purchased now with the intention of paying later. A record must be made immediately after the purchase is made. In the case of assets we need to record the fact that the item now belongs to us and also that we owe that value to the supplier.

The rules learned apply as follows.

1 We receive the value of the asset—therefore debit the asset account.

2 The supplier 'gives' the value of the asset—therefore credit the supplier's account.

Sooner or later we will have to pay the supplier, and when that happens:

3 We pay cash—therefore credit the Cash (or Bank) Account.
4 The supplier receives the money—therefore debit his account.

Example
On 1 May we buy a pair of scales from Measure Right Ltd at a cost of £58 and on 30 May we pay the bill by cheque. The ledger entries are:

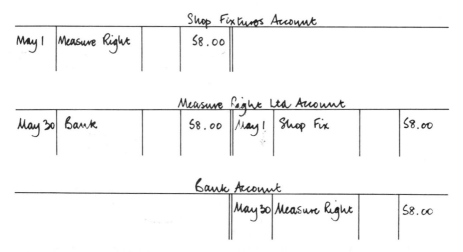

Between 1 May and 30 May the account of Measure Right Ltd had a credit balance. He was a *creditor* (someone to whom we owed money). Creditors are liabilities.

Asset purchases in a book of original entry

In Chapter 4 (*Joe's Rule No 4*) you were told that all transactions should first be entered in a book of original entry—and this includes the purchase and sale of assets. If assets were purchased and paid for immediately, then the payment would be first recorded in the Cash Book or Bank Book (both books of original entry) and posted to the asset account in the ledger. Assets purchased on credit are first entered in either the Journal or the analysed Bought Day Book. Since both of these books are dealt with at a later stage, you must assume, for the time being, that entries for assets purchased on credit are entered directly to the two ledger accounts concerned, that is—debit the asset account and credit the supplier's account.

Capital expenditure

Assets purchased are going to be used in the business. No doubt they will wear out eventually, but they will be kept until such time as they are no longer useful. All expenditure on assets to be retained in business for a long period of time (i.e., fixed assets) is called *capital expenditure*.

Revenue expenditure

Expenses incurred in operating the daily affairs of the business—such as rent, wages, travelling, insurance, advertising, and so on—are called *revenue expenditure*.

Capital and revenue expenditure are further considered in Chapter 17.

7.07   Enter the name of the account to be debited and the account to be credited for the following transactions. (Use a sheet of paper for writing your answer.)

(a) Motor van purchased on credit from R A Garage Ltd
(b) Display cabinets purchased on credit from Shop Fitters Ltd
(c) Cheque paid to Shop Fitters Ltd
(d) Cash deposit paid to B Worth for purchase of office desk yet to be delivered
(e) Cheque received for the sale of old office equipment

7.08   Enter the following details into the Cash Book, Bank Book, and Sales Day Book and make the double entry posting to the Sales Ledger and General Ledger. Total the Sales Day Book and balance the accounts.

			£
Apr	1	Balance at bank	400.00 (credit)
		Cash balance	50.00 (debit)
	2	Cash sales	175.00
	7	Sold goods on credit to M Miller	45.00
		" " " " " P White	85.00
	9	Paid wages in cash	77.00

Apr	10	Purchased loading truck on credit from Forklifts Ltd	1950.00
		Paid a deposit by cheque to Forklifts Ltd	150.00
	12	Received a cheque from M Miller	45.00
	15	Paid all cash in hand into the bank	
	16	Sold goods on credit to P White	56.00
		" " " " " S Bond	19.50
		Cash sales	167.40
		Paid wages in cash	75.80
	18	Standing order payment for office machine rental	18.70
	19	Credit transfer receipt from P White	85.00
	20	The owner drew a cheque	35.00
	22	Paid cheque, on account, to Forklifts Ltd	100.00
	23	Cash sales to date	342.90
		Paid wages in cash	78.65
	28	The owner drew cash	40.00
	30	Bank made interest charge	28.50

NA.7.09 Which of the following items are revenue expenditure and which are capital expenditure?

(a) Office desks and chairs
(b) Repairs to plant and machinery
(c) Motor vans
(d) Painting the factory
(e) Spare parts for factory machinery
(f) A new piece of equipment that will enable a machine to be more efficient
(g) A stock of stationery bought for the office
(h) A new business sign to be displayed outside the factory

Nominal accounts for cash discounts

Cash discounts are given to encourage a debtor to pay his bills promptly. By so doing he is entitled to reduce the bill by the agreed amount. These discounts are quite different from *trade discounts*. The invoice sent by the supplier will usually contain details of the *terms of trade*. These contain the conditions under which the supplier is selling goods to the buyer. If a discount is to be offered, it will state this on the invoice. For example: 'Terms—2½ per cent 7 days'. This means that the debtor can deduct 2½ per cent from the invoice total if he pays within 7 days. Look at the effect on the accounts in the example below.

Example

Joe sells to Bis Ltd, carpets costing £100 and offers a cash discount, for prompt payment, of 5 per cent within seven days.

In Joe's books the accounts for Bis Ltd will be:

			Bis Ltd Account			B1
Mar 1	Sales	SDB3	100.00			

If Bis Ltd pays the amount due within the period for claiming discount, he will send Joe a cheque for £95 (£100 less 5 per cent discount). Since a cheque for £95 has been received it will be debited to the Bank Account and posted to the credit side of Bis Ltd's Account. Bis Ltd's Account now becomes:

			Bis Ltd Account				B1
Mar 1	Sales	SDB3	100.00	Mar 5	Bank	BB8	95.00

It still appears from Bis Ltd's Account, that he owes £5 to Joe. This is not true, so the £5 must be taken out of Bis Ltd's Account by entering the discount as a credit and posting the discount to a Discount Allowed Account (as a debit). Joe allowed a discount to Bis Ltd and therefore Joe has made a loss of £5. The final position is:

			Bis Ltd Account				B1
Mar 1	Sales	SDB3	100.00	Mar 5	Bank	BB8	95.00
				Mar 5	Discount allowed	GL D3	5.00

			Discount allowed Account			
Mar 5	Bis Ltd	B1	5.00			

What would the ledger entries be in Bis Ltd's books? The records in Bis Ltd's books show:

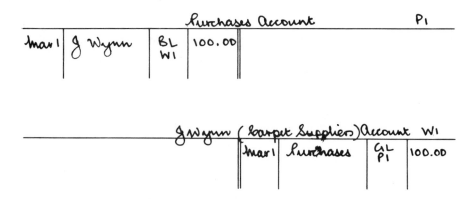

The records in Bis Ltd's books show that Bis Ltd has bought the goods costing £100 and this figure will be posted to the Purchases Account— the credit being entered in J Wynn's Account. If Bis Ltd has only paid £95 for £100 of goods, the company has made a profit, or received a discount of £5. The entries for discount received will be as follows:

Remember   Discount allowed is a loss and a debit balance on the Discount Allowed Account.

Discount received is a profit and a credit balance on the Discount Received Account.

NA 7.10 (a) Enter the following transactions in the Cash Book, Bank Book, and the Sales Day Book and post the entries to the ledger accounts.

Discounts and credit purchases should be entered directly in the ledger, as the books for these transactions have not yet been explained.

Aug	1	J Taylor started business with £500 borrowed from High Finance Ltd
	1	She opened a current account and paid in £450, keeping £50 for office cash
	3	Cash purchases of £32.00 and purchases by cheque of £140.00
	5	Cash sales of £87.00
		Advertising expenses paid in cash £15.00
	7	Credit sales to P Barr of £82.00; B Parr of £65.00
	9	Shop display units bought on credit from Design Fittings Ltd £460.00
	12	P Barr paid his account, deducting 5 per cent cash discount, by cheque
	14	Purchases on credit from H Milton & Co £60.00
	18	Paid stationery expenses in cash £4.50 and motoring expenses £7.80 in cash
	22	Credit sales to H Wilson & Partners £45.00
	23	Paid a cheque to H Milton & Co for £57.50 in full settlement of the account
	24	H Wilson returned goods and was allowed a credit of £2.50
	28	Paid advertising expenses in cash £25.00
	31	Paid all but £10 cash into bank

(b) Balance the accounts and draw up a list of accounts with a debit balance and a list of accounts with a credit balance.

(c) Total each list.

Cash discounts in a book of original entry

You have seen how the ledger accounts are entered for cash discounts. *Joe's Rule No 4* was that no ledger account should have an entry made in it unless it is a posting from a book of original entry. Sometimes it is easier to understand how the ledger accounts are entered before trying to understand the original recording in a book, and this is the case regarding cash discounts. In Chapter 10 you will learn how cash discounts are recorded *before* being posted to the ledger accounts.

Asset accounts and expense accounts

When an asset is purchased the entries are:

Debit the asset account: Credit Cash or Bank Account or creditor's account.

When an expense is paid the entries are:

Debit the expense account: Credit the Cash or Bank Account.

Therefore an account with a debit balance can be either an *asset account* (something the business owns) or an *expense account*.

How do you know which type of account it is? An asset account will have the name of the asset in its title—for example, Machinery Account, Buildings Account, Motor Vehicles Account. The expense account will also have the description of the expense in its title—Rent Account, Wages Account, and so on. A debtor is also an asset—in this case his name will be the title of the account, and it will have a debit balance.

Liability accounts and income accounts

If cash is received from sales the entries are:
Debit Cash Account: Credit Sales Account.

If cash is received from the person who rents some of our warehouse space:
Debit Cash Account: Credit Rent Received Account.

If cash is received from someone who lends us money:
Debit Cash Account: Credit the account of the lender.

If an asset is purchased on credit:
Debit the asset account: Credit the supplier's account.

If purchases are made on credit:
Debit the Purchases Account: Credit the supplier's account.

Therefore an account with a credit balance can be either an *income account* or a *liability account* (something the business owes).

A creditor is a liability—his account will have a credit balance.

What you should remember
1 An account can only have either a credit balance or a debit balance.
2 If it has a debit balance, it is either an asset or an expense.
3 If it has a credit balance, it is either an income or a liability.

Revenue incomes and receipts
Earnings from business activities are called *revenue incomes*—and when the cash is received it is a *revenue receipt*.

Capital incomes and receipts

Earnings from the sale of assets are called *capital incomes*, and when the cash is received it is a *capital receipt*. Money received from a loan is also a capital receipt.

How can you tell which type of account it is? By its title.

NA 7.11   Enter the name of the account to be debited and the account to be credited for these transactions. (Use a sheet of paper for writing your answer.)

Account to be
debited   credited

(a)   Rent received from subletting premises
(b)   Carpet cutting machine purchased on credit
(c)   Cheque received from a debtor
(d)   Discount received from W A Smith Ltd
(e)   Interest paid on a loan
(f)   Cash withdrawn by the owner
(g)   Insurance payment by credit transfer
(h)   Office typewriter paid for by cheque
(i)   Dividends received by the bank
(j)   Goods sold on credit to P Hood

NA 7.12   Tick the column whose heading is the correct type of account for the following.
(Use a sheet of paper for writing your answer.)

	Asset	Liability	Expense	Income
(a) Motor vehicle				
(b) Bank overdraft				
(c) Supplier (of a motor vehicle purchased on credit)				
(d) Rent paid				
(e) Rent received				
(f) Commissions received				
(g) Sales				
(h) Bank charges				
(i) Office equipment and fittings				
(j) Repairs to office equipment				
(k) Cash				
(l) Motor repairs				
(m) Redecorating the office and factory				
(n) Customer to whom we have sold goods on credit				
(o) Loan-a-lot Ltd, from whom money has been borrowed				
(p) Drawings				

8. Capital and Drawings

Capital

When Joe started the business, he must have put some money into the business Bank Account (or Cash Account), otherwise the business could never have bought any stock, fixtures, premises, or other assets such as motor vans. Although it is Joe's business, you must remember that it is the *business records* that we are keeping—not Joe's records. After all, Joe may have several different businesses, and each one would need to have its own separate books and accounts. We need to know how much money Joe has put into *this* business. This is called *capital* and represents the amount that Joe has invested in the business. The *Capital Account* is the personal account of the owner and shows exactly how much the business owes the owner.

A liability

If capital is the amount of money put into the business, how can it be a liability? Capital is a liability of the business, not the owner. The bookkeeping records are those of the business, and the business has received the money (or value of assets) from the owner. Exactly the same position arises if the business borrows money from a bank or other money-lending firm. Our business receives the money—so debit the Cash Account (or Bank Account) and credit the account of the company or person lending the money. That person's account has then a credit balance and a credit balance on a personal account is a liability.

Like anyone who lends money, the owner would hope someday to have it repaid, and therefore an accurate record must be kept of how much the business owes him.

Drawings

If Joe works in his business full-time, he will need to use some money for his own private expenses. Therefore he will take money out of the business, either in cash or from the bank, probably every week. The record of what he takes out is kept in the *Drawings Account*, and the bookkeeping entries are simple:

Credit the Bank (or Cash) Account: Debit the Drawings Account.

Drawings are made by the owner because the business is (one hopes) making a profit. Of course, the business may be making a loss—in which case drawings represent a repayment to the owner of some of his original capital.

Capital Account

The amount originally put into the business was credited to the Capital Account. Any additional amounts subsequently put into the business and any profit owing to the owner are also credited to the Capital Account (increasing his capital). Since Drawings reduce the amount owed by the business to the owner, the total amount of Drawings during the year are transferred to the Capital Account.

Look at this example of how a Capital Account might appear.

Capital Account

Dec 31	Drawings	NL	13 800	Jan 1	Bank	BB	10 500
		DI		Dec 31	Profit	1	
	Balance	c/d	10 900		for year	NL	14 200
			24 700			T	24 700
				Jan 1	Balance	b/d	10 900

This account shows that on 1 January the owner introduced £10 500 into the business by paying it into the business Bank Account.

> Dr Bank Account: Cr Capital Account.

During the course of the year, the business made a profit of £14 200 which it now owes to the owner:

> Dr Trading and Profit and Loss Account: Cr Capital Account.

Also during the year, the owner withdrew £13 800, and this was recorded in the Drawings Account in the Nominal Ledger (D1) and is now transferred to the Capital Account. The owner has, at the end of the year, capital of £10 900.

> Opening capital plus profit less Drawings = Closing capital. Why is profit credited to the Capital Account?

The business operates to make a profit on behalf of the owner. He benefits if a profit is made, but he also suffers any loss that arises. The accounts required to calculate profits or losses are explained in Chapter 14, but you should remember that since a profit is owed by the business to the owner it increases his capital. Obviously, therefore, a loss decreases his capital. Profit is a liability of the *business*, since the business now owes that profit to the owner.

Example

Look at the example below.

Step 1   Janis Pale starts a business with £50 cash. Therefore Dr Cash Account: Cr Capital Account.

Step 2   Goods costing £50 are bought for cash. Therefore Dr Purchases Account: Cr Cash Account.

Step 3   All the goods purchased are sold for £60 cash. Therefore Dr Cash Account: Cr Sales Account.

Step 4   Compare the costs with the incomes: the £50 cost and £60 income give a £10 profit. This profit is not shown in any account so far. In order that the purchases can be compared with sales both of these accounts are closed by transfer to a Trading Account. Therefore Dr Trading Account: Cr Purchases Account.

Dr Sales Account: Cr Trading Account.

Step 5   Income in excess of costs (i.e., profits) is transferred to the owner's Capital Account. Therefore Dr Trading Account: Cr Capital Account.

Cash Account

STEP 1 →	May 5	Capital		50.00	May 6	Purchases	50.00 ← STEP 2
STEP 3 →	May 10	Sales		60.00			

Capital Account

				May 5	Cash	50.00 ← STEP 1
				May 31	Profit	10.00 ← STEP 5

Purchases Account

STEP 2 →	May 6	Cash		50.00	May 20	Trading	50.00 ← STEP 4

Sales Account

| STEP 4 → | May 20 | Trading | | 60.00 | May 10 | Cash | | 60.00 ← STEP 3 |

Trading Account

| STEP 4 → | May 20 | Purchases | | 50.00 | May 20 | Sales | | 60.00 ← STEP 4 |
| STEP 5 → | May 31 | Capital | | 10.00 | | | | |

If you look at the Capital Account, you will see that £60 is owing to the owner. (Original capital £50 + £10 profit.) *Therefore the business has a liability of £60.* If you look at the Cash Account you will see that £60 is in hand. *Therefore the business has an asset of £60.*

So the business assets equal the business liabilities. In fact the business assets *always* equal the business liabilities.

Look at the example again. After each bookkeeping step—what were the assets and liabilities?

Step 1   Started business.   Asset   = Cash   = £50
                                  Liability = Capital = £50

Step 2   Bought goods.   Assets   = Cash   = Nil
                                            + Stock = 50

                                            Total = £50

                                  Liability = Capital = £50

Step 3   Sold goods.   Assets   = Cash   = 60
                                            + Stock = Nil

                                            Total = £60

                                  Liability = Capital = 50
                                            + Profit = 10

                                            Total = £60

Joe's Rule No 8
The total of the business assets always equals the total of the business liabilities.
    You should also remember that since every debit entry has a credit entry (and vice versa):

Assets plus Expenses (debit balances on accounts)	*always equal*	Liabilities plus Incomes (credit balances on accounts)

Assets introduced by the owner

When a person starts a business, he may bring into it assets other than cash. If you, for example, owned a motor car, and then you started business as a freelance photographer, you would use the car to carry your equipment and to go to various appointments. The car is being used in the business. Similarly, tools, equipment, stocks of materials, and even premises can be brought into the business by the owner.
    If a person started a business on 15 March with the following assets

Premises	£12 500
Stock	550
Motor van	1 850
Equipment	400

then his capital at that date would be the total of all the assets he has introduced into the business, i.e., £15 300. The entries in the accounts would be as shown below. If he then paid £200 into the bank on 18 March, his capital is increased to £15 500.

Capital Account				C1
	Mar 15	Premises	P6	12 500
		Stock	S4	550
		Motor van	M6	1 850
		Equipment	E2	400
	18	Bank	B B1	200

Premises Account			P6
Mar 15 Capital	C1	12 500	

Stock Account   S4

Mar 15	Capital	C1	550		

Motor Van Account   M6

Mar 15	Capital	C1	1 850		

Equipment Account   E2

Mar 15	Capital	C1	400		

Bank Account   BB1

Mar 18	Capital	C1	200		

Note the Stock Account is used only to record the value of stock at the specific date entered in the account. Purchases of stock (cash or credit) are recorded in the Purchases Account.

Drawings by the owner

The value of whatever the owner takes out of the business is debited to his Drawings Account and credited to:

1 Sales Account in the case of stock.
2 Bank Account if taken out by cheque.
3 Cash Account if taken in cash.
4 The appropriate expense account if the business has paid a private expense.

Perhaps item 4 needs a little more explanation. Imagine that the owner lives in a flat above his shop. He owns all the premises and pays rates to the local council. He receives a rates bill for £800. This represents £650 for the shop premises and £150 for his flat.

The following could happen:

1 The business pays £650 to the council and the owner withdraws £150 as Drawings and pays it to the council.

or

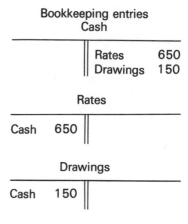

2 The business pays £800 to the council. *But*—since £150 relates to the owner's flat—the business has really paid it on behalf of the owner. Although it has saved the owner from paying it himself, he must be charged with that sum. Therefore: Dr Drawings: Cr Rates.

The result is the same either way.

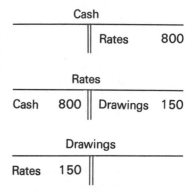

A business may pay many bills on behalf of the owner—electricity, gas, motor expenses, rents, telephone, and so on. Whatever proportion of the bill relates to the owner must be charged to his Drawings Account and credited to the expense account. The effect of this is to leave in the expense account only the amount chargeable to the business.

The Private Ledger

Where a business employs a number of people recording transactions in the books, the owner may not wish employees to see exactly what he has put into the business by way of capital. Also, he will probably not wish to disclose just how much profit (or loss) the business is making. Therefore, his Capital Account, Drawings Account, and the business Trading and Profit and Loss Accounts will be kept in a separate ledger which he himself (or his accountant) will maintain. This is the Private Ledger.

Try the following exercises:

8.01 T Taylor started a business by paying £5000 into the Bank Account of the business on 1 September. On the same date, he also brought into his business a motor car valued at £1450 and stock worth £500. The following transactions took place in September.

Sept	2	Cash sales £250; rent paid £55 by cheque
	3	Credit sales to R Haskall £42.00; P Rowler £93.00
	8	Purchased on credit from London Supply Company, office equipment costing £425.00
	11	Purchases by cheque £195.00
		Paid £150 into the bank from office cash
	12	Paid £3500 by cheque as a deposit on a shop lease
	14	Cash sales £231. Cheque received from R Haskall £39, £3 discount was allowed
	18	Sundry expenses paid in cash were: stationery £4.25; postage 85p; packing materials £12.45
	25	Purchases by cheque £442
	28	Owner withdrew stock for his own use £26
	29	A bank loan of £2500 was agreed by the bank manager and paid into the business Bank Account
	30	Petrol paid by cash £36 (£9 of this was for T Taylor's own personal use)

(a) Enter the transactions in the books of original entry, and post to the ledger.
Balance the accounts at the end of September.
(b) Make up a list of the debit balances and credit balances.
(c) Total the debit balances and total the credit balances.

8.02 On 1 September Roger Bell had £2845 in his Capital Account. During the following year he drew out a total of £1980 in cash and the following transactions also took place.
Expenses paid by the business:

Rates	£400	(one-half chargeable to Roger Bell)
Motor expenses	£750	(two-thirds chargeable to Roger Bell)
Heating	£240	(one-third chargeable to Roger Bell).

The profit for the year was £3150 after allowing for the adjustments above. Draw up Roger Bell's Drawings Account and Capital Account at the end of the year. (His Capital Account should show what his capital is at the end of the year.)

8.03 The business of Paula Meadowbank has the following assets and liabilities on 1 November. Calculate the owner's capital at that date.

Stock	450	Motor vans	2800
Cash	25	Bank overdraft	390
Premises	9850	Owing to creditors	850
Debtors	630	Mortgage	5000

The following questions require you to enter the opening balances in the ledger accounts. The total debit balances should equal the total credit balances. Where no Capital Account balance is given, the total of the credit balances, deducted from the total of the debit balances will give you the Capital Account balance. Enter the transactions in the books of original entry, and post to the ledger accounts. Balance the Cash and Bank Books and ledger accounts. Total the debit accounts and total the credit accounts.

8.04

Feb	1	*Debit balances*	Cash	£36.25	Fixtures	£290.00
			B Rush	82.50	Motor van	800.00
			S Bade	48.75	Bank	137.00
			Stock	285.00		
		Credit balances	K Hick	93.00		
			S Hoe	33.45		
			C Camp	?		

Feb	2	Cash sales £185.30
		B Rush paid his account by cheque
	4	C Camp withdrew £25 stock for his own use
	5	Paid trade expenses in cash £19.50
	8	Sold goods on credit to T Tymm £98.42
	10	Wages paid in cash £41.75
		Purchases by cheque £438
		Sold goods on credit to F Fynn £147 and P Pynn £64.40
	11	A cheque value £50 was sent to K Hick as payment on account
	18	Dividends of £16.80 received and paid into bank
		The owner drew a cheque value £35 as **Drawings**
		Wages paid in cash £42.50
		Credit sales to P Pynn £43.25 and M Minn £57.60
	21	Telephone bill paid by cheque £46.75
		Cash sales to date £288.00
	25	Wages paid in cash £43.95
	28	C Camp drew stock for his own use £43
		All cash except £25 was paid into bank
		Bank charges were incurred of £5.50

NA.8.05

Mar 1 *Credit balances*

	C Toms	£186.00
	Bank loan	550.00
	T Twigg—Capital	?

Debit balances

	Cash	10.00
	Bank	341.00
	Plant and machinery	4 250.00
	Buildings	10 800.00
	A Short	38.50
	G Rose	76.30
	Stock	891.00

Mar 5 Cash sales to date £436.75
Trade expenses paid in cash £49.00
Motor running expenses paid by cheque £77.65
 8 Office equipment bought on credit from West End Office Supplies £188.40
 10 Purchases by cheque £350.00
Amount of £50 paid by standing order towards repayment of loan
 15 Cash sales £295.00, Cash paid to bank £375.00
 17 Cash withdrawn by owner £50
 21 Cheque of £100 paid to West End Office Supplies
 26 Trade expenses paid in cash £34.50
Insurance premium of £116.00 paid by cheque
 27 Rent received in cash £25.00
 28 Owner withdrew stock value £16.00 at selling price
 30 Cash sales to date £526.85
 31 All cash was paid into the bank
Cheque paid, in full settlement of his account, to C Toms for £180.00
Balance of West End Office Supplies account paid by cheque
Cheque for £38.00 received from A Short

9. The Trial Balance

Proving double entry

Can you remember *Joe's Rule No 7?*
For every debit entry there is a corresponding credit entry in another account.

If this rule is properly followed, then all entries made on one side of the accounts will exactly equal all entries made on the other side of the accounts. By now you are using several books—the Cash Book, the Bank Book, the Sales Ledger, and the Nominal Ledger and naturally the more books and accounts that need to be kept, the greater the likelihood of errors arising. If our double entry principle is put into practice correctly, it should be easy to check that the books are correct, by adding up all the debit entries and all the credit entries. If the totals are not the same, an error has been made. Let Joe demonstrate with this example.

Transactions

(1) Started business by paying £700 into the bank
(2) Paid cheque £85 for purchases
(3) Paid cheque £28 for wages
(4) Withdrew £90 by cheque for office cash
(5) Cash sales of £160
(6) Cash purchases £42

Bookkeeping entries

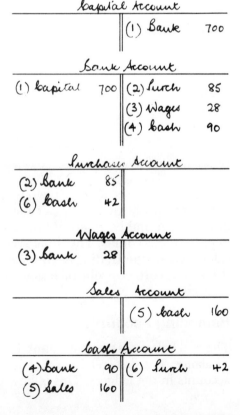

Capital Account

| | (1) Bank | 700 |

Bank Account

(1) Capital 700 | (2) Purch 85
| (3) Wages 28
| (4) Cash 90

Purchases Account

(2) Bank 85
(6) Cash 42

Wages Account

(3) Bank 28

Sales Account

| (5) Cash 160

Cash Account

(4) Bank 90 | (6) Purch 42
(5) Sales 160

A total of entries would show the following:

	Debit entries £	Credit entries £
Capital		700
Bank	700	203
Purchases	127	
Cash	250	42
Wages	28	
Sales		160
	£1105	£1105

However, it is the practice not to show all the entries but merely the *balance* on the accounts, and such a test of balances is called a *trial balance.* The above example then becomes

Trial Balance as at (. . . *)

	Dr £	Cr £
Capital		700
Bank	497	
Purchases	127	
Wages	28	
Cash	208	
Sales		160
	£860	£860

*Always enter date on which the balances are prepared.

The trial balance is always drawn up at the end of a trading period and before the profit or loss is calculated. Also, the trial balance may be drawn up monthly, quarterly or half-yearly, just to check the entries made in the accounts. The 'final accounts' in which the profit or loss is calculated are the Trading Account and the Profit and Loss Account, and if I wish a correct profit or loss to be calculated, the records must be accurate.

Balancing accounts

The trial balance is *not* an account. It is only a list of accounts which have a balance. The first step in taking out a trial balance is to balance all the accounts in the ledgers. This is how you should balance the accounts.

1 *Cash Account and Bank Account*   Balance in the normal way and carry down the balances on the accounts.
2 *Debtors' accounts in the Sales Ledger*   Balance as normal and carry down the balances on each account.
3 *Expenses and income accounts*   Since these accounts normally have entries on one side only, it is necessary merely to pencil in the total of that side underneath the last entry, or by its side. See the illustration below.

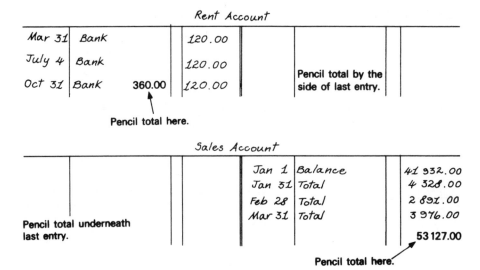

Rent Account

Mar 31	Bank		120.00			
July 4	Bank		120.00		Pencil total by the side of last entry.	
Oct 31	Bank	360.00	120.00			

Pencil total here.

Sales Account

Pencil total underneath last entry.			Jan 1	Balance		41 932.00
			Jan 31	Total		4 328.00
			Feb 28	Total		2 891.00
			Mar 31	Total		3 976.00
						53 127.00

Pencil total here.

The reasons why pencil totals should be used will be explained later, when you start learning about adjustments required at the end of the year. If an account has only one entry then that entry represents the balance, and no further balancing is required.

Difference in totals of the trial balance

If the total debits do not equal the total credits, it could mean that *either* the books and accounts contain an error *or* that you have made an error in preparing the trial balance. This is what you should do.

1 Double check your arithmetic in adding up the debit and credit columns.
2 Check that each item in the trial balance is entered in the correct column. (*Remember*   Assets and expenses are debits, but liabilities and income are credits.)
3 Check from the accounts in the ledger that you have entered the

correct balance—and not transposed a figure—and that it is in the correct column.

4 Check that *all* the ledger balances plus the Cash and Bank Accounts are in the trial balance.

5 Check the arithmetical accuracy of the balances in the ledger accounts.

If the totals still do not agree, the books contain an error.

Errors not shown by the trial balance

If the total debits agree with the total credits, then the arithmetical accuracy of the books is proved correct. However, the books and records may still contain errors, since some types of mistakes are not shown up by the trial balance.

1 *Errors of misposting (or commission)*   These arise where expenses are posted to the wrong expense account or assets purchased are posted in the wrong asset account. For example, rent posted to the Rates Account in error. The wrong account has been entered, but the account wrongly entered is the *same class* as the correct one.

2 *Errors of principle*   These occur when assets are posted to a revenue account or a revenue item (expense or income) is posted to a capital account. For example, when a van (asset) is sold and the sale value is credited to the Sales Account, this is an error of principle. The Sales Account should only be credited with the sales value of goods sold or services provided.

3 *Errors of omission*   If an entry is completely omitted from a book of original entry, then neither a debit nor a credit entry will have been made.

4 *Compensating errors*   These arise in the unlikely circumstances of the same arithmetical inaccuracy arising on both the debit and the credit side of two accounts.

How errors affect the accounts

Which errors are the most serious? All errors are serious! However, errors of misposting are the least serious as the profits/losses shown by the accounts will not be affected.

Errors of omission may result in large sums being missed out of the accounts—in which case the accounts are inaccurate and will be misleading. Similarly errors of principle will cause profits to be under- or overstated—again giving a misleading picture of the state of affairs of the business.

Joe's Rule No 9
A trial balance can be prepared at any time in order to show that the books are correct,
but it is always taken out before preparing the Trading and Profit and Loss
Accounts.

Use of trial balance in examinations

You have already learned that total debits equal total credits. Often in
examination questions you are asked to calculate the owner's capital.
This can be calculated, since the rules say:

$$\underbrace{\text{Assets} + \text{Expenses}}_{\text{Debit Balances}} = \underbrace{\text{Liabilities} + \text{Incomes}}_{\text{Credit Balances}}$$

And since owner's capital is a part of the total liabilities then:

Assets + Expenses = Capital + Other Liabilities + Incomes

So if we know all these values except capital then:

Capital = (Assets + Expenses) − (Other Liabilities + Incomes)

If in the question there are no values given for expenses and
incomes then:

Capital = Assets − Other Liabilities

Example
Teresa Bullock's business has the following assets and liabilities on 1
May: Cash at bank £185; Fixtures £250; Stock £4850; Debtors £592;
Loan from Easicome Ltd £750; and Creditors £670. What is the
owner's capital?

Total the assets:	£	Total the liabilities:	£
Bank	185	Loan	750
Fixtures	250	Creditors	670
Stock	4850		
Debtors	592		
	£5877		£1420

Since   Assets = Capital + Other Liabilities
£5877 = Capital + £1420

Therefore Capital = £5877 − £1420 = £4457

9.01 Prepare a trial balance as at 31 December from the following details.

	£
Premises	14 500
Motor vehicles	6 800
Fixtures	975
Wages	7 855
Purchases	14 982
Sales	22 468
Rents received	420
Lighting and heating	370
Telephone	450
Motor expenses	1 420
Creditors	3 400
Debtors	4 805
General expenses	948
Bank overdraft	1 402
Capital	28 000
Drawings	2 585

9.02 The following trial balance has been prepared incorrectly. Draw up a correct trial balance.

R Saunders & Son
Trial Balance as at 28 February 19--

	£	£
Capital		14 000
Plant and machinery		12 000
Wages	3 800	
Purchases	17 400	
Sales		28 650
Rents received	346	
Debtors	3 895	
Creditors	2 450	
Stock		750
Cash in hand	125	
Bank overdraft		503
Drawings	2 199	
Motor vehicles	3 500	
Motor running expenses		855
Rent and rates	1 425	
	35 140	56 758

9.03 Enter the following transactons in the books of account of J F K & Co, balance the accounts, and take out a trial balance at the end of the month.

Nov 1 Started business with £4800 cash
     2 Put £4500 of the cash into a bank account
     3 Purchased shop fixtures by cheque £750
     5 Bought goods by cheque £650
     8 Cash sales £92
     9 Paid rent in cash £20
    11 Sold goods on credit to A Hill £145
    13 Cash sales £130. Paid £100 cash into bank
    15 Bought a secondhand motor van, paying by cheque £1650
    16 The owner withdrew cash £45
        Paid motor expenses: petrol £50 and insurance £82, both by cheque
    17 A Hill paid his account by cheque £140, having been allowed a £5 discount
    19 Sold more goods on credit to A Hill £38
    20 Purchases by cheque £290
    21 Advertising bill of £15 paid in cash
    24 Owner withdrew £55 from the bank
    29 Cash sales £94
    30 Banked all cash in hand

9.04 The balances in a trader's account on 1 June 19-7 were as follows: Land and buildings £14 000; Fixtures and fittings £580; Motor van £2000; Bank balance £1420; Loan on mortgage of land and buildings £10 000; Creditors £170.

During the year ending 30 May 19-8 he drew nothing out of the business and paid in no additional capital. On 30 May his position was: Land and buildings £14 000; Fixtures and fittings £650; Motor van £2000; Bank balance £1200; Stock £480; Cash in hand £250; Loan on mortgage £9800; Creditors £245.

You are required to calculate the business profit or loss for the year

(a) Using only the information above.
(b) If the owner had withdrawn £1715 during the year.
(c) If, in addition to drawing £1715 he had paid in additional capital of £2500.

9.05 The debiting of the purchase of a fixed asset to the purchases account is an error of

A commission
B omission
C compensation
D principle

(AEB 'O' June 1984)

9.06 Which of the following errors would be revealed by the trial balance?

A A sale for £10 to C Jones is posted to the debit of B Jones's account.

B A cheque received and entered in the cash book as £25 is entered in B Green's account as £52.

C The purchase of a new van for £520 is entered in the debit of the purchases account as £520.

D An invoice from J Smith is received but is not entered in the purchase day book or J Smith's account.

(AEB 'O' Nov 1984)

9.07 Gerry Shoman is a central heating engineer and consultant whose accounts contain the following balances on 31 May 19-6:

	£
Debtors	1 600
Rent and insurance	355
Stock on hand 1/6/-5	5 500
Bank (credit)	760
Salaries and wages	8 100
Cash	60
Loan	1 590
Sub-contract expenses	3 100
Materials purchased	11 206
Creditors	2 746
Misc office expenses	405
Servicing/installation	26 432
Drawings	7 360
Stationery	20
Fees received	520
Building/tools/equipment	19 600
Motor expenses	1 428

These balances do not include Shoman's capital on 1 June 19-5.

Prepare the trial balance as at 31 May 19-6 including the owner's capital account.

NA 9.08 A trial balance agreement does not necessarily mean that the books of account are entirely correct. Explain why this is so and give examples of errors which may not be shown up by a trial balance.

(RSA 1)

NA 9.09 The following trial balance was extracted from the books of J Sanders on 30 October 19-4.

	Debit £	Credit £
Premises	84 000	
Office equipment	2 190	
Fixtures and fittings	1 240	
Trade debtors	2 790	
Trade creditors		1 870
Stock 1 Nov 19-3	2 455	
Purchases	41 000	
Sales		87 257
Wages	3 000	
Insurance	235	
Cash in hand	384	
Bank overdraft		583
Capital 1 Nov 19-3		47 584
	137 294	137 294

Further examination of the books revealed the following:

(i)   A typewriter bought on 5 Oct 19-4 for £85 had been posted to the purchases account.
(ii) A payment in cash of £25 had been made to a creditor, entries of £52 had been made in the books.
(iii) J Sanders had taken £200 from the firm's bank account, the amount had been debited to the wages account.
(iv) A standing order for £5 had been paid by the bank for insurance, no entry had been made in the book.

You are required to:

(1) Redraft the trial balance after making the corrections.
(2) Explain and give an example of each of the following:
   (i) Compensating error
   (ii) Error of omission

(RSA 1)

10. The Cash Books

The term 'Cash Books' refers to a range of different styles of book used in practice, from single column to analysed multi-column ones, recording either cash only transactions or cash and bank transactions.

Joe wishes to use a three-column Cash Book, but since we have been using only a one-column Cash Book, let Joe first explain how a two-column Cash Book works.

The two-column Cash Book

Rather than keeping the Cash Account and Bank Account apart from each other, the two-column Cash Book enables us to keep them both side by side. This is more convenient and we can quickly see how much money we have got altogether.

Open the Cash Book you should now have bought to the first double page. The illustration below shows how it is ruled and what the columns are used for.

CASH BOOK

Dr			Columns 1	2	3	Dr			Columns 1	2	3
Date	Details	Folio		Cash	Bank	Date	Details	Folio		Cash	Bank

When we use only two of the three columns on each side we have a two-column Cash Book. In the illustration you can see that the book has three columns on each side. I will explain the use of column 1 later. Columns 2 on both sides are used for cash receipts and payments and columns 3 on both sides are used to record receipts into the bank and payments from the bank. Look at the following illustration.

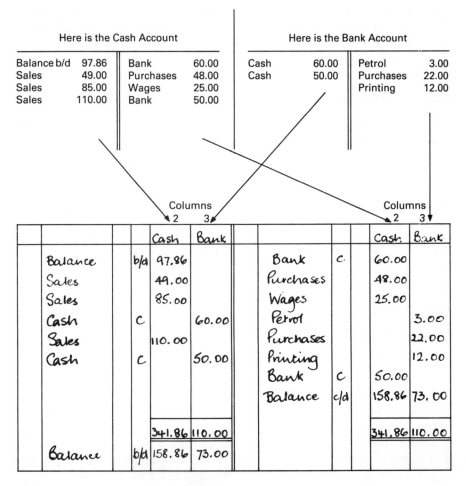

Here is the Cash Account

Balance b/d	97.86	Bank	60.00
Sales	49.00	Purchases	48.00
Sales	85.00	Wages	25.00
Sales	110.00	Bank	50.00

Here is the Bank Account

Cash	60.00	Petrol	3.00
Cash	50.00	Purchases	22.00
		Printing	12.00

Columns 2 3   Columns 2 3

			Cash	Bank					Cash	Bank
Balance	b/d	97.86			Bank	c.	60.00		
Sales		49.00			Purchases		48.00		
Sales		85.00			Wages		25.00		
Cash	c		60.00		Petrol			3.00	
Sales		110.00			Purchases			22.00	
Cash	c		50.00		Printing			12.00	
					Bank	c	50.00		
					Balance	c/d	158.86	73.00	
		341.86	110.00				341.86	110.00	
Balance	b/d	158.86	73.00						

This is how they will now look in the Cash Book.

You can see how the two separate accounts fit into one book. Previously we have had two separate books—one for cash and the other for the bank. When these two accounts are kept in one book, quite separately to the ledger, the book becomes the Cash Book—this is a *two-column* Cash Book.

Balancing the Cash Books

This means balancing both the Cash Account and the Bank Account. To balance the Cash Account, imagine the Bank columns do not exist. Then imagine that the Cash columns do not exist when you balance the Bank

Account. All you are doing is balancing a Cash Account and a Bank Account as you have already learned. Just remember to leave a line for the balances to be entered when you total the columns (it is the practice to put the totals on the same line).

Contra entries

In the example above, you will see two entries on both sides of the Cash Book that have a C written in the narrow Folio column. C is the abbreviation for *contra* (Latin for 'opposite'). It is used where an entry in the Cash Book on one side has a corresponding entry in the Cash Book on the other side. Look at the first item on the credit side of the Cash Account. It shows that £60 has gone out of Cash and into Bank. Obviously, the £60 must be recorded as going out of Cash (that is a credit entry) and into Bank (that is a debit entry). Both entries are in the Cash Book—one in the Cash Account and the other in the Bank Account.

Making entries in the Cash Book

The principles used are the same as those you learned in Chapters 2 and 3. It will be useful here to summarize the source documents of entries in the Cash Book.

Receipts
1 Copy of receipt note given to the customer.
2 Total of till roll (which should correspond to the total of cash in the till).
3 Cheques received from customers, postal orders.
4 The bank statement, which shows interest and dividends received and payments made by customers by Bank Giro transfer, should be used to verify the receipts recorded from dividend warrants and credit transfer, and Bank Giro slips. (The bank statement would be used for entry purposes only if the original documents had been lost in the post.)

Payments
1 Records of payments made in cash—e.g., receipt slips, wages sheets.
2 Postal order counterfoils.
3 Cheque book counterfoils.
4 Bank statement showing bank charges and interest paid to the bank, payments made under standing orders, amounts collected by direct debit.

Entries should be made in strict date order and no blank lines should be left between entries.

Learn Figure 10.1 to help you to remember how to enter cash sales and cash purchases.

Try these exercises. Enter the transactions in a two-column Cash Book and balance both the Cash Account and the Bank Account after making all the entries.

10.01

Mar 1 Cash sales £40.00
     3 Cheque received from J Smith £200.00
     5 Wages paid in cash £25.00
     7 Cash sales £120.00
     8 Paid £85.00 cash into bank
    10 Postages paid by cash £1.50
    15 Cash sales £171.00
    18 Drawings by the owner by cheque £25.00
    23 Purchases by cheque £48.00
    31 Cash sales £149.00

10.02

Jan 1 Balance at bank £400.00
        Balance in cash £100.00
     2 Purchased goods with cheque £50.00
     3 Received cheque from B Taylor and paid into bank £35.00
     4 Paid cash—wages £14.00
            —stationery £7.50
     5 Cash sales to date £44.00
     6 Banked £30.50
     7 Paid D Harvey cheque £35.00
     8 Cash sales to date £84

10.03

Mar 1 Balance in cash £2000.00
     2 Paid cash into bank £1500.00
     3 Bought motor van by cheque £1250.00
     4 Paid cash—wages £125.50
            —rent £114.50
     5 Cash sales to date £189.00
     6 Paid cheque to P White £142.25
     7 Received a cheque from T Blake and paid into bank £78.65
     8 Paid cash for purchases £163.80
    11 Paid wages in cash £143.45
        Paid stationery in cash £38.65
    12 Withdrew cash from bank £90.00
        Purchased office equipment by cheque £500.00

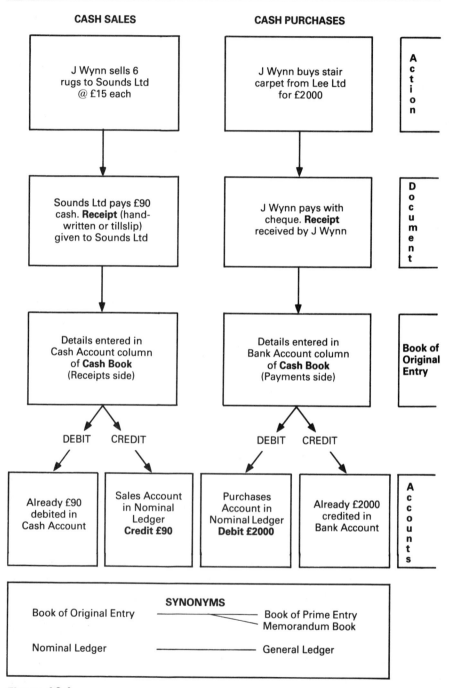

Figure 10.1

Cash discount

Let Joe recall what he said in Chapter 7. When we sell goods to our customers, we state the terms of the sales on the invoice, which may include terms for early settlement of the account. For example, an invoice for sales of £120.00 to Sounds Ltd could show that if the company settles the account within 14 days it can deduct 10 per cent from the net invoice price, this 10 per cent deduction being a *cash discount* which we allow. The idea is to encourage our customers to pay their accounts quickly. If we can get the cash quickly we can use it to buy and sell more goods, or use it to pay our own bills.

Recording the cash discount

Consider the invoice for £120 which we sent on 4 April to Sounds Ltd, and let us suppose that on 11 April the company sends us a cheque for the amount less the 10 per cent discount: 10 per cent of £120 is £12, so the cheque should be for £108. We will pay this cheque into the bank and debit the Bank Account. The corresponding credit entry will be in Sounds Ltd's account in the Sales Ledger.

Sounds Ltd   SL no

Date		Folio	£	p	Date		Folio	£	p
Apr 1	Sales	SDB	120.00		Apr 11	Bank	CB2	108.00	
					11	Discount	CB2	12.00	

The cash discount of £12 allowed to Sounds Ltd has been entered in the Discount Allowed column in the Cash Book and is credited to Sounds Ltd's account as a gain. Since it is a gain to Sounds Ltd (it owed us £120 but need only pay £108), it is a loss to us, because we have given away the value of £12 which will not be repaid. So it will be recorded in the Discount Allowed Account as a debit.

However, to save making a number of individual entries in the Discount Allowed Account, the column in the Cash Book is added up, when the Cash Book is balanced, and the total is posted as one entry to

Cash Book

Dr

Date			Disc Allow	Cash	Bank
Apr 1	Balance	b/d		13.50	491.00
11	Sounds Ltd	SL 51	12.00		108.00
28	Bow Furnishings	SL B6			150.00
29	Funfare Centre	SLF6	3.00		21.00
30	Balance	c/d			90.00
30	Disc Allowed Dr	NL D3	15.00	13.50	860.00
May 1	Balance	b/d		13.50	

Cr

Date			Disc Recd	Cash	Bank
Apr 15	Jill Taylor	SL 72	5.00		45.00
30	Trade Subs s/o	NL 54			12.00
30	Bank Charges	NL B5			5.00
30	Motor Van	NL M3			800.00
30	Balance	c/d		13.50	
30	Disc Received Cr	NL D4	5.00	13.50	860.00
May 1	Balance	b/d			90.00

the account in the ledger. The illustration opposite shows the details entered on 30 April against the total of £15 for Discount Allowed.

Similarly, if we receive discounts from our creditors, they will be gains to us and so we shall record them in the Discount Received column. For example, on 15 April we paid Jill Taylor £45 by cheque in full settlement of £50 owed to her. The entries will be as shown in the Cash Book. You should note that the Discount columns are *not* ledger *accounts*. They are memorandum columns similar to a day book. So at the end of the month we add up the columns and open ledger accounts in the Nominal Ledger for them as shown.

The entries for the monthly totals appear on the same side as in the Cash Book because they are not a double entry, but a posting from memorandum columns.

The Cash Book and double entry

The Cash Book is a book of original entry. The first record of cash received or paid is made in this book. Unlike the Sales Day Book, the Cash Book is not merely a *book of original entry*. It also contains the *accounts* for the cash and bank transactions. The entry made in the Cash Book is one half of the double entry record. Can you remember the double entry rule?

Every debit entry must have a corresponding credit entry.
Every credit entry must have a corresponding debit entry.
Cash received is *debited* in the Cash Account and *credited* to the account which records its origin.

Here are some examples.

Cash is received from a debtor:	*debit* Cash Account and *credit* the debtor's account.
Cash is received from subletting a part of the office:	*debit* Cash Account and *credit* Rent Received Account.
A cheque is paid for insurance:	*credit* Bank Account and *debit* Insurance Account.
Cash is paid to a creditor:	*credit* Cash Account and *debit* the creditor's account.

If you look back at the illustration on page 80 you will see that each entry has a reference number against it in the Folio column. The fact that such a number appears means that the corresponding (double) entry has been made in the account in the ledgers. The first entry shows that a cheque for £45 was paid to Jill Taylor. The debit has been made to her account in the Bought Ledger—account no T2 (BL T2).

Credit transfers, standing orders, bank charges

In Chapter 3 the use of standing orders and credit transfers was discussed. Our bank may receive a payment direct from some of our debtors. This is a *credit transfer* (or Giro transfer, as it is sometimes called). We may also instruct our bank to pay some of our bills, say, quarterly or yearly. This instruction to our bank is called a *standing order*. When we receive our bank statement it will show any credit transfers, standing orders, and bank charges—see below.

Bank charges are the amounts the bank deducts for the services it offers us.

J Wynn   Bank Statement

Date	Details	Dr	Cr	Bal.
Apr 28	Bow Furnishings Ltd C T		150.00	150.00
30	Sundries: Standing order			
	(Trade subs)	12.00		
	Charges	3.00		135.00

These entries on the bank statement will be recorded in the Cash Book as shown in the illustration on page 80.

Bank overdrafts and bank loans

Joe has arranged with his bank manager that the business may draw more money than it actually has in its account. The limit of the amount we can overdraw is £200. This overdrawn amount is called an *overdraft*.

10.04 Enter the balances in the Cash Book and then enter the following transactions and balance the Cash and Bank Accounts. (Do not post the double entry.)

Apr   3   Cash balance brought forward £33.50, bank overdraft £90.00
        3   Cash paid for expenses £28.00
        4   Cash sales paid direct to bank £114.00
        6   Cash sales £49.50
        7   Paid wages in cash £25.40
        8   Received a cheque from Betta Bake Co for £80.00 in full settlement of a debt of £88.00
            Cash sales £51.40
      10   Received a cheque from Sounds Ltd in payment of its debt of £120.00 less 15 per cent discount
      15   We paid Wholesale Suppliers by cheque £48.00 after deducting £2.00 discount
      16   Paid for purchases by cheque £203.00
            Bought postage stamps by cash £2.13
      21   Bow Furnishers Ltd was paid by cheque £48.00 after deducting £6.00 discount
      25   Dividend received by the bank £315.00
      28   Cash sales £112.50

While both bank loans and bank overdrafts are liabilities, there is a difference between them. When the loan is received, the amount is debited to the Bank (Current) Account and credited to a separate Bank Loan Account in the Nominal (or private) Ledger. Interest is payable on this loan for the period of the loan and usually is deducted by the bank from the Current Account, in the same way that interest on an overdraft is deducted. The bookkeeping entry for interest is to credit the Bank Account and debit the Bank Interest Payable Account.

As previously explained, an overdraft (which is another form of loan) appears in the Cash Book as a credit balance on the Bank Account.

Interest is usually charged each day on the actual amount overdrawn.

The importance of the Cash Book

Originally a Cash Account and a Bank Account were kept in the ledger. Due to the number of entries required and the importance of knowing the cash position exactly, a separate Cash Book is usually kept by a cashier, who is held responsible for its accuracy.

Joe's Rule No 10
The Cash Book is both a book of original entry and a record book, since it contains the Cash and Bank Accounts.

Dishonoured cheques

Cheques received from debtors are paid into our bank and our bank will usually enter the amount immediately as a receipt in our account. Our bank will then proceed to collect the amount stated on the cheque from our customer's bank. If our customer does not have sufficient money in his account to pay this cheque then, naturally, his bank will not pay our bank. The return of a cheque unpaid is referred to as the *dishonouring* of a cheque, and our bank will return it to us and take out of our account the amount originally entered. The cheque will usually have R/D written across it, meaning *Refer to Drawer*. We must now remember to credit the Bank Account and debit the customer, who now still owes us the sum.

10.05   In which one of the following will cash discount allowed be originally recorded?
　　　　A   Ledger
　　　　B   Journal
　　　　C   Purchases Book
　　　　D   Cash Book

(AEB 'O' June 1984)

10.06   Walter Gardner, a sole trader, enters all his cash and bank transactions in a three-column Cash Book. His transactions for the month of February 19–4 were as follows:

Feb　1　Cash in hand £37. Cash at bank £194
　　　4　Received cash from H Robins £47, in full settlement of a debt of £51
　　10　Paid by cheque to F Johnson the sum of £152, in full settlement of a debt of £160
　　11　Received from N Wilson a cheque for £32, in full settlement of a debt of £37. *This cheque was paid into the bank the same day.*

12   Paid wages in cash £44
22   Drew a cheque for £50 for office cash
25   Drew a cheque for £60 in favour of 'self', being in respect of
     Drawings
26   Paid wages in cash £42
29   Paid salaries by cheque £51
29   Paid by cheque to R Church the sum of £65 in full settlement of a
     debt of £70

Required:

(i)   Draw up the three-column Cash Book of Gardner to record the above
       transactions.
(ii)   Balance the Cash Book as at 29 February 19–4 and carry down the
       balances.
(iii) Total the two discount columns and state to which *side* of the ledger each
       entry should be made.

Note   Ledger accounts are *not* required.

(LCCI Elem)

NA 10.07   Abel Cass is a sole trader who keeps records of his cash and bank
transactions in a three-column Cash Book. His transactions for the
month of February 19–5 were as follows:

Feb   1   Cash in hand £37, Cash at bank £244
      6   Received cash £39 from D Young in full settlement of a debt of £42
     11   Paid wages in cash £41
     15   Paid by cheque £68 to J Edwards in full settlement of a debt of £75
     19   Received from H Shipley a cheque for £63. *This was paid directly into
          the bank.* The cheque was in full settlement of a debt of £68 due
          from Shipley
     21   Paid salaries by cheque £74
     23   Drew £50 from the bank for office cash
     23   Paid wages in cash £40
     28   Paid by cheque £60 to F Gill in full settlement of a debt of £65

Required:

(i)   Enter the above transactions in the three-column Cash Book of A Cass
       and balance the Cash and Bank columns.
(ii)   Carry down the balances of the Cash and Bank columns.
(iii) Total the two Discount columns and state to which account in the ledger
       each total should be posted and also which *side*.

(LCCI Elem)

NA 10.08   The books of C Baker showed the following balances on 1 July.

Cash	£40.50	*Debtors*	P Steele	£150.00
Bank	£185.00 (Dr)		K Hoe	£75.00
Stock	£931.00	*Creditors*	SRS Ltd	£185.00
Fixtures	£1010.00		J Dove Ltd	£96.50

Enter these balances in the ledger accounts. Calculate Baker's opening capital and post also to his account. Enter the following transactions in the books of original entry and post the memorandum totals to the ledger accounts at the month end. Balance all the accounts at the month end and take out a trial balance at that date.

July	1	Credit sales of £90.00 to M Hart
	2	Cash sales of £72.50; cash purchases of £65.00
	3	Paid rent in cash £25.00; stationery expenses £2.15 in cash
	4	C Baker withdrew stock value £43.00, at selling price
	5	K Hoe paid his account, deducting 5 per cent cash discount, by cheque. The cheque was entered in the Cash column
	6	A cheque value £180.00 was paid to SRS Ltd in full settlement of its account.
	7	Cash sales to date £532; cash paid to bank £571.25 (this included the cheque from K Hoe)
	8	Credit sales to P Steele £72.00 and R Reeves £86.50
	9	Motor expenses paid by cheque £33.00
	10	Paid rent in cash £25.00; cash sales £69.00
	11	Bank advised that P Steele had paid into the bank account £145 by Bank Giro. Purchases by cheque £325.00
	12	Received a cheque £90.00 from M Hart and paid direct to bank
	14	Shop display units purchased by cheque £287.65
	15	Credit sales to L Rodgers £58.00
	16	Bank advised Baker that cheque from M Hart had been returned with 'No Funds' marked. Cash sales £172.54
	17	Rent paid in cash £25.00
	21	Baker drew £19.00 cash for his own use
	24	Rent paid in cash £25.00
	25	Purchases by cheque £297.00
	26	Motor expenses paid in cash £42.50
	28	Advised by the bank that bank charges of £14.86 had been made. Cash sales £141.00
	29	Standing order payment, for hire charge of equipment, made by bank of £46.00
	30	A customer returned goods previously bought and complained about the quality. £10 cash was refunded to him. (Debit a Sales Returns Account)

31   The bank agreed to make a loan of £750.00. This was entered into our
      Current Account on this date
31   A cheque for £860.00 was paid for a secondhand motor van
31   L Rodgers paid a cheque of £55.00 in settlement of his account. £3.00
      discount was allowed. The cheque was entered into the Cash column

NA 10.09   William Smith records all his cash and bank transactions in a three-
               column Cash Book. The following are his transactions for the month of
               May 19–5.

May   1   Cash in hand £19. Cash at bank £427
      5   Paid by cheque the amount due to F Gardner (£70) less £4 discount
      8   Received from H Evans cash £38 in full settlement of the debt of
           £40
      10   Received from W Bidmead a cheque for £68 in full settlement of his debt
           of £72. This cheque was placed in Smith's cash box
      14   Paid into the bank the sum of £99—including the cheque received from
           W Bidmead on 10 May
      19   Paid wages in cash £11
      21   Paid by cheque the amount due to N Jackson (£55) less £3 discount
      28   Drew cheque for £25 for office cash

           Required:
           Draw up the three-column Cash Book for the month of May 19–5. The
           two Discount columns should be totalled. You should state to which
           ledger account these totals should be posted and on which side of the
           ledger account the entry should be made.

                                                                  (LCCI Elem)

11. Credit Purchases

Whenever goods are bought on credit, the buyer will need to record the value of the goods purchased and the amount now owing to the supplier. The supplier to whom money is owed is called a *creditor*.

Creditors have accounts in the Bought Ledger (or Creditors' Ledger) and, as you would expect, they have credit balances on their accounts. Compare these two illustrations.

Bookkeeping entries for cash purchase

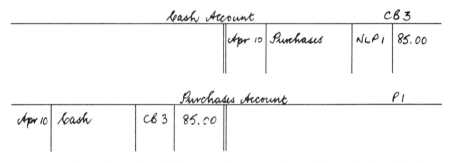

Goods are bought and paid for in cash. A receipt will be obtained by Joe. The payment is posted to the Purchases Account.

Bookkeeping entries for credit purchase

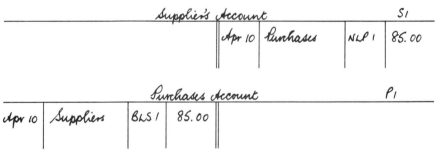

Goods are bought on credit. An invoice will be received by Joe showing how much he owes to the supplier, as shown in the ledger entries.

In both cases, the Purchases Account is debited because we have received the value of the goods. In the case of the cash purchase, cash was given, therefore credit the Cash Account. In the case of a credit purchase, the supplier has given the goods (until he is paid) and therefore his account is credited.

11.01 If the supplier were to be paid cash of £85.00 on 11 April what two entries would be required to record the payment?

Joe's Rule No 4 (learned in Chapter 4) is that no entry should be made in a ledger unless a record first appears in a book of original entry. Let Joe continue the explanation regarding the credit purchases of carpets and accessories.

Let me draw you a simple diagram, which shows a page of the Bought Day Book (which is another book of original entry). It is entered from invoices received. Only the date of invoice, the supplier's name, and the invoice total are entered.

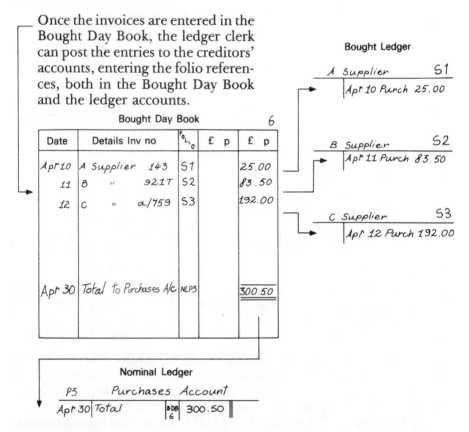

Once the invoices are entered in the Bought Day Book, the ledger clerk can post the entries to the creditors' accounts, entering the folio references, both in the Bought Day Book and the ledger accounts.

Bought Ledger

A Supplier   S1
Apr 10 Purch 25.00

B Supplier   S2
Apr 11 Purch 83.50

C Supplier   S3
Apr 12 Purch 192.00

Bought Day Book   6

Date	Details Inv no	Fo.	£ p	£ p
Apr 10	A Supplier 143	S1		25.00
11	B " 921T	S2		83.50
12	C " a/759	S3		192.00
Apr 30	Total to Purchases A/c	NLP3		300.50

Nominal Ledger

P3   Purchases Account
Apr 30 Total |BDB 6| 300.50

At the end of the month the total of all the invoices is posted to the Purchases Account in the Nominal Ledger.

You can see that the three credit entries in the individual creditors' accounts (totalling £300.50) have a corresponding debit entry in the Purchases Account.

Detailed entries in the Bought Day Book

Look at the invoice below, and see how it may be entered.

Inv no B/1735	Wearing Co Ltd 21 Farr Drive Greenway
Invoice to: J Wynn	
22 m A1 Tufted @ £3 per m	66.00
10 m B1 Beige @ 50p per m	5.00
	71.00
25% trade discount	17.75
Net total	53.25

Bought Day Book

Date	Details Inv no	£ p	£ p
Apr 12	Wearing Co 81735		
	22 m A1 @ £3 per m	66.00	
	10 m B1 @ 50p per m	5.00	
		71.00	
	Less 25% trade disc	17.75	53.25

Here is another invoice. See how this one is entered.

BKW Carpets To: Joe Wynn	Inv no 77/1934 Date April 15		
		£ p	£ p
10	metres Broadloom @ £4 per metre *Less* 20% trade discount	40.00 8.00	32.00
20	metres Underlay @ £1 per metre *Less* 50% trade discount	20.00 10.00	10.00
	Net Invoice Total 2½% 7 days		42.00

Bought Day Book

Apr 15	B K W Carpets	£ p	£ p
	10 metres of Broad-loom @ £4 per m	40.00	
	Less 20% t disc	8.00	
		32.00	
	20 metres Underlay @ £1 per m	20.00	
	Less 50% t d 10.00	10.00	42.00

In the above illustration the calculation on the invoice is shown within the details section in order to show the two separate calculations and yet leave in the right-hand column the amount that is to be posted to the Bought Ledger. *Only one figure* should appear in the right-hand column for each invoice. This figure will be added to all the other invoice totals in that column to obtain the weekly or monthly total of credit purchases.

Totalling entries in the Bought Day Book

Instead of copying all the details from the purchase invoices into the Bought Day Book, only the invoice *total* is entered. So the two invoices illustrated above will appear in the Bought Day Book as follows:

	Bought Day Book			**BDB3**
Apr 12	Wearing Co Inv no B1735			53.25
Apr 15	BKW Carpets Inv no 77/1934			42.00
Apr 30	Dr Purchases A/c			95.25

The general rule is that the Bought Day Book is entered with the invoice totals only. If anyone wishes to see the details of the amount owing to each supplier, it is necessary only to refer to the invoice, which will have been filed away. It is because the invoice is usually readily available for reference that the time-consuming job of copying all the invoice details is avoided.

Joe's Rule No 11
The Bought Day Book records only credit purchases of goods for resale and is not an account—it is a memorandum book.

Remember Only the *net total* is entered in the creditor's account since it is only the *net amount* that is owed.

11.02 Make detailed entries of the following invoices received in the Bought Day Book.

May 2 Allweather Covers Ltd
60 metres narrow plastic sheet @ £1.50 per metre net
100 metres coated gauge @ 50p per metre net

3 Allday Protectors Ltd
12.5 metres heavy duty tarpaulin @ £10.00 per metre less 10 per cent trade discount

5 Allpurpose Sheeting Ltd
60 metres printed cotton @ 45p per metre less 40 per cent trade discount
150 metres ribbed polythene @ £3.00 per metre less 33⅓ per cent trade discount

Total the Bought Day Book.

11.03 On 1 May Circular Tracks started business with a bank balance of £2505 and cash in hand of £143.00. Enter these amounts and also the transactions below in the books of original entry. Post entries to the ledger accounts, and balance the Cash Book. Balance the accounts and prepare a trial balance.

Remember The capital should be entered with the total of the bank balance and cash in hand at 1 May.

May 2   Cash purchases £48.50
          Invoice received from Square Way Dealers £73.00
          Rent paid by cheque £19.50
     3   Invoice no 313 issued to Sampson Brothers for goods sold on credit, value £98.00
     4   Motor repairs paid by cheque £49.50
          Wages paid in cash £85.40
          Cash sales £133.45
          Purchase by cheque £600.00
     5   Invoice received from Round Wheels Ltd—net invoice total £256.00
          Invoice no 314 issued to Tubular Poles Ltd for goods totalling £76.00
          Petrol paid in cash £5.50
     6   Invoice no 315 issued to Wheeltappers Institute for goods totalling £100.00
     8   Cash sales £68.50
          Invoice received from Rollover Blind Ltd—total £157.00
     11   Wages paid in cash £81.45
     12   Sampson paid his bill by cheque deducting 5 per cent for cash discount
          All cash was paid into bank

11.04 Which of the following documents does a bookkeeper need to record a purchase of goods in the purchases day book?

A   The purchaser's order
B   The delivery note
C   The credit note
D   The supplier's invoice

(AEB 'O' Nov 1984)

11.05 The following information has been extracted from a firm's records at the end of an accounting period:

	£
Opening trade creditors	1 100
Closing trade creditors	1 200
Cash paid to suppliers	20 000
Discount received	1 000

What is the total figure for purchases for the accounting period?

A   £22 300
B   £21 100
C   £20 900
D   £19 800

(AEB 'O' Nov 1984)

NA 11.06   Which of the following would *not* be classified as revenue expenditure?

A   Building an extension to a warehouse
B   Legal costs of collecting debts
C   Rent
D   Purchases of stock

(PEI Elem)

NA11.07   A special trade allowance operating between firms in the same trade is a

A   trade discount
B   cash discount
C   nominal account
D   credit account

(PEI Elem)

NA 11.08   A creditor is

A   someone to whom the business owes money
B   someone who is in debt to the business
C   a type of shareholder
D   the owner of a business

(PEI Elem)

12. Bought Ledger (or Creditors' Ledger)

Joe has demonstrated the use of the Bought Day Book. From this book postings are made to the accounts of the suppliers which are credited. All suppliers' accounts are kept together in a separate ledger and, since suppliers are people to whom we owe money, the ledger is often called a *Creditors' Ledger*. Another common name for it is the *Bought Ledger*. Remember, then, that these two titles refer to the same ledger—the one in which creditors' accounts are kept.

As Joe says, I need to know how much I owe to suppliers, so a separate ledger account for each supplier records what I have purchased (on credit), what payments I have made to the supplier, what goods were sent back to him (called 'returns'), and what discounts (if any) I was allowed. Each account will have its own Bought Ledger reference number. In a bound ledger each page is numbered consecutively, and BL3 would be the third account, on the third page of the Bought Ledger. As I have a large number of suppliers' accounts I group them alphabetically as follows:

Allyn Displays Ltd	Account A1
American Pile Carpets	Account A2
BKW Carpets PLC	Account B1
Bemrose & Co	Account B2
Books Galore	Account B3
⋮	
Dalton Tin Tacks	Account D5
⋮	
Wearing Co Ltd	Account W1

I use a loose-leaf binder which forms the ledger so that new accounts can be entered in the appropriate place.

Let us look at Wearing Co Ltd's account in the Bought Ledger.

Wearing Co Ltd				W1
	Apr 12	Purchases	BDB 3	53.25

The credit entry shows that the supplier has 'given' the value of £53.25

12.01 Can you remember where we record the value 'received'?
The folio reference is BDB3—showing that the entry has been posted from
the Bought Day Book page 3.

Payments to creditors

Authorization for payment
Before I sign any invoice I need to be sure that:

1 The carpets or carpet fittings have been received.
2 The items received correspond to those ordered.
3 The items received were not in any way damaged.
4 The proper discount has been given.

The following procedures are in operation to do this:

1 When goods are received they are noted in the Goods Received Book,
kept by the storeman. This is the proof of receipt by us.
2 A copy of each purchase order is given to the storeman so that he can
see whether or not the items received correspond to those ordered.
3 If any damaged carpets are received the storeman will make out a
separate 'Damaged Goods' slip and note this in the Goods Received
Book. The slip comes into the office and I can then telephone the
supplier immediately. If the goods are correct then the storeman signs
his copy of the purchase order and sends it to me.
4 When I receive the invoice I check it against the copy of the purchase
order signed by the storeman. I can check the price charged and if
everything is in order I sign the invoice. It will then be used to enter
the Bought Day Book. At the end of the month the signed invoice is
the basis for paying the supplier.

Bookkeeping entries for payment
When we pay Wearing Co Ltd the double entry will be:

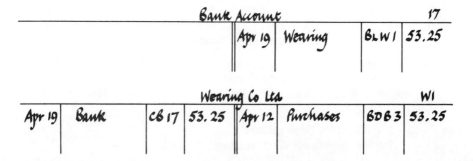

Bank Account			17
	Apr 19 Wearing	BLW1	53.25

Wearing Co Ltd				W1
Apr 19 Bank	CB17	53.25	Apr 12 Purchases	BDB3	53.25

Joe's Rule No 12
Credit the supplier's account with the value of the goods we have purchased on credit, and debit the supplier's account with amounts paid to him.

Before Wearing was paid the amount owing, the account had a credit balance of £53.25. An easy point to remember—a creditor has a credit balance on his account in the Bought Ledger. A credit balance means that we *owe* that sum to the supplier, therefore creditors equal *liabilities*. A liability is an amount owing by our business. The Bought Ledger therefore contains accounts of creditors and shows the liabilities of the business for the credit purchases of goods, the credit purchases of assets, and amounts owing for services (but you will have to wait until later to learn more about the last aspect).

Learn Figure 12.1 to help you remember how to enter credit transactions.

Cash discounts received

Many of our suppliers offer a cash discount for prompt payment of the bill (discount received), as our business would offer a cash discount to our customers (discount allowed) to encourage them to pay us quickly.

Using BKW Carpet's invoice on page 90 as an example, we may deduct 2.5 per cent if we pay the bill within seven days. Our cheque will be for £42 less 2.5 per cent = £42 less £1.05 = £40.95. The discount of £1.05 will be shown in the Discount Received column (memorandum only) in the Cash Book—and posted to BKW's account in the ledger at the same time as the payment. The total of the entries in the Discount Received column in the Cash Book will be posted to the credit of the Discount Received Account in the Nominal Ledger at the end of the week or month, or whenever the Cash Book is balanced.

Learn Figure 12.2 to help you remember entries for discounts.

12.02   The balances in the Bought Ledger of Ann Royal are All Weather Covers £678.32, BKW Carpets £26.00, Yates £3.26.

  (a) Enter the following invoice in the Bought Day Book and state the total value posted to the Purchases Account.
  (b) Post the entries to the Bought Ledger and list the creditors' balances on 15 January.

Jan   2   Inv 991 from Yates £63.92
          Inv 901B from All Weather Covers £32.88

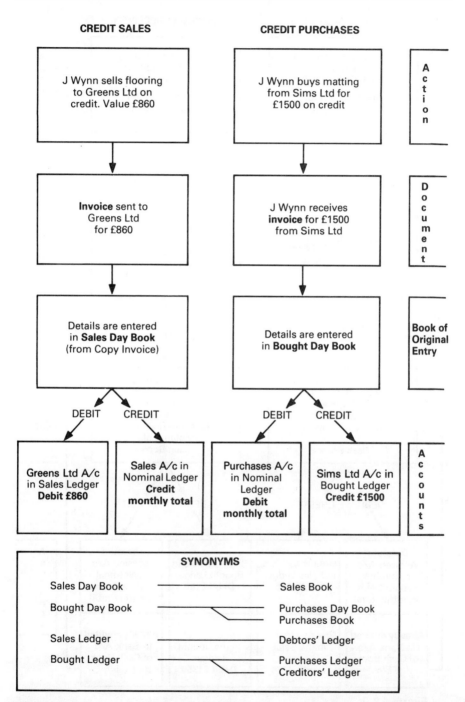

Figure 12.1

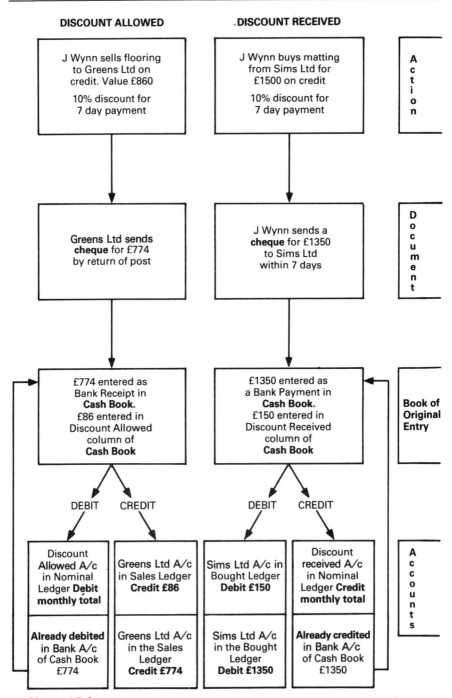

Figure 12.2

Jan 5   Inv 6100B from BKW Carpets £212.08
          Inv 86Z1 from Easi-File £12.83
          Inv 006 from Yates £81.63
          Inv 87Z6 from Easi-File £16.29
      9   Inv 7165C from BKW Carpets £212.08
     10   Inv 012 from Yates £2.32
     13   Inv 9018D from BKW Carpets £212.08
          Inv 116 from Yates £13.96

12.03 Draw up the statement that Bill Byer will expect to receive at the end of
October from his supplier, Susan Cellar, in respect of the following transactions. Make out the statement with the correct headings and names.

Oct   5   Goods invoiced to Byer at a net value of £36.00 on Invoice no SC/432.
     12   Byer sent a cheque in respect of his purchases on 5 October deducting
          5 per cent cash discount.
     18   Goods invoiced to Byer (Invoice no SC/443) for a catalogue value of £90
          less 30 per cent trade discount.
     21   Byer received a debit note from Cellar for £10.00, being a charge for con-
          tainers used in dispatching the goods invoiced on 18 October.

12.04 (a) Record the following transactions in the Cash Book and other books of
              original entry.
         (b) Total and post the subsidiary books to the ledger.
         (c) Balance all the accounts and extract a trial balance at 30 September.

Sept 1   L Hockey started business as a painter and decorator under the name of L
          & H Painters and paid £580 into a newly opened business bank account.
          He also brought into the business his motor van, valued at £800.
      2   The business purchased ladders and brushes by cheque costing £340.
          Tables and other equipment costing £250 were bought on credit from
          N Evans & Co Ltd
      4   Materials costing £80 were purchased on credit from P & D Supplies Ltd
          and costing £42 from Allday Services Ltd
      8   A cheque was drawn from the bank for £55, £35 being paid as wages,
          £7.50 for miscellaneous materials, £2.50 for stationery, and the
          reminder being kept by L Hockey
     10   Invoices were sent to T Hawker for £88 and C Hat for £59
     15   A cheque was sent in payment of P & D Suppliers Ltd's account and the
          servicing costs of £50 was paid by cheque for the motor van
     18   Materials were purchased on credit from P & D Supplies for £166 and a
          cheque for £65 was drawn for cash. Cash was paid for wages £35 and
          Hockey took £20 for his own use
     21   Cash sales of £15.00 were received out of which miscellaneous
          materials costing £6.50 were purchased
     22   Invoices were sent to S Pecker for £185.00 and Mr and Mrs Voyce
          for £248.00

Sept 24   Cash withdrawn from bank totalled £106: £38.00 was paid as wages, £4.50 was spent on stationery and postage, and materials cost £33.50. L Hockey retained £30 for his own use
   25   Invoices were sent to L Affter for £175.00, W Hisper for £70.00 and Cylant Receivers Ltd for £200.00
   29   Cheque for £88 received from T Hawker
          Cash sales totalled £22.00
   30   Invoice, for petrol and oil used in the month, for £39.50 was received from A Garage Ltd
          A cheque for £80.00 was drawn and paid as follows: wages £45.00, Drawings £30.00, £5 casual labour

NA 12.05   The trial balance of Ken Stevens on 30 April 19–4 was as follows:

Ken Stevens
Trial Balance as at 30 April 19–4

	Dr £	Cr £
Sales		20 750
Purchases	13 170	
General expenses	4 972	
Fixtures	2 500	
K Gibson	1 130	
T Lowe		700
Bank	1 720	
Drawings	2 800	
Capital		7 228
Stock	2 386	
	28 678	28 678

During the month of May the following transactions took place:

May   1   Bought goods on credit from T Lowe £85
   2   Sold goods on credit to K Gibson £105
   18   Banked cash sales £400
   20   K Gibson paid £680 by cheque in part settlement of his account
   26   Paid general expenses by cheque £97.
          Sent a cheque value £300 to T Lowe in part settlement of his account
   28   Paid general expenses by cheque £275
   30   Withdrew £300 from the bank for his own use.

You are required to:

(a)   Open the accounts at 1 May 19–4.
(b)   Record the transactions directly in the accounts by means of double entries. *Do not* use subsidiary books.
(c)   Extract a trial balance at 31 May 19–4.   (RSA 1)

NA 12.06 The basic principle of double entry bookkeeping is that 'for every debit entry there must be a corresponding credit entry'.
Explain how this statement is followed when posting from:

(a) The Purchases Day Book
(b) The Sales Returns Book
(c) The Cash Book

Give an example of each to illustrate your answer.

(RSA 1)

NA 12.07 (a) The ledger of your firm is subdivided into the cash book, sales ledger, purchases ledger, the general ledger and the private ledger.
In which subdivision of the ledger would you expect to find each of the following accounts?

(i) J Allsop, a customer
(ii) J Smith, a supplier
(iii) sales account
(iv) purchases account
(v) the proprietor's capital account
(vi) bad debts account
(vii) bank account

(b) State the sources of information from which the sales ledger account is compiled.

(RSA 1)

12.08 On 1 June the following balances were in the Bought Ledger books of Sheila Hogg Co, an office furniture manufacturer: Ark Ltd £210.03; Barons £26.32; Office Supplies Ltd £426.00; Sevenways Garage £90.00; Woodman Timber £8.63.
During the month of June the following transactions occurred.

June 2   £34.50 of desk handles was bought from Office Supplies Ltd (Inv 931)

5   Middlewich Looms supplied £834.60 of materials of which £60 was for containers (Inv 106)

8   £66.23 of material was supplied by Barons (Inv 1011B), £142.36 of timber from Woodman Timber (Inv 9604) and hinges from Sevenways Garage (Inv 89901) for £12.99

15   Cheques were sent to Woodman Timber for £150.99, to Barons for £26.32 and to Ark Ltd for £200.00

16   Drawer slides were bought for £37.90 from Office Supplies Ltd (Inv 1061), material from Blackmore Wholesale for £92.26 (Inv B491), and brackets for £20.50 from Sevenways Garage (Inv 99004)

June 22   Cheques were sent to Office Supplies Ltd for £426.00 and Sevenways
           Garage for £90.00.
           Castors, nails, and glue were supplied by Blackmore Wholesale for
           £67.91 (Inv B649)
      23   Hinges bought from Sevenways Garage (Inv 99864) cost £12.32
           (a) Enter the invoices in the Bought Day Book.
           (b) What is the total to be posted to the Purchases account for
                June?
           (c) Record payments in the Cash Book and post to the ledger
                accounts.
           (d) Post the Day Book entries to the Bought Ledger and balance the
                suppliers' accounts.
           (e) List the suppliers' balances at the end of June.

NA 12.09   Enter the following transactions in the purchases and sales books of
               T Stubbs and post to the ledger.

Jan   6   Sold goods to J Black for £65 less 20% trade discount
       8   Purchased goods from R Smith £59
       9   Bought goods from N Jackson £34
       9   Sold goods to P Shore £48
      11   Invoiced P Townsend goods £84, less 25% trade discount
      12   C Carr purchased goods £57

                                                              (PEI Elem)

13. Further Consideration of Debtors/Creditors

Recording sales returns

Sales returns are sometimes called *returns inwards*. Customers may not be satisfied with the goods we have sold them; we may, in error, have dispatched incorrect goods; or the goods may be damaged in transit. Whatever the reason, some record will be kept of goods returned to the business.

From the bookkeeping viewpoint, we must know the value of the returns, otherwise we cannot make any entries in the books. Two situations arise frequently.

1 Customers return goods which have been bought previously for cash. The bookkeeping entries for the actual amount refunded are:

Credit Cash Account (or Bank Account, if paid by cheque): Debit Sales Returns Account.

2 Customers return goods which have been bought previously on credit; the customer having been invoiced. Since the customer's account has been debited in the Sales Ledger with the original invoice value, any refund needs only to be credited to his account in the ledger (which reduces the amount owing to us). The double entry in the accounts will be:

Credit the customer's account in the Sales Ledger: Debit the Sales Returns Account.

Sales Returns Book

Before these entries above can be made, you will need to know the actual amount to be credited. This can be found in the Sales Returns Book (or Returns Inwards Book) which is a book of original entry and is a record of *credit notes* (with an abbreviation of C/N) sent to customers. The Sales Returns Book is a memorandum book in the same way as the Sales Day Book.

The procedure is as follows—goods returned by the customer are noted by our storekeeper, who sends the details to me. If I agree to the refund I arrange for a credit note to be prepared and sent to the customer. Our credit notes are printed in *red* so that they do not become confused with invoices. The credit note is sent to the customer to tell him of the amount which has been credited (in our books) to his account.

In a larger business the Sales Manager will authorize the Accountant to prepare and issue credit notes. The copy of the credit note is used to enter our Sales Returns Book with the details of the customer, the goods returned, and the total of the credit note. The total of each credit note is posted to the credit of the customer's account in the Sales Ledger and the monthly total of the Sales Returns Book is posted to the debit of the Sales Returns Account in the Nominal Ledger.

Allowances, containers, errors

There are many reasons why we will need to credit customers' accounts even though we do not actually receive goods returned. The customer may wish to keep damaged goods if we reduce the price to him. Such a reduction is called an *allowance*, and requires a credit note. Customers previously overcharged will need a reduction equivalent to the overcharge; customers previously invoiced for returnable containers will expect a refund when the containers are returned. In all such cases, a credit note is prepared and sent to the customer.

Example

July   3   B Baker returned seven rugs that were badly stained. He had previously been charged £35.0 each and was now given full credit on C/N 093

     18   P Edwards returned a length of carpet which had damage marks and was unsuitable for use. We allowed him a credit of £114.0 on C/N 094

     21   C Woolerton informed us that we had overcharged him £4.00 on Invoice no A/1643. This was checked and the error agreed. C/N 095 for £4 was sent to him

     28   C/N 096 was sent to B Baker for £15 for containers returned

	Sales Returns Book				16
July 3	B Baker Rugs returned	C/N 093	SL		245.00
			B3		
18	P Edwards Damaged carpet	C/N 094	E1		114.00
21	C Woolerton Overcharge	C/N 095	W2		4.00
28	B Baker Containers	C/N 096	B3		15.00
31	Sales Returns Account	Dr	NL S6		378.00

In the Sales Ledger the accounts would be entered as follows.

			£ baker				*B 3*
June 21	Sales	SDB 6	350	July 5	Sales Returns	SRB 16	245
				July 28	" " (containers)	"	15.00

			£ Woolerton				*W 2*
July 16	Sales	SDB 7	84.00	July 21	Sales Returns (Overcharge)	SRB 16	4.00

			Sales Returns Account				*S 6*
July 31	Total	SRB 16	378.0				

			P Edwards				*E 1*
May 28	Sales	SDB 5	1814.0	July 18	Sales Returns	SRB 16	114.0

Note the following points.

1 The reason for the credit is written in the Details column of the ledger account.
2 The Sales Returns Book is entered in exactly the same way as the Sales Day Book.
3 The double entry is completed when the total in the Sales Returns Book is posted at the month end to the ledger account.

Recording purchases returns

Purchases returns (or *returns outwards*) arise when we find that goods supplied to us are faulty, incorrect, or damaged. The goods may be sent back by us to the supplier, or we may wish to retain them if the supplier will give us an allowance. We may also return to him containers with which we have previously been charged. In all these cases we expect him to credit our account in his books with the amount of the allowance or refund. We will receive his *credit note* showing us the amount credited to our account in his Sales Ledger. This document is recorded in our *Purchases Returns Book* (or *Returns Outwards Book*). This book is ruled in the same way as the Bought Day Book, and it too is a book of original entry. In posting to the ledger, remember that the supplier's account in the Bought Ledger is *debited* (since we now owe him less), and the total of the Book is posted to the *credit* of the Purchases Returns Account.

Learn Figure 13.1 to help you remember entries for returns.

Bad debts and credit control

In this business our credit customers are usually traders. A business relies on customers paying their debts, so I try to avoid taking on customers who cannot pay. If I have a new trade customer I sometimes say that the invoice must be paid before I send the goods—then I know I have been paid. Mostly if credit is required I ask the customer for two references to check both his genuineness as a trader and his creditworthiness. One of these should be a *'trade' reference*, that is from another business man. I always check with the persons given as referees that the new customer is known personally to them. I ask how long the new customer has been in business, whether or not his creditworthiness is as much as I am prepared to allow him, and what is his connection with the trader.

Sometimes I go to see a new customer to look at his business and premises and talk to the owner or manager. I have occasionally used the services of an agency which specializes in assessing the creditworthiness of people and firms.

Even so, some customers may not pay their debts. If it is known that a debtor cannot pay, it is incorrect for his account to be kept in the Sales Ledger—since the asset is no longer an asset! The amount which cannot be obtained from him is lost and must be considered as a loss. It is transferred from his account in the Sales Ledger to a Bad Debts Account in the Nominal Ledger. The double entry in the account is:

Credit customer's account: Debit Bad Debts Account

The authority to do this will be an entry I will make in the Journal (to be explained later). In a bigger business the accountant would be the only person authorized to make this Journal entry.

Overdue accounts and new orders

When a customer's order is received there is a check made on his account. If his account has an outstanding overdue amount or has reached its credit limit then the order is not processed and the customer is notified to this effect. As debtors receive our statement every month

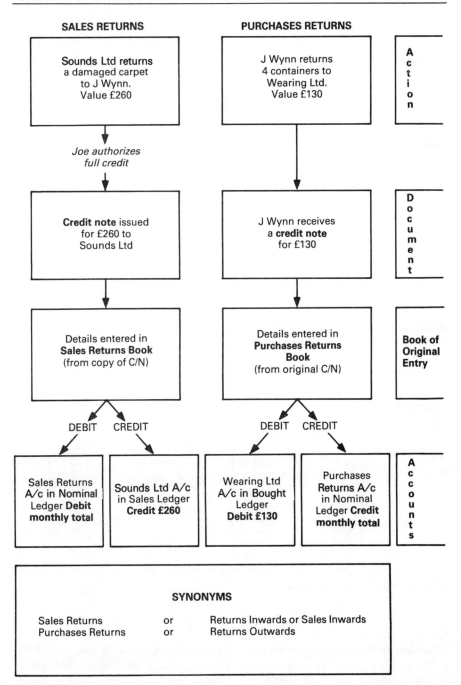

Figure 13.1

they can see exactly how much they owe us. If payment hasn't been received by the second month a rubber stamp is used to show on the statement

> # OVERDUE ACCOUNT
> ## Please Pay Immediately
> ## NO FURTHER ORDER ACCEPTED

If nothing happens I usually ring up the customer and ask for payment, and state that if no payment is forthcoming I will have to take legal action.

Dividends in bankruptcy

It often happens that when a business goes into liquidation, or an individual goes bankrupt, the business debts cannot be paid in full, but there is some money available. This is distributed proportionately among the creditors. For example, if one of our debtors owes in total £10 000, but can only raise £4000, then the amount each creditor will receive will be a *dividend* of 40p in the pound. So if we are owed £120 we will actually receive 120 x 40p = £48. The entry in our Sales Ledger Account will be:

A Debtor Account

Feb 1	Balance	b/d	120.00	Feb 16	Bank	CB 16	48.00
				Feb 16	Bad Debts A/c	J 3	72.00
			120.00				120.00

The authorization for Bad Debts entry will be an entry in the Journal, which I shall explain later.

Dishonoured cheques

Cheques from customers are paid into the bank account and our bank collects this sum from the customer's bank. Should our bank not be able to collect this, because the customer's account has insufficient money in it, then our bank returns the cheque to us marked R/D (Refer to Drawer).

The amount previously entered into our Bank Account has now not in fact been received, so we must take it out of our Bank Account and debit the customer who still owes this sum. This was discussed in Chapter 10 on the Cash Book and mentioned here because it can cause a situation to arise which is discussed below (Disallowed discounts).

The following two sections explain the double entry postings to the ledger accounts. The book of original entry used to record these details is the Journal.

Disallowed discounts

These usually arise because a debtor's cheque has been dishonoured (see Chapter 10). The dishonoured cheque is credited in the Cash Book but no discount (previously allowed and now disallowed) is entered. *Remember* There are no memorandum columns in the Cash Book for discounts disallowed.

1. (a) If a discount previously allowed to a customer is now disallowed, then the original ledger entries have to be reversed. The original double entry was:

   Debit Discount Allowed Account: Credit customer's account.

   Obviously, therefore, the reverse (since he now owes this sum) is:

   Debit customer's account: Credit Discount Allowed Account

   The point to note here is that the discount disallowed is not shown in the Cash Book.

   (b) Discounts not allowable, but claimed. If a customer pays his account and deducts discount to which he is not entitled—then the actual amount received posted to his account will leave the amount unpaid as a balance.

   The monthly statement sent to the debtor will show him that the discount he claimed has not been allowed.

2. Discounts previously received from creditors. It may arise that we pay a creditor and deduct a cash discount, when in fact we are not entitled to do so. The original entries for the discount received will need to be reversed:

   Credit supplier's account (we owe this amount to him): Debit Discount Received Account (to cancel the original credit entry).

Offsetting accounts

We may buy goods from, and sell goods to the same person. In this case this person will have two accounts in our books—one in the Sales Ledger and another in the Bought Ledger. This is necessary to show exactly what the position is between us, and the two sets of transactions should be kept quite separate. We pay him for goods bought; he pays us for goods we have sold him. However, even if we want to do this, he may wish to offset one account against the other. For example, if we owe Wearing Ltd £50 and Wearing Ltd owes us £60, rather than pay us the £60 (and wait for us to pay it £50) it may simply pay us £10, which is the difference owing to us.

If this happens, it will be necessary to effect what is sometimes called a *contra* entry (*contra* means within the same account), that of transferring £50 from his account in our Bought Ledger to his account in our Sales Ledger, as shown below.

Wearing Ltd (Sales Ledger) Account

| Bal | b/d | 60.00 | Transfer from Bought Ledger A/c | J6 | 50.00 |
| | | | Bank | CB10 | 10.00 |

Wearing Ltd (Bought Ledger) Account

| Transfer to Sales Ledger A/c | J6 | 50.00 | Bal | b/d | 50.00 |

Credit transactions other than goods for resale

The Bought Day Book used so far has recorded only credit purchases of goods for resale. Many services are provided on credit and assets are also often bought on credit. Any invoice received represents a credit 'purchase' be it stationery, decorating, telephones, assets or goods. It is possible to operate a simple three-column Bought Day Book, which analyses purchases between 'Goods for Resale' and 'Others'. The personal accounts of creditors are entered as normal, and so is the Purchases Account. The column headed 'Others' will need analysing for posting to the nominal accounts. An example is shown below.

Example

Bought Day Book

Date	Details	Folio	Goods for Resale	Others	Total
Oct 4	ABC Ltd	BLA1	149.00		149.00
5	Sevenways Garage Ltd (Petrol)	BL53		25.00	25.00
10	Office Supplies Ltd (Desk)	BLD1		83.00	83.00
18	Printing Company (Stationery)	BLP6		15.75	15.75
	Dr Purchases A/c	NLP1	149.00	123.75	272.75
	Dr Motor Running A/c	NLM3		25.00	
	Dr Office Fixtures A/c	NLD1		83.00	
	Dr Stationery A/c	NLS2		15.75	

As an alternative to the analysed Bought Day Book a credit transaction (other than goods for resale) could be entered in the Journal.

Joe's Rule No 13
If a record is made in a book of original entry, it must have a document as evidence of the transaction.

Costing jobs

What is job costing?

This is working out the price to charge to customers. Since each customer represents a separate job of work the term used is 'to cost a job'.

So far, in dealing with customers, all you have seen is the invoice made out to them for the goods and services we have supplied. How do I determine the price to be charged? The salesman who sees the customer and gives a quotation for the job needs to know:

1 The amount of carpet and accessories (underlay or felt, gripper rods, door strips, etc.) and their prices.
2 The time it will take for the carpet fitters to lay the carpet—and their rate of pay.
3 The extra amount to be added to cover all the other costs incurred by

the business (salesman's salary, warehouse employees' wages, your salary, rent, insurance, and so on)—called overheads.
4 The amount to be added for profit.

Let us deal with each point in order.

1 *Direct materials*   If I know the sizes and quantities of carpets and other items to be charged to a job these materials are called *direct materials*. The prices paid by us for these are known so the salesman keeps an up-to-date price list to enable him to calculate the cost of them—when he has worked out the quantities required.
2 *Direct labour*
   (a) *'Man hours'*   The salesman who visits the customer has to work out the time it will take to complete the job. He calculates the 'man hours' required. With the contracts for large areas he will decide that perhaps three carpet fitters will need to work together. With a smaller job he will know whether or not one man alone can do the job. Having decided the 'man hours' required, he multiplies the figure by the hourly rate of pay to give the direct wages or direct labour cost.
   (b) *Wage rate per hour*   You know that the carpet fitters earn £200 per week and since five of them are employed the total wages for the year are $5 \times £200 \times £52 = £52\,000$. However, although they are paid for 52 weeks they each have four weeks' holiday in the year so the effective working weeks are 48. The working week is 40 hours per man but since they have to travel to the customer's premises the effective working hours per week are only 30. (This also allows for illness and time lost for other reasons.)

     Consequently the effective working hours during the year are $5 \times 30 \times 48 = 7200$.

     Therefore the direct labour rate per man hour = $£52\,000 \div 7200 = £7.22$.
3 *Overheads*
   (a) *What they entail*   In order to provide the service we do, our business has to use a warehouse, a shop, motor vans, tools, equipment. It employs warehousemen, a shop assistant, salesmen, carpet fitters, and office staff. It pays insurance, rates, postage and stationery, vehicle running expenses, advertising, and a lot more. The cost of employing carpet fitters can be charged directly to the jobs they do, but all the other expenses cannot be directly charged to jobs. How much of the motor van's road fund licence should be charged to one particular customer? How much of your salary should be charged to the same

customer? The way we charge overheads is explained below but try to understand why the customers' jobs have to be charged with overheads. Remember that the income of the business has to be sufficient to pay *all* the expenses. Therefore all customers will have to pay sufficient to cover not only the direct costs (carpet fitters and materials) but also a proper proportion of all the other costs. Charging overheads to jobs is referred to as 'overhead recovery', i.e., recovering overheads by charging them to the jobs completed.

(b) *Overhead recovery rate per hour*   I have calculated that the total overhead expenses for the year are £60 000. The customers for whom we do work will have to be charged this amount and one way to do it is to base the charge on the direct labour hours worked. As we have already calculated the direct labour hours to be 7200 the overhead rate per direct labour hour will be £60 000 ÷ 7200 = £8.33.

4 *Profit*

(a) The final part of working out how much to charge customers is to add to the cost determined above an amount for profit. To do this I have to think about how much profit I want to make in the year and then charge this, in some way, to the customers.

(b) Since I have a large amount of capital tied up with stock and premises and other assets, I expect a profit that will represent both a fair return on capital and a fair reward for the work I do. I have calculated that I need £30 000 per year and if this is divided by 7200 (the direct labour hours) the additional rate to charge customers is £30 000 ÷ 7200 = £4.12.

Job Cost Sheet

When the salesman is discussing an order with a customer he will need to prepare a quotation. To help him do this—and to act as a permanent record—he completes his part of the Job Cost Sheet. You will see that the one illustrated on page 114 is divided into two halves. The left-hand side shows the details entered by the salesman. The right-hand side has details entered by the foreman of the carpet layers to show the actual quantities used and the actual time taken. I can then complete the actual costs to see whether or not the price we charged was either more or less than the cost we incurred.

The far right-hand column shows the variances between the quoted prices and the actual prices. In the case shown the actual cost is £50.45 more than the estimated cost. You will see, though, that the customer is to be charged the extra £50 and so the real difference (or

J Wynn (Carpet Suppliers)	**JOB COST SHEET**			No 567 Job no: 942
Customer: Star Hotel		**Date of Quotation:** 23 September		
Location: Quayside, Book		**Salesman** John Patel		
Estimate	Cost £ p	Actual	Cost £ p	Var
Direct Materials				
1. Carpets				
Style/manuf. Ax 11		✓		
Colour Brown				
Qty 100 ☐ metres		✓		
Price per metre 14.50				
Total carpet	1450.00		1450.00	
2. Others				
Underlay/felt Card	50.00	100 ☐ metres felt	100.00	(50.00)
Gripper rods 110 m	165.00	✓	165.00	
Door strips 5 m	5.00	✓	5.00	
Others 1 can Super	16.00	2 cans	32.00	(16.00)
Direct Labour				
Man hours 10		9		
Rate £7.22				
Total labour	72.20		64.98	7.22
Overheads				
Hours 10				
Rate 8.33		9		
Total overheads	83.30		74.97	8.33
Margin	1841.50		1891.95	(50.45)
Hours 10				
Rate £4.12		9		
Total margin	'41.20		37.08	(4.12)
	1882.70		1929.03	
Price quoted £1885				
Notes Extra cost of felt to be	changed to customer			

variance) is a figure of £0.45 (£50 − £50.45), which is more than the estimated cost. This is made up as follows:

Adverse variance on glue	(£16.00)
Favourable variance on labour	7.22
Favourable variance on overheads	8.33
Total adverse variance =	£0.45

An adverse variance is one which is not in our favour, for example, we have paid out more than expected. A favourable variance is one that benefits us, in the example above labour and overhead costs were less than we expected. The margin variance is adverse—we are earning less than expected.

Process costing
Calculating the cost per unit of output
I am thinking of buying a series of machines and equipment that will press/mould rubber car mats. I have collected together some figures—let me show you. The machines and equipment will cost £6000 and I expect them to last four years. They will be operated by one man and he will earn £8500 p.a. It will cost £1200 p.a. to operate the machines (power, maintenance, and so on).

Other overheads chargeable to the machines will be £560. The machines should produce 9800 mats per year. The cost of the raw material will be £2450 per year. The annual cost of operating this small process will be:

Depreciation (capital cost written off)	£1 500
Labour cost	8 500
Overheads	560
Operating costs	1 200
Material costs	2 450
Total costs:	£14 210

$$\text{Cost per mat} = \frac{£14\ 210}{9\ 800} = £1.45$$

As you can see it is a self-contained activity or 'process'. Having collected all the costs associated with that process—direct costs such as materials and labour and indirect (overhead) costs allocated to the process (such as a proportion of the rates for the space it will occupy)—then, by dividing the total cost by the output, it is possible to calculate the cost per unit of output. This is the main difference between process costing and job costing. You know that the cost of each job in providing and laying carpets is different. With any process it is the total costs incurred in producing a total quantity that need to be measured.

Scrap and wasted units
I did not tell you that some of the mats produced will be defective. Occasionally the odd mat will be pressed with perhaps a hole in it. Since only the good output can be sold it is this figure which is divided into the

total cost. The cost of the wasted materials is therefore automatically included in the cost of the good units of output.

Some terms to remember

Cost unit   A quantity of the product in relation to which costs are determined (e.g., box of chocolates, ream of paper). In my case—a rubber car mat.

Cost centre   A person, or a machine or an area which has the costs relating to it determined. In our case, the new 'process' machines would be a cost centre and the rest of the business would be split into a cost centre for the shop (selling carpets) and a cost centre for the carpet laying department.

Direct costs   Costs which can be measured as being specifically related to a job or process. Our carpet fitters measure their time spent on jobs and this is therefore a direct cost.

Overheads   These are costs—material, labour or others, which cannot be measured as a direct cost to a job or process. Take the carpet salesman who meets customers to discuss what the customer wants and then to give a quotation. For many of the jobs he quotes it is wasted time—we do not get the order! His salary cannot therefore be charged to jobs we don't get. It has to be recovered by being charged to the jobs we do.

Overhead recovery   The charging of overheads to either jobs or processes. Carpets sold in the shop have to be sold at a price which will pay for both the cost of the carpet and the cost of operating the shop. Putting an extra 'charge' on to the carpets is referred to as 'recovering' overheads.

Cost sheet   A detailed record of the estimated and/or actual cost of a job or cost unit. See page 114.

Cost classification   The process of collecting and recording costs. While wages are calculated and paid as one total every week, they do relate to different parts of the business. The shop assistants' wages need to be 'charged' to the shop; the carpet fitters' wages we recorded as being charged to jobs and, any person employed on the new rubber mat process will be charged to that process. Meanwhile, all other wages/salaries are 'overheads'. All costs have to be recorded in a way which will enable us to measure what our costs are for different jobs or products supplied.

13.01   On 1 May the following balances were in the books of A King.

Sales Ledger	T Price £49.00; A Thomas £313.00; D Goodall £137.00
Bought Ledger	C Carter Ltd £98.50; M Nash & Co £148.60; F Hulse & Son Ltd £75.00
Cash Book	Bank Account £491.50 (Dr)

During the month the following transactions occurred.

Invoices were issued to:
B Cutts £65.00; T Jones £36.00; J Bright £92.00
Credit notes were sent to:
T Jones for containers returned £6.00
A Thomas for damage allowances £25.00
Invoices were received from:
D Spencer £166.00; P Sharrock £61.00; C Carter Ltd £98.50
Credit notes were received from:
M Nash & Co £16.80, for goods returned
F. Hulse & Son Ltd £10.00, for container returned

Cheques were received from:	*Cheques were sent to:*
A Thomas £288.00	C Carter & Co £94.00 in full
D Goodall £134.00, being	settlement of the balance on
allowed £3.00 discount	1 May
B Cutts, less 5 per cent cash	M Nash & Co £131.80
discount	D Spencer—deducting 2½ per cent
	cash discount

A dividend of 50p in the £ was received from the court on behalf of T Price. It was decided to write off the balance of his account as a bad debt. You are required to:

(a) Open personal accounts for debtors and creditors and enter the transactions for May.
(b) Open the Cash Book and make the entries required during the month.
(c) Balance the personal accounts and the Bank Account.

Note   Do *not* open the Day Books.

13.02   Enter the following balances into the ledger of T Roome as at 1 Jan 19–8.

Cash in hand £30.00; Cash at bank £192.50; Stock of goods £889.00; Premises £10 800.00; Fixtures and equipment £1500.00
Debtors A Cowley £49.50; J Plant £118.00; P Sharp £94.00
Creditors Allday Services Ltd £245.00

Calculate and post T Roome's capital to his Capital Account. Enter the following transactions in the books of original entry and post to the ledger, completing the double entry at the end of the month. Balance the three-column Cash Book, rule off the ledger account and take out a trial balance on 31 January.

Jan 1   Received an invoice from G Groves for goods at a net price of £166.00

2   Cash sales £143.50. Paid sundry expenses in cash £15.25

4   Sold goods on credit to L Butler £75.00 and R Rawson £132.00

5   J Plant returned goods that had been wrongly supplied and a credit note for £22.00 was sent to him

8   Wages paid in cash £48.55

9   T Roome withdrew goods for his own use valued £18.70 at selling price

15 Cash sales to date £391.00. Wages paid in cash £46.15. Paid into bank £300.00

18 Sold goods on credit to R Rawson £87.50.
L Butler returned goods unsuitable and a credit note for £35.00 was sent to him
J Plant paid his account at 18 January by cheque

20 P Sharp paid his account at 1 January by cheque, deducting £4.00 for discount. This was not allowable

22 Purchase by cheque £250.00. Wages paid in cash £46.30.
Cash sales to date £272.00

24 Invoice received from Allday Services Ltd for goods purchased valued £845.00. A cheque was sent to pay their account at 1 January

25 T Roome withdrew cash £25.00 for own use

27 L Butler paid his account by cheque deducting 2½ per cent cash discount

28 Goods valued at £16.50 were returned to Allday Services Ltd and a credit note received for this sum

29 Cash sales to date £314.00. Wages paid in cash £46.50

31 T Roome drew £35.00 cash for his own use
All cash except £30.00 was banked

NA 13.03 The following statement is received by E Wise from E Southport Ltd.

E WISE: North Street Hornford			STATEMENT
To: E Southport Ltd		Date	
July 1 Balance			245.00
6 Goods Inv no B/164	30.00		275.00
12 Bank		240.00	
Discount		5.00	30.00
18 Credit–Returns C/N D12		2.00	28.00
19 Goods Inv no B/178	95.00		123.00
24 Credit–Containers		10.00	113.00

Explain the purpose of the statement and the meaning of the entries shown on it.

13.04 The following balances were extracted from the books of D Armstrong at 1 January 19-5.

Trial Balance as on 1 January 19-5

	Dr	Cr
	£	£
Purchases	2600	
Sales		3750
Returns outwards		29
Returns inwards	63	
S Moran	120	
K Wilson	175	
J Davis		95
H Worth		105
Cash at bank	890	
General expenses	1020	
Drawings	1140	
Capital at 1 January 19-5		2029
	£6008	£6008

The following transactions took place in the month of January:

		£
(i)	*Purchases Day Book*	
	Jan 5 J Davis	35
	17 H Worth	60
(ii)	*Sales Day Book*	
	Jan 9 S Moran	65
	12 K Wilson	200
(iii)	*Sales Inwards Day Book*	
	Jan 22 K Wilson	20
(iv)	*Payments* (all by cheque)	
	Jan 4 Electricity (analysed under General expenses)	135
	24 H Worth (for goods purchased)	105
	26 Drawings	200
(v)	*Receipts* (all banked)	
	Jan 3 K Wilson (for sales)	100
	S Moran (for sales)	80
	Cash sale to P Jones	20

Required:
(a) Open up the accounts as they would appear in the books of D Armstrong as on 1 January 19-5.
(b) Make entries in the accounts to record the transactions which took place in the month of January.
(c) Balance off the accounts at 31 January 19-5.

(RSA 1)

NA 13.05 The personal account of C Street in the purchase ledger of E Farm showed there was an amount of £273.36 owing to Street on 31 May 19-4. However, the statement received from Street by Farm on 1 June 19-4 showed a balance outstanding of £312.54.

On comparing the two documents the following differences were found:

(a) Credit note CN22 for £28 in respect of an overcharge had not been received by Farm.
(b) A cheque for £78.28 dispatched by Farm on 28 May had not yet been received by Street.
(c) Street had dispatched goods as per Farm's order number ON 276 value £27.64 on 30 May; these had not yet been received by Farm.
(d) Street had offset a *contra* invoice of £38.74 from Farm against the account. Farm had recorded this separately in the Sales Ledger.

You are required to reconcile Street's statement with his ledger account in Farm's Books.

(RSA 1)

13.06 T Pitt owes you £59.00 on 1 January. He pays you £29.00 on 31 January but ignores all further requests for payment. On 6 May you hear that he has been made a bankrupt, and his trustee in bankruptcy announces that a dividend of 25 per cent in the £ will be paid on 30 September. This payment is received in due course.

Show Pitt's ledger account and the bad debts account at 31 December, the end of your financial year.

(PEI Elem)

13.07 Post the following transactions from the sales day book and the sales returns day book to the ledgers.

SALES DAY BOOK

Date			Folio	Details	£
January	3	M Jones	L2		60
	7	B Buston	L3	200	
		less 10%		20	180
	10	M Jones	L2		70
	15	M White	L4	180	
		less 10%		18	162
	21	M Jones			70
					542

SALES RETURNS DAY BOOK

January 20	M Jones	L2		12
				12

(PEI Elem)

NA 13.08 Ben Charles, a wholesaler, has an account in his ledger for Doddy and Co, and T Rash Ltd. On 1 June 19-7 these accounts showed the following balances:

	£
Doddy and Co—debit balance	1360
T Rash Ltd—credit balance	380

(a) Enter these balances in the personal accounts, make entries in these accounts which record the following transactions, and balance the two accounts at 30 June 19-7.

June 3 Paid cheque to T Rash Ltd for the amount of its account less 5 per cent cash discount
   10 Sold goods to Doddy and Co at list price £400 less 20 per cent trade discount
   11 Received from Doddy and Co cheque which was paid into the bank for the amount of the balance on the company's account at 1 June 19-7 less 2½ per cent cash discount
   18 Purchased 14 boxes of goods from T Rash Ltd at £20 per crate. These boxes are returnable and are charged at an additional £1 each

20   Doddy and Co returned part of the goods sold to the company on 10 June, list price £80, and a credit note was sent

28   Eight empty boxes at £1 each were returned to T Rash Ltd and a credit note was received.

(b) What do the closing balances on each of the two accounts mean to Ben Charles?

(c) Show the discount amounts for the month of June.

NA 13.09

STATEMENT

In account with

J Hunt
24 Coventry Road
Nuneaton C4

Mr R J Cook
14 Thorn Street
Derby DE3

31 March 19–7

		£	£	£
February	1 Balance			130.42
	6 Invoice	140.64		271.06
	8 Cheque		127.16	
	Discount		3.26	140.64
	12 Returns		16.30	124.34
	26 Invoice 540	184.42		308.76
	28 Undercharge	3.60		312.36

Study the statement above.

(a) Name the person who is supplying goods.

(b) Explain in simple terms the meaning of each item in the statement from 1 to 26 February and state the document used for the item on 28 February and the names of the sender and the receiver.

(c) Give the names of the debtor and the creditor and the amount owed on 28 February 19–7.

(RSA 1)

NA 13.10 The following ledger accounts appear among many others in the books of R Cope:

T Brown (credit limit £500)	Dr	Cr	Balance
December 1 Balance			250
4 Sales*	110		360
9 Returns		20	340
10 Bank		245	
Discount		5	90

R Fisher	Dr	Cr	Balance
December 1 Balance			150
8 Purchases		450	600
9 Cash	150		450

(i) Study the above accounts and answer the following questions:
  (a) Which of the accounts is that of a customer?
  (b) What is the significance of the entry 'credit limit £500'?
  (c) Why is there no credit limit written on R Fisher's account?
  (d) What is the name of the document associated with the entry marked *?
  (e) What is the rate of cash discount allowed to T Brown?
  (f) Which entry would be associated with a credit note?
  (g) Which of the accounts would appear in a creditor's ledger?
  (h) What is an advantage of writing out accounts in three column form?
(ii) Write up T Brown's account in the traditional form.

(London 'O')

13.11 Peter Hoff is a central heating engineer. He employs a young assistant whom he pays £85 per week. He estimates that during the next year he will

1 incur motor expenses of £2400
   bookkeeping and accounting fees of £600
   telephone, insurance, and other general expenses £840
2 work on average 30 hours per week for 48 weeks (so will his assistant)
3 wish to earn himself £8 per hour

Calculate the rate per hour that Peter Hoff will need to charge his customers during the forthcoming year. Now answer 13.12.

13.12 Peter Hoff has obtained an order to install a new central heating system in a house. He estimates that the work will take him and his assistant, working together, 60 hours. He estimates that the materials will cost £1600 and he always adds 5 per cent to this cost as a handling charge. Calculate the price that Peter Hoff should quote for this job.

13.13 Complete the following Process Accounts

Process Account

(a)

	Units	£		Units	
Direct materials	500	500	Completed units		
Direct wages		1200	transferred	300	£
Overheads		300	WIP c/d	200	£
		———			———
		———			———

Note Work in process is half completed.

Process Account

(b)

	Units	£		Units	
Direct materials	500	1500	Completed units		
Direct wages		2000	transferred	260	£
Overheads		1000	WIP c/d	240	£
		———			———
		£4500			£4500

Note WIP is one-sixth complete.

Process Account

(c)

	Units	£		Units	
Direct materials	500	500	Completed units		
Direct wages		1200	transferred	300	£
Overheads		300	WIP	200	£
		———			———
		═══			═══

Note WIP is fully completed regarding materials and half completed regarding labour and overheads.

14. Trading and Profit and Loss Accounts

Joe needs to know whether his business is making a profit or a loss. Apart from Joe, there are other interested parties who would like to know whether or not the business is profitable—for example, the Inland Revenue (Tax Office) would like to know, so that it can work out how much tax Joe will have to pay. Also the Bank Manager of the business would like to know the results of trading, should Joe want a loan or overdraft. The Trading Profit and Loss Accounts are usually referred to as 'the final accounts'. We can prepare final accounts for any period of time— for example, every six months. However, it is usual to prepare final accounts for a 12-month period, because tax assessment is based on annual profits.

Before preparing the final accounts

To be of any value the final accounts must be correct. The results can only be based on the accounts and records maintained by the business, and therefore these accounts must be accurate. To check the arithmetical accuracy of the accounts, a trial balance is always taken out before preparing the Trading and Profit and Loss Accounts. The trial balance should be balanced before proceeding further.

Finding the profit

Now, let Joe explain.

We buy a roll of carpet for £800 and sell the same carpet for £1000—we have £200 more than we paid for it (selling price minus cost price) and if we do not incur any other expenses on the carpet before selling it, then we say our profit is £200 (£1000 − £800 = £200). You do remember that when the carpet was bought we debited our purchases account as shown in the illustration on page 126. As we have sold the whole carpet, we credit sales and there will be no stock of carpets left in the warehouse.

If these were the only transactions in that period we would transfer the total of the entries to the Trading Account.

Debit Trading Account: Credit Purchases Account.
Debit Sales Account: Credit Trading Account.

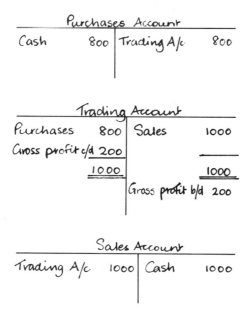

When the Trading Account is balanced, the 'balance' is the gross profit.
Remember that if the sales income is less than the cost of purchase the
result is a gross loss. A profit results in a credit balance on the account,
and a loss in a debit balance.

Often it happens that all the carpets will not be sold at the end of the
year when we prepare the Trading Account. For example, let us say that
during the period from 1 January to 31 December Joe's total purchases
of carpets came to £3500 and his total sales came to £3000. If you
compare these two figures it appears that he has made a loss. However,
the stock of carpets left in the warehouse is worth £1800, so we can say
that Joe has sold £1700 of the carpets (£3500 − £1800 = £1700) for
£3000. So the cost of the carpets he has sold for £3000 is £1700.
Look at it again.

Cost of the whole stock of carpets = £3500
Cost of stocks left over on 31 Dec = 1800

Therefore, cost of the carpets sold = 1700

The stocks left will be transferred to the Stock Account by debiting the

Stock Account and crediting the Trading Account. This is shown in the accounts as follows:

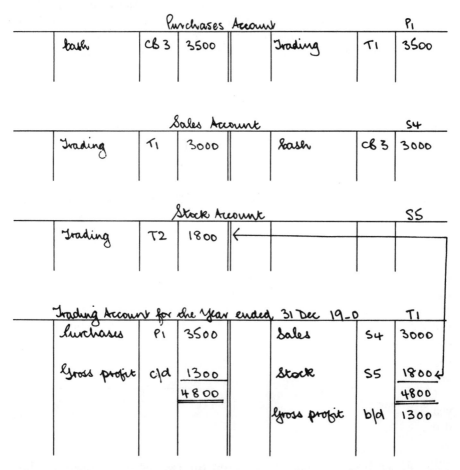

The 'balance' on the Trading Account is the profit and it is called *gross profit* because it is the profit made on the trading transaction *before* any deduction of expenses in connection with running the business. The heading of the Trading Account shows that the account is for a one-year period of trading: 'Trading Account for the year ended 31 December 19–0'.

Closing stocks

All goods purchased for resale are recorded in the Purchases Account at cost prices. All the goods sold are recorded in the Sales Account at selling prices. Nowhere in our accounts do we have any record of the actual stock that is still held in the business. How can Joe find out *exactly* what stocks of carpets there are in the warehouse—and what value should be put upon these carpets? The only way to do this is to have a *stocktake*. This means an actual count of the stock and recording the quantities on stock sheets. When it has all been checked, reference can be made to the original invoices from the suppliers and the cost price applied to the quantity in stock to give a stock value. This value is the closing stock entered in the Trading Account.

The double entry for closing stock

Having counted and valued the stock at the year end, that value is the actual asset value at that time. Assets are recorded as debit balances and therefore the value must be debited into a Stock Account. Since every debit has a credit, the corresponding credit is usually made in the Trading Account. The reason for this is as follows: the purpose of the Trading Account is to determine the gross profit, which is the difference between the selling price and the cost price *of the goods sold.* So far you have transferred the sales value of the goods sold to the Trading Account, but the Purchases Account, also transferred, shows the value of the goods *bought*, and since some of them are left in stock the purchases figure does not show the cost price of the goods sold. If you look at these two entries in the Trading Account—

Trading Account for the...			
Purchases	3500	Stock	1800

you will see how the balance between the two figures represents the purchase cost of the goods that have been sold. To show this more clearly the Trading Account is usually laid out as follows:

Trading Account for the...		
Purchases	3500	
Less Closing stock	1800	
Cost of goods sold	1700	

Trading expenses

Joe may have incurred some expenses directly connected with buying the goods for resale—i.e., in connection with the purchases—such as the amount paid to bring the goods to Joe's warehouse (carriage inwards or freight and insurance charges). Such expenses can also be deducted from the sale proceeds to arrive at the gross profit.

Let us use the following figures to prepare the Trading Account for the year ended 31 December 19-0.

Purchases £3500; Sales £3000; Carriage charges on purchases £145; Closing stock £1800.

Trading Account for the year ended 31 December 19-0

Purchases		3500	Sales		3000
Carriage charges		145	Closing stock		1800
Gross profit	c/d	1255			
		4800			4800
			Gross profit	b/d	1255

The Trading Account shows the profit made by the business on the goods bought and the expenses directly connected with the goods. Since the Trading Account is usually prepared so as to show the 'cost of goods sold', as previously explained, the layout above is not preferred and so you are recommended to prepare the Trading Account in the form shown below. This approach is preferred by examiners and so students should prepare the Trading Account in this way.

14.01 Prepare the Trading Account for the year ended 31 December 19-0 in the preferred style.

Continuing from the above illustration, let us suppose that in the following year, ended 31 December 19-1, the following trading transactions took place:

Purchases £4200; Sales £7300; Carriage charges on purchases (carriage inwards) £150; Stock at the end of the year £2000.

The Trading Account will be prepared as:

Trading Account for the year ended 31 December 19–1

Opening stock (see below)	1800	Sales	7300
Purchases	4200		
Carriage inwards	150		
	6150		
Less Closing stock	2000		
Cost of goods sold	4150		
Gross profit c/d	3150		
	7300		7300
		Gross profit b/d	3150

Opening stock

The closing stock of the previous year ended 19–0 becomes the opening stock of year 19–1. The value of the closing stock on 31 December 19–0 was £1800 and this was the value after the close of trading on the last day of the financial year. When the business opened on 1 January 19–1 (the following day) the stock already in hand to begin that year was, of course, the same stock valued at £1800. The Stock Account would then look like this.

Stock Account

19–0 Dec 31 Trading A/c (1)		1800	19–1 Dec 31 Trading A/c (2)		1800	
19–1 Dec 31 Trading A/c (3)		2000				

(1)   Debit the closing stock value: Credit the Trading Account.
(2)   Transfer the closing stock of the previous year to the Trading Account for the current year. Entries Dr Trading Account: Cr Stock Account.

(3) Debit closing stock value on 31 December 19–1: Credit the Trading Account.

If you were asked to calculate the cost of goods sold for 19–1 the method would be:

	£
Value of stock held on 1 Jan 19–1	= 1800
+ Cost of purchases made during 19–1	= 4200
+ Cost of carriage on purchases	= 150
	6150
− Value of stock held on 31 Dec 19–1	= 2000
Cost of goods sold during year	= 4150

Sales returns and purchases returns

Look at the following trial balance extract (i.e., some of the items that appear in the trial balance).

Trial balance (extract) as at 31 Dec 19–3

	£	£
Sales		28 950
Purchases	16 940	
Opening stock 1 Jan 19–3	2 800	
Sales returns	600	
Purchases returns		185

We also know that the stock value on 31 December was £3750.

Using the principle of double entry the nominal accounts are closed by transferring the balance to the Trading Account.

The Trading Account will then look as follows.

Trading Account . . .

Purchases		16 940	Sales	28 950
Sales returns		600	Purchases returns	185
Opening stock (1 Jan)		2 800	Closing stock	3 750
Gross profit	c/d	12 545		
		32 885		32 885
			Gross profit b/d	12 545

This layout does not show cost of goods sold, net sales, or net purchases, but such information makes the Trading Account much more informative. The layout below is the one that you should adopt to show these details.

Trading Account . . .

Opening stock		2 800	Sales	28 950	
Purchases	16 940		Less Sales returns	600	
Less Purchases returns	185				
*Net purchases		16 755	*Net sales		28 350
		19 555			
Less Closing stock		3 750			
		15 805			
Gross profit	c/d	12 545			
		28 350			28 350
			Gross profit	b/d	12 545

*The terms Net purchases and Net sales are not normally shown.

14.02 Can you remember why opening stock is an expense at the end of the year and not an asset?

Profit and Loss Account

If Joe wants to know the 'true' profit (or loss) made by the business he would have to deduct from the gross profit all of the other revenue expenses incurred in running the business—for example, light and heat, telephone, stationery, and salaries.

Example
Suppose the following information is known to you at the end of 19–1.

	£		£
Wages	850	Light and heat	120
Telephone	175	Stationery	42
Salary (clerk)	720	Interest received	32
Opening stock	1800	Carriage inwards	150
Sales	7300	Closing stock	2000
Purchases	4200		

Transfer of expenses to Trading and Profit and Loss Account

Trading and Profit and Loss Account
for the year ended 31 December 19–1

Opening stock	1800		Sales		7300
Purchases	4200				
Carriage inwards	150				
		6150			
Less Closing stock		2000			
Cost of goods sold		4150			
Gross profit c/d		3150			
		7300			7300
Wages		850	Gross profit b/d		3150
Salary		720	Interest received		32
Light and heat		120			
Telephone		175			
Stationery and printing		42			
Net profit c/d		1275			
		3182			3182
			Net profit b/d		1275

Carriage Inwards A/c

Balance	150	Trading A/c	150	

Wages A/c

Balance	850	Profit & Loss A/c	850	

Salary A/c

Balance	720	Profit & Loss	720	

Light and Heat A/c

Balance	120	Profit & Loss	120	

Telephone A/c

Balance	175	Profit & Loss	175	

Stationery and Printing A/c

Balance	42	Profit & Loss	42	

Interest Received A/c

Profit & Loss	32	Balance	32	

We can find the 'true' profit, called the *net profit* for the year, by preparing a Profit and Loss Account. The Profit and Loss Account is a continuation of the Trading Account. We bring down the gross profit to the credit side of the Profit and Loss Account and transfer these revenue expenses to the debit side of the account as shown on page 133.

The net profit of £1275 made by the business belongs to the owner of the business and so it will be transferred to his Capital Account (or Current Account, if there is one) as below.

Profit and Loss (extract)

Capital Account	1275	Net profit b/d	1275

Capital Account

	Balance 1 Jan	8000
	Net profit for year	1275

Remember   The Trading and Profit and Loss Accounts compare all revenue incomes with all revenue expenditure

14.03   Why are Drawings not in the Profit and Loss Account?

14.04   Can you remember the definitions of capital expenditure, revenue income and revenue expenditure?

Closing nominal accounts in the ledger

When entries are made for expenses and incomes in the nominal accounts, the rule is:

Debit expenses: Credit incomes

Each income and expense account in the Nominal Ledger is totalled at the end of the trading period and transferred to either the Trading Account or the Profit and Loss Account. The result of this is that expenses and losses which appear as *debits* in their respective accounts are shown as *debits* in the final accounts. Also, incomes and gains that appear in the Nominal Ledger as *credits* are shown as *credits* in the final accounts. The final accounts summarize the total activities of the business.

Transfers to the final accounts are made by closing each income and expense account. To close an account means making an entry on the side *opposite* to the existing balance—if you refer to the example on page 133 you will see that in the case of the expense accounts which contain debit balances, they have been closed by credit entries. Following the rules of double entry, these credit entries must have corresponding debit entries—which are those in the Trading and Profit and Loss Accounts.

As an example, this is how the Advertising Account will appear in the ledger.

Advertising Account							
Mar 31	Bank	48.00		Dec 31	Profit and Loss A/c		174.00
July 4	Bank	51.00					
Sept 25	Bank	31.00					
Dec 31	Bank	44.00					
		174.00					174.00

The effect of all this is that all income and expense accounts are *closed* (no balances appear on these accounts in the ledger) and the totals of each account are shown in the final accounts. The final accounts are in turn 'closed' as follows: any gross profit or loss is transferred (carried down) to the Profit and Loss Account: any net profit or loss is transferred to the owner's Capital Account.

Procedure for preparing final accounts

1 Balance all accounts and prepare a trial balance, which must be balanced as a check on the accounts before proceeding further.
2 Conduct a stocktake and calculate the value of closing stock—Debit the Stock Account: Credit the Trading Account.
3 Close off all nominal accounts by transfer to the Trading and Profit and Loss Accounts.
4 Calculate the gross and net profits (or losses) and close the final accounts by transfer to the owner's Capital Account.
5 Verify that remaining balances in the ledgers are correct by preparing a Balance Sheet (Chapter 15). These balances consist of personal accounts—i.e., debtors and creditors—and real accounts—i.e., assets.
Transfer Drawings to Capital Account.

Here is an example:

Step 1   Balancing the accounts will result in the trial balance.

Trial Balance as at 31.12.19–2

	Dr	Cr
	£	£
Premises	15 000	
Capital		19 275
Machinery	6 600	
Purchases	16 800	
Sales		24 650
Returns inwards	150	
Carriage inwards	78	
Salaries	3 600	
Advertising	165	
Rent and rates	985	
Interest received		240
General expenses	698	
Debtors	1 500	
Creditors		2 800
Vehicles	3 500	
Stock 1 Jan 19—2	2 000	
Bank		911
Drawings	1 800	
Bank loan		5 000
	52 876	52 876

Step 2   Calculating the closing stock results in two extra entries shown *under* the trial balance.

Stock 31 Dec 19–2	3800	
Trading Account (closing stock)		3800

Step 3   Deciding the items in the trial balance that require to be transferred to either the Trading Account or the Profit and Loss Account. These will be incomes and expenses.

(The remaining accounts are assets and liabilities and these will be used for preparing the Balance Sheet.)

Trial Balance Items	*Action*
Premises	Asset (BS)
Capital	Liability (BS)
Machinery	Asset (BS)
Purchases	Expenses—Trading Account
Sales	Incomes—Trading Account
Returns inwards	Expenses—Trading Account
Carriage inwards	Expenses—Trading Account
Salaries	Expenses—Profit and Loss Account
Advertising	Expenses—Profit and Loss Account
Rent and rates	Expenses—Profit and Loss Account
Interest received	Incomes—Profit and Loss Account
General expenses	Expenses—Profit and Loss Account
Debtors	Asset (BS)
Creditors	Liability (BS)
Vehicles	Asset (BS)
Stock 1 Jan 19-2	Expenses—Trading Account
Bank O/D	Liability (BS)
Drawings	Asset (BS)
Bank loan	Liability (BS)

(Stock 31 Dec 19-2 = Asset (BS): Trading Account − Closing Stock credited.)

Step 4   Having transferred incomes and expenses the Profit and Loss Account will appear as follows:

Trading and Profit and Loss Account for the year ended 31 December 19-2

Opening stock	2 000	Sales	24 650	
Purchases	16 800	*Less* Returns inwards	150	24 500
Carriage	78			
	18 878			
Less Closing stock	3 800			
Cost of goods sold	15 078			
Gross profits c/d	9 422			
	24 500			24 500
Salaries	3 600	Gross profit b/d		9 422
Advertising	165	Interest received		240
Rent and rates	985			
General expenses	698			
Net profit to capital A/c	4 214			
	£9 662			£9 662

Step 5   You will have to see Chapter 15 to learn about the Balance Sheet, but the position regarding the accounts in the ledgers after *Step 4* above will be as shown by the trial balance *after* preparing the final accounts.

Trial Balance as at 31 December 19–2
(after preparation of the final accounts)

Capital		23 489
Drawings	1 800	
Bank loan		5 000
Machinery	6 600	
Debtors	1 500	
Creditors		2 800
Vehicles	3 500	
Stock	3 800	
Bank O/D		911
Premises	15 000	
	£32 200	£32 200

(Note beside Capital/Drawings/Bank loan: } See *Step 6*)

Step 6   Transfer Drawings Account to the owner's Capital Account. (Note that the balance of £23 489 consists of opening capital and net profit—i.e., £19 275 + £4214.)

(Although the balance on the owner's Capital Account can now be shown as one figure (£21 689), it is usual to show, in the Balance Sheet how this figure has been calculated.)

Profits due to owner

You have had to learn many bookkeeping rules in this chapter concerned with the preparation of the final accounts. Always remember the *purpose* of preparing such accounts is to determine the profit or loss of the business. The business operates to make profits for the owner and when the profit is determined it appears as a liability of the business (credit balance on the Profit and Loss Account)—since the business now *owes* that profit to the owner. Should the business suffer a loss, then the owner must bear that loss, the bookkeeping rule that summarizes the position is *Joe's Rule No 14.*

Joe's Rule No 14

The owner of a business receives the profits, but also has to bear the losses. Therefore profits *are* credited *to the owner's Capital Account, and* losses *are* debited *to the owner's Capital Account.*

14.05 Prepare the Trading and Profit and Loss Account from the following trial balance.

Fiona Williamson & Co

Trial Balance as at 31 May 19-8

	£	£
Opening stock 1 June 19-7	1 240	
Capital		5 873
Purchases and sales	10 260	16 840
Returns	190	210
Discounts allowed	45	
Commission received		82
Rent received		364
Wages and salaries	3 675	
General expenses	942	
Carriage inwards	156	
Debtors and creditors	3 455	1 862
Motor vans	3 010	
Cash at bank	383	
Drawings	1 875	
	£25 231	£25 231

Closing stock is valued at £2845.

14.06 J Jones had a stock consisting of 500 articles of £5 each on 1 September 19-6. He purchased during September: 1000 articles at £5.25 each on 9 September, and 2500 articles at £4.55 each on 20 September. On 25 September he sold 3000 articles at £6.25 each. On 28 September 50 of the latter were returned to Jones in perfect condition.

You are required to:

(a) Calculate the quantity in stock at 30 September 19-6.
(b) Value the stock at this date.
(c) Prepare the Trading Account for the month of September 19-6.

(RSA 1)

14.07 From the following list of balances prepare:

(a) a trial balance, and (b) the Trading and Profit and Loss Account for the year ended 31 December 19-4.

Stock 1 January 19-4 £1800; Shop fittings £750; Capital £2360; Sales £6850; Purchases £4100; Wages £2865; Commission received £255; Discounts received £168; Sales returns £42; Debtors £1008; Creditors £1400; Bank £92 (overdrawn); General expenses £560.

Stock on 31 December was valued at £875.

NA 14.08 From the following list of balances prepare the trial balance and the Trading and Profit and Loss Account for the year ended 31 May 19-5.

Capital 1 June 19-4 £10 865; Stock 1 June 19-4 £3800; Plant and equipment £6500; Vehicles £2850; Sales £38 672; Purchases £20 431; Carriage inwards £640; Wages and salaries £8760; Sales returns £98; Discounts allowed £140; Interest received £16; Debtors £2219; Creditors £2477; Drawings £3540; Bank £1104; Advertising £550; General expenses £1398.

One-third of the wages and salaries should be charged to the Profit and Loss Account. Closing stock was £2650.

NA 14.09 You have prepared the accounts of a delicatessen for the year ending 31 December 19-6. The sales for the year amounted to £75 000. The owner explains that during the year a small quantity of stock, which cost £200, was thrown away, and she is wondering why there is no charge against the profits in respect of this amount.

1   Explain the position to the owner.
2   Say how the treatment of stock losses would have differed if the amount involved had been £2000.

NA 14.10 Stephen Crowther, a sole trader, extracted a trial balance at the close of business on 31 March 19-5. The two sides of the trial balance did not agree but, in spite of this, Crowther prepared Trading and Profit and Loss Accounts for the year ended 31 March 19-5. The net profit as shown in this Profit and Loss Account was £1860.

Subsequently, the following errors were discovered in Crowther's books and these accounted for the whole of the difference in the trial balance:

1   In the Purchases Day Book one page totalled £1420 but this had been carried forward to the next page as £1240.
2   The Discount Allowed total in the Cash Book—£135—had been credited to the Discount Received Account.

3 Cash received from a debtor, W Johnson—£84—had been correctly entered in the Cash Book but Johnson's account had been credited with £48.
4 An item of £166 in respect of salaries paid had been shown in the Cash Book but the double entry had not been completed.

Required:
(i) Indicate how, and the extent to which, each of the above errors affected the trial balance. Your answers should be in the form of the following table:

ERROR	DEBIT		CREDIT	
	Understated	Overstated	Understated	Overstated
(1)				
(2)				
(3)				
(4)				

(ii) Calculate the correct net profit.

Note Calculations must be shown.

(LCCI Elem)

NA 14.11 The following trial balance was extracted from the books of a sole trader on 31 December 19–4:

	£	£
Capital		15 015
Fixed assets	10 500	
Stock	1 726	
D Smith	238	
R Brown	425	
L Edgar	247	
Cash in hand	197	
Cash in bank	918	
T Williams		217
R Wilkins		415
Sales		17 310
Returns	139	
Purchases	18 482	
Returns		415
Rates	500	
	33 372	33 372

Study the above trial balance and

(a) write down the names of the trader's customers.
(b) write down the names of the trader's suppliers.
(c) find the total amount owed by the business to suppliers.
(d) find the total amount owed to the business.
(e) name two accounts which should have the date 1 January 19-4 written by the side.
(f) calculate the difference which would appear between the debit and credit sides of the trial balance if the clerk making the extraction had entered the sales returns and the purchases returns on the wrong side.
Write down the debit and credit totals if the error indicated above had occurred.
(g) calculate the net sales and net purchases.
(h) indicate the minimum of extra information necessary to compile a trading account for the year ended 31 December 19-4 and state how that information would be obtained.

(London 'O')

NA 14.12 From the information below, you are required to extract the necessary details to work out the gross profit on September's trading of David Tomms (Wholesalers) Ltd.

	£
Stock 1 September	620
Stock 31 September	640
Cash balance	120
Drawings	150
Purchases for month	2160
Sales for month	3275
Carriage inwards	30

(PEI Elem)

15. The Balance Sheet

The Balance Sheet is a summary of the balances of the accounts remaining open in the ledgers after the Trading and Profit and Loss Accounts have been prepared. It seeks to show the financial state of affairs of a business at one point in time. The Balance Sheet does not relate to a period, but sets out the book values of the assets, liabilities, and capital *as at a particular date*. The heading for a Balance Sheet should therefore be 'Balance Sheet as at . . . [the date] and *not* 'Balance Sheet for the year ended . . .', which is used in the heading of the final accounts. The Balance Sheet shows on the one hand the amount of capital put (invested) into the business by the owner (and sources of borrowed money), and on the other hand the form in which such capital is employed. So the liabilities side of the Balance Sheet will show, for example:

1 The capital put into the business by the owner.
2 Loans from other people.
3 The amount of money the business owes to other people (creditors).

The other side of the Balance Sheet will show the assets divided into *fixed* assets and *current* assets.

Balance Sheet layout

On one sheet of paper the assets are compared with the liabilities. The layout can be similar to the entries in the accounts and the Trading and Profit and Loss Account:

Assets on the left-hand side
Liabilities on the right-hand side

Or the layout can be 'vertical'. However, *it is not an account*, and entries are *not* posted to the Balance Sheet. It is a *list* of assets and liabilities of the business at one particular date. The different forms of layout are illustrated on pages 144 and 147.

Accounts in the ledgers at the year end

When the net profit or loss has been calculated, the income and expense accounts have all been closed. The only accounts remaining 'open', i.e., containing balances, are those for assets and liabilities, plus the owner's Drawings and Capital Accounts.

Look at the trial balance below (which was shown on page 138), this was prepared after the preparation of the final accounts; it contains only assets and liabilities.

Trial Balance as at 31 December 19–2

Capital		23 489
Drawings	1 800	
Bank loan		5 000
Machinery	6 600	
Debtors	1 500	
Creditors		2 800
Vehicles	3 500	
Stock	3 800	
Bank		911
Premises	15 000	
	32 200	32 200

This trial balance is really a Balance Sheet, except that a Balance Sheet is laid out as follows:

Balance Sheet as at 31 December 19–2

Fixed assets				*Capital*			
Premises	15 000			Bal 1 January		19 275	
Machinery	6 600			*plus* Net profit			
Vehicles	3 500	25 100		for year	4 214		
				less Drawings	1 800	2 414	
						21 689	
Current assets							
Stock	3 800			*Long-term liability*			
Debtors	1 500	5 300		Bank loan		5 000	
				Current liabilities			
				Creditors	2 800		
				Bank overdraft	911	3 711	
		30 400				30 400	

This presentation is called a *Horizontal Balance Sheet*. In practice the style of layout can vary to convey useful summarized information to both owners and interested parties.

Assets
Fixed assets are the assets which the owner of the business buys to use in the business for more than one accounting period and which he does not intend to sell as part of his stocks or turn into cash.

Current assets are those assets which are bought with the intention of turning them into cash, and they include debtors and cash.

Examples of fixed assets	*Examples of current assets*
Land	Stock of raw materials
Buildings (premises)	Stock of goods being processed
Plant and machinery	Stock of finished goods, and other materials (e.g., stationery)
Fixtures and fittings	Debts owed to the business (debtors)
Motor vehicles	Cash in bank
	Cash in hand
	Prepayments

Although there is no statutory order for arranging the items in the Balance Sheet, they should be grouped under the heading of fixed and current assets to show the financial position to people who know little about accounts. Remember that these assets would appear in the asset accounts in the ledgers.

Liabilities
On the liabilities side, the capital shown first is the balance of capital at the beginning of the year. Added to this is the net profit which the business owes to the owner (but take away any loss), and then the total Drawings are subtracted, leaving the figure representing the owner's capital at the date of the Balance Sheet. This figure corresponds to the balance in the Capital Account in the ledger. In preparing accounts for small businesses it is usual to show the transactions on Capital Account in the Balance Sheet as shown in the illustration on page 144. The figure

of £21 689 is the liability to the owner—and he can see how that has been worked out.

Examples of long-term liabilities	*Examples of current liabilities* (Items expected to be repaid within the next year)
Bank loan	Trade creditors
Mortgage	Bank overdraft
Loans from other sources	Sundry creditors, e.g., amounts owing for rent, wages, etc.

Realizability

Except for limited companies, there is no statutory order about how particular items in a Balance Sheet should be arranged. Usually the assets are arranged in descending order of *liquidity*. In other words, they are arranged in order of how quickly the asset can be turned into cash, with the most liquid asset at the bottom and the most fixed asset at the top. (Turning an asset into cash is called 'realizing the asset'.) So that cash comes last and premises are listed on top. We do the same for the liabilities.

Current liabilities are shown at the bottom, to match the current assets. They are current because they will have to be settled fairly soon—usually within 12 months. The current liabilities are followed by the long-term liabilities in ascending order, because long-term liabilities (such as loans) are normally taken out for several years. Finally, the amount due to the owner of the business (Capital *plus* Net profit *less* Drawings) is put on top of the liabilities because, unless the business is being discontinued, this amount of money will not be repaid.

Vertical presentation

The assets and liabilities can also be arranged with one group on top of the other instead of one beside the other. The most usual vertical layout is as shown on the next page.

In this layout we start with the assets, grouping them under fixed assets and current assets, as usual in subtotals. These are followed by the current liabilities, which are deducted from the total current assets to show the net amount of *working capital* available to the business. Working capital is the fund available to the owner for running the business. It does not include funds which have been used on fixed assets. Therefore working capital is current assets *less* current liabilities.

Balance Sheet as at 31 December 19-2

Fixed assets	£	£	£
Shop premises		15 000	
Machinery		6 600	
Vehicles		3 500	25 100
Current assets			
Stock		3 800	
Debtors		1 500	
		5 300	
Less current liabilities			
Creditors	2 800		
Bank O/D	911	3 711	
Working capital			1 589
			26 689
Represented by			
Capital:			
Balance 1 January			19 275
Add Net profit for year		4 214	
Less Drawings		1 800	2 414
			21 689
Long-term liability			
Bank loan			5 000
			26 689

Summary of Balance Sheet purposes

By the proper grouping of assets and liabilities, the owner can see the exact financial state of affairs of the business at the financial year end. Other people are interested in this financial summary—for example the Income Tax Inspector, the VAT officer, and prospective buyers of the business. If the owner wishes to borrow money, the prospective lender will also want to see the latest Balance Sheet. Where repayments have to be made to creditors, the effect on working capital can be seen. Also the fact that the Balance Sheet balances is good evidence that all the bookkeeping has been correctly carried out.

Other uses of a Balance Sheet

1. To determine the owner's capital where double entry records have not
   been kept. The assets and external liabilities (that is, creditors, bank
   overdrafts/loans, and loans from other sources) can usually be
   established fairly easily. Since Assets = Liabilities, the owner's capital
   can be calculated. (Remember that Liabilities = External liabilities +
   Capital.)

Example 1

Total assets are valued at £3975 and liabilities to external creditors
amount to £1015.

> Assets   = External liabilities + Capital
> Therefore £3975   = £1015 + Capital
> Therefore Capital = £2960

2. To calculate the business profit or loss where double entry records
   have not been kept. When goods are bought and sold at a profit, the
   assets of the business must increase. Conversely, if the business is
   making a loss, the assets will decrease. The profit or loss for a trading
   period can be calculated by reference to the increase or decrease in net
   assets over that trading period. (Note that net assets are total assets *less*
   external liabilities.)

Example 2

On 1 January 19-2 the assets of Henry Pells totalled £8963 and on that
date his capital was £6850. On 31 December 19-2 the assets totalled
£10 801 and the only liabilities were to trade creditors for £2075. A
Balance Sheet drawn up in the normal way will show:

Balance Sheet of H Pells as at 31 Dec 19-2

Assets	10 801	Capital 1 Jan	6 850
		Profit for year	1 876
			8 726*
		Trade creditors	2 075
	10 801		10 801

*Assets (£10 801) = Liabilities (£2075) + Capital (£8726).

The figure of £8726 is calculated first. Since capital on 1 January was £6850, the profit added must be £1876.

What is the effect of Drawings?

It is unlikely that Henry Pells has drawn nothing at all from his business during the year. If it can be established that he drew £2125 during the year, then the Balance Sheet would appear as follows.

Balance Sheet of H Pells as at 31 Dec 19-2

Total assets	10 801	Capital 1 Jan	6 850
		Add Profit (3)	4 001
		(2)	10 851
		Less Drawings	2 125
		(1)	8 726
		Trade creditors	2 075
	10 801		10 801

1 The capital at the year end is calculated as before.
2 Since £8726 is the capital *after* deducting the Drawings of £2125, the capital *before* deducting the Drawings must be the total of the two, i.e., £10 851.
3 £10 851 is the capital *after* adding the profit, and since the capital before adding the profit was £6850, then the difference must equal the profit, i.e., £4001.

Joe's Rule No 15
All *assets and* all *liabilities, together with* capital *must be shown in the Balance Sheet. It is called a Balance Sheet because assets of the business should balance with the capital plus liabilities.*

In all answers lay the Balance Sheet out in the horizontal method, unless the question specifically states otherwise.

15.01 The following balances remained in the books of P Jarvis after the preparation of the Trading and Profit and Loss Account for the year ended 31 December 19-5

	£
Sundry debtors	1965
Stock	2412
Balance at bank	900
Freehold premises (at cost)	5460
Mortgage (repayable over 30 years)	5000
Drawings	2360
Profit for year 19-5	4670
Trade creditors	1520
Expense creditors	340
Furniture and equipment (cost £3000)	2620
Rates in advance	150
Capital 1 January 19-5	4337

Prepare the Balance Sheet of P Jarvis at 31 December 19-5.

(RSA 1)

(*Authors' note*   Rates in advance should be treated as a current asset.)

15.02 On 1 July 19-5 D Loss commenced business with £6000 in his Bank Account. After trading for a full year, he ascertained that his position on 30 June 19-6 was as follows.

Plant	£3600	Fixtures	£360
Creditors	£720	Bank balance	£600
Debtors	£930	Stock in trade	£1350
Cash in hand	£135	Drawings	£1600

You are required to:
(a) Calculate D Loss's capital at 30 June 19-6.
(b) Prepare D Loss's Balance Sheet at 30 June 19-6 (assuming a profit of £1855), set out in such a manner as to show clearly the totals normally shown in a Balance Sheet.

(RSA 1)

15.03 From the following trial balance prepare the Trading and Profit and Loss Account for the year and the Balance Sheet as at 30 November 19-4.

Amy Jones (Jewellery)
Trial Balance as at 30 November 19–4

	£	£
Capital 1 December 19–3		11 650
Purchases/sales	26 841	35 492
Debtors/creditors	4 815	3 076
Returns inwards	149	
Discounts		36
Wages and salaries	6 941	
Advertising	562	
Postage and stationery	79	
Rent and rates	1 436	
General expenses	849	
Premises	5 600	
Vehicles	1 500	
Stock 1 December 19–3	2 300	
Drawings	1 300	
Bank and cash		2 118
	52 372	52 372

The closing stock on 30 November 19–4 was valued at £2150.

15.04 A sole trader has prepared the following 'Balance Sheet'.

Balance Sheet for the year ended 31 May 19–5

	£		£
Bad debts written off	80	Net profit	870
Fixtures and fittings	560	Creditors	1470
Cash	30	Provision for bad and	
Drawings	800	doubtful debts	70
Discount allowed	110	Bank overdraft	190
Debtors	1380	Capital 1 June 19–4	1900
Stock	1540		
	£4500		£4500

Required:
Redraft the above statement to conform with modern commercial practice.
If you consider the net profit figure of £870 to be incorrect, you should
correct the figure but show your calculation.

(LCCI Elem)

(*Author's note* The provision for bad debts should be shown in the
Balance Sheet as a deduction from debtors, so that debtors will appear as
£1380 − 70 = £1310.)

15.05   Redraft the following Balance Sheet of Kandy Stores in its correct form.

Balance Sheet for the year ended 31 December 19-5

	£		£
Cash	248	Capital	20 000
Bank overdraft	1 500	Trade debtors	6 420
Trade creditors	5 140	Prepaid expenses	460
Stock in trade	4 656	Net profit for the	
Drawings	3 000	year	7 364
Freehold premises	12 000		
Furniture and fittings	2 500		
Motor vehicles	4 960		
Accrued expenses	240		
	£34 244		£34 244

(RSA I)

(*Author's note* Accrued expenses should be treated as a current liability.)

15.06   Arthur Adams is a sole trader who does not use the double entry method of bookkeeping. His records, however, are accurate and from them the following information has been obtained:

	31 Oct 19-3	31 Oct 19-4
Debtors	2930	3260
Bank	–	930
Bank overdraft	790	–
Creditors	640	1030
Stock	1520	1870
Fixtures and fittings	600	500
Bills payable	200	–
Bills receivable	–	300

The figures quoted for fixtures and fittings are valuations made at the dates given.

During the year ended 31 October 19-4 Adams had drawings as follows:

Cash	£1430
Goods at cost price	£110

Required:
(i) Calculate Arthur Adams's Capital as at 31 October 19-3 and 31 October 19-4.

(ii) Calculate Arthur Adams's Net Profit for the year ended 31 October 19–4.

(LCCI Elem)

(*Author's note*   Bills payable is a liability;
                   Bills receivable is an asset.)

15.07   The following list of balances remain in the books of J Seymour following the preparation of Trading and Profit and Loss Accounts which revealed a net profit for the year of £5200.

	£
Rent received owing	75
Cash at bank and in hand	850
Stock (at 31 December 19–4)	3 600
Trade debtors	1 750
Fixtures and fittings	2 000
Drawings	6 000
Bank loan (over five years)	2 000
Freehold land and buildings	22 000
Trade creditors	3 000
Capital account 1 January 19–4	29 000
Motor vehicles	3 000
Insurance prepaid	50
Electricity bill outstanding	125

Required:
(a) Prepare the Balance Sheet for J Seymour at 31 December 19–4, paying particular attention to presentation and order.
(b) Write up the Capital Account as it would appear in Seymour's private ledger.
(c) Briefly comment on any differences between short- and long-term liabilities.

(RSA 1)

NA 15.08   A sole trader, whose knowledge of bookkeeping is very poor, prepared the following document from his records.

Balance Sheet for the year ending 31 October 19–6

	£		£
Cash in hand	40	Capital 1 Nov 19–5	1980
Debtors	1670	Bank balance	480
Office furniture	300	Net profit for year	1380
Drawings	1160	Creditors	930
Bad debts	90	Discount received	80
Discount allowed	120		
Stock	1470		
	£4850		£4850

The items shown in the above document have been correctly extracted from the ledger, i.e., those on the left-hand side are debit balances whereas those on the right-hand side are credit balances.

Required:
(a) Commencing with the incorrect net profit figure of £1380, calculate the correct net profit.
(b) Redraft the above document so that it conforms with modern practice.

(LCCI Elem)

NA 15.09 Complete the following table.

Business	Capital at 1 January	Profit for year	Drawings	Capital 31 Dec
W	2170	(A)	620	1775
X	(B)	920	170	2175
Y	2195	630	320	(C)
Z	6270	1340	(D)	7250

(PEI Elem)

NA 15.10 Which of the following would you *not* need to take into account in calculating working capital?

A Cash   B Debtors   C Creditors   D Motor vehicles

(PEI Elem)

16. End of Year Adjustments

Matching expenses and incomes

The trade and activity of a business continue irrespective of the end of year accounting date. Problems arise because on this date, some bills will not have been paid, some may have been paid for next year, and money is probably owed to us. Joe intends to explain how adjustments are made in the books to deal with these problems. The idea is to match the expenses for the year with the incomes for the year. Let us look firstly at the problem of cash payments.

Payments and expenses

Cash payments do not always correspond exactly with expenses. Take a simple example with which you are already familiar. In May, cash purchases are £492.00 and credit purchases (for which payment has not yet been made) are £768.00. All the goods have been sold for £1582.00 cash.

The accounts look like this:

	Cash Account						CB 16
May	Sales	S1	1582	May	Purchases	P1	492
					Balance	c/d	1090
			1582				1582
	Balance	b/d	1090				

				Supplier's Account			S2
				May	Purchases	P1	768

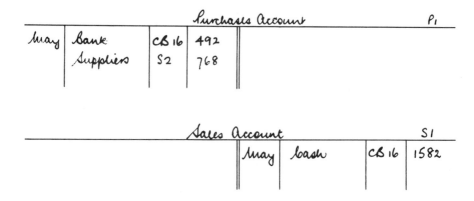

If you were asked to calculate the profit, you would say:

Sales	=	1582.00
Purchases	=	1260.00
Profit	=	322.00

You would *not* say that, because the cash is now £1090 more at the end of the month, your profit is £1090. What has actually been paid during the month is not what the total expenses are for the month.

But you already know this and practise it with regard also to credit sales and stocks when you prepare the Trading and Profit and Loss Accounts. What I now expect you to learn is how this rule of matching expenses with revenues is applied to all expenses and revenues in addition to sales and purchases. Remember the rule so that you can apply it to all transactions.

Joe's Rule No 16
When preparing the accounts for a trading period, the expenses and revenues to be included are those expenses that should be charged to the period and those revenues that should have been received in the period.

Adjustments

In applying this rule you must always ask yourself the question: What *should* be charged into the accounts for this expense, and what *should* have been received as income? These adjustments are made after the trial balance is extracted.

Example 1

If the local council charges £475 rates for the year, what should be charged into the Profit and Loss Account for rates? Answer: £475. If, however, we pay only one-half of the rates bill, the Rates Account in the ledger will show only £237.50. Only this amount will appear in the trial balance. Obviously, therefore, some adjustments are needed *after* the trial balance has been taken out.

Example 2

Another example will help to explain this point. Let us say that our business rents a factory and pays £1000 per quarter, at the end of each quarter. While payments ought to be made promptly, a few days' difference at the end of each quarter may arise because of holidays, illness, or weekends. The Rent Account at the end of the year may appear as follows:

	Rent Account			R4
Mar 30	Bank	1000		
July 2	Bank	1000		
Oct 3	Bank	1000		

Obviously, the last quarterly payment due on 31 December has been missed. The Rent Account in the trial balance will appear with a total of £3000—after all, only £3000 has actually been paid at 31 December. When preparing the Profit and Loss Account, it is important that £4000 is charged because that is what the expenses for the year *should* be—and indeed *will* be, since the £1000 due on 31 December will be paid in January or thereafter. The position on 31 December is that we have paid £3000 and owe £1000.

Bookkeeping entries

The trial balance, once taken out and balanced, will not itself require alteration. But adjustments will need to be entered in the ledgers as a double entry. You have already learned how to deal with closing stock—that is an adjustment after the trial balance has been proved. Remember that it is credited to the Trading Account and debited to a Stock Account. Take the example of rent above. What double entry is required to record the fact that £1000 is owed for rent on 31 December?

There are two ways of recording this:

Method 1

Rent Account   R4

Mar 30	Bank	CB 4	1000	Dec 31	Profit & Loss A/c			4000
July 2	Bank	CB 4	1000					
Oct 3	Bank	CB 4	1000					
Dec 31	Balance	c/a	1000					
			4000					4000
				Jan 1	Balance	b/a	1000

Method 2

Rent Account   R4

Mar 30	Bank	CB 4	1000	Dec 31	Profit & Loss A/c		4000
July 2	Bank	CB 4	1000				
Oct 3	Bank	CB 4	1000				
Dec 31	Landlords A/c	L 16	1000				
			4000				4000

Landlord's Account   L 16

				Dec 31	Rent	R4	1000

Both methods are correct and can be used. In the second method, what is owed at the end of the year is debited in the Rent Account and credited to the personal account of the person to whom it is owed. The balance on the Rent Account is then the sum that should be taken to the Profit and Loss Account.

You might believe that the second method is preferable—after all, you do owe the landlord £1000 on 31 December and the double entry is easy to understand. When you pay the rent due at the year end, the debit will be made to the landlord's account—which will then be cleared.

The first method may not appear so simple, but I use it because it saves opening a landlord's account. The thought process to use is as follows:

How much *should* be charged to the Profit and Loss Account for the year? Answer = £4000. Therefore credit the Rent Account and debit the Profit and Loss Account with this amount. The result of the credit entry in the Rent Account will be that a balance arises of £1000 (NB a *credit* balance). You have already learned that a credit balance is either an income or a liability. Since rent (that we pay) cannot be income, the balance must be a liability—£1000 of rent is *owed*. This liability will appear in the Balance Sheet under current liabilities.

Accruals

Expenses underpaid are called amounts owing or accruals, sometimes they are added to other accruals and called *sundry creditors*. Other examples of accruals at the year end are:

Wages owing
Rates outstanding
Telephone bills unpaid
Electricity owed

Expenses prepaid

While some expenses may not have been paid, others may have been paid in advance. This is the reverse of the above situation. Someone owes us money, because we have paid them before the due time. Therefore an asset will appear in the books.

Example

We pay rent quarterly in advance (i.e., at the beginning of each quarter) at the rate of £500 per quarter. You would expect four payments in the year. Due to dates of holidays, it may be that the Rent Account appears as follows.

Rent Account   R4

Jan 1	Bank	CB 4	500	Dec 31	Profit and Loss A/c		2000
Mar 30	Bank	"	500		Balance	c/d	500
July 4	Bank	"	500				
Oct 2	Bank	"	500				
Dec 30	Bank	CB 5	500				
			2500				2500
Dec 31	Balance	b/d	500				

Note the following points.

1 The actual rent payable for the year of £2000 is transferred to the Profit and Loss Account.
2 Since £2500 has actually been paid during the year, a balance of £500 appears as a debit balance.
3 A debit balance is either an expense or an asset. In this case on 31 December, the balance is an asset, since the landlord has received the sum in advance of the actual date.
4 Prepayments should appear in the Balance Sheet under the heading *Current assets*, as prepaid expenses, or payments in advance, or simply prepayments. Sometimes the various prepayments are added together and shown under the title Sundry debtors.

Other examples of prepayments are:

Rates paid in advance
Telephone rental prepaid
Insurance premiums paid in advance

Revenue adjustments

Just as expenses can be prepaid or owing, so can income be outstanding (i.e., owing to us) or paid to us in advance (and thereby owing by us). You are already familiar with the fact that debtors' accounts enable our business to record sales on credit—the revenue earned is in the Sales Account (which is transferred to the Trading Account) although the money has not been received. Debtors are assets and appear in the Balance Sheet. The same type of treatment is required at the year end when we are owed rent by persons to whom we have sublet premises, commissions by persons for whom we have worked, interest by persons to whom we have lent money, dividends on investments made, and similar revenues.

Remember the rule regarding those items that need adjustment: the amount to be taken to the Profit and Loss Account is the amount that *should* have been received in the year, not the actual amount that appears in the account and in the trial balance.

Example
Interest is receivable on a loan made by our business on 1 January 19–8. The Interest Received Account has only the following entry:

4 July (for half year to 30 June) £120.

On 8 January 19–9 the business received £120 interest for the half year ended 30 December 19-8. If our business makes its accounts up to 31 December, this is how the Interest Receivable Account will appear.

	Interest Receivable Account							
Dec 31	Profit and Loss A/c		240	July 4	Bank			120
				Dec 31	Balance	c/d		120
			240					240
Jan 1	Balance	b/d	120					

Up to 31 December our business earned £240 in interest—£120 up to 30 June and £120 for the six months up to 31 December.

The borrower owed us £120 on 31 December and this item will appear as an asset in the Balance Sheet under Current assets. These amounts are shown as Sundry debtors.

Other examples of *Revenues due* are:

Commission and fees receivable due
Interest on investments due
Rent receivable due
Insurance claims agreed but not yet paid to us

It is unusual to receive *income in advance* of its due date. One example, however, is when rents receivable are paid before the end of one year, for the following year. In this case, we owe the money to the person renting the property. The Rent Receivable Account will have a credit balance after transferring the correct sum for the trading period to the Profit and Loss Account. This balance is a liability and will be shown in the Balance Sheet under the title Sundry creditors.

A Balance Sheet summary

Balance Sheet as at . . .

Current assets	*Current liabilities*
Stock	Trade creditors (4)
Trade debtors (1)	Sundry creditors (5)
Sundry debtors (2)	Accrued expenses (6)
Payments in advance (3)	Customs and Excise (VAT) (7)
Bank	Inland Revenue (PAYE) (8)

(1)   Debtors for goods sold on credit.
(2)   Amounts due to us from transactions other than goods sold on credit.
(3)   Expenses that we have paid in advance of when they should have been paid.
(4)   Creditors for goods and services purchased.
(5)   Amounts due by us for transactions other than specifically connected with buying and selling.
(6)   Expenses that were owing at the Balance Sheet date.
(7)   Amounts due to Customs and Excise for Value Added Tax (explained later).
(8)   Tax and National Insurance contributions, deducted from employees' wages, owing to the Inland Revenue.

The effect of adjustments

Always remember to account for the two effects of end of year adjustments. One effect is on the Trading or Profit and Loss Accounts, the other is on the Balance Sheet. The adjustment, since it is made *after* the trial balance is prepared, will obviously affect the amount of that item to be charged to the Profit and Loss Account.

Example

The trial balance shows that rent actually paid totals £490. If we owe £50 for rent, then the bookkeeping entries (using Method 1 on page 158) will be:

Dr Rent Account Balance c/d £50: Cr Rent Account Balance b/d £50

So beneath the trial balance we show the adjusted entries:

Trial Balance as at . . .

	£	£
Rent	490	
Rent	50	
Rent owing		50

The Profit and Loss Account will show a total of £540 for rent, and £50 liability will appear in the Balance Sheet.

Depreciation

The methods of providing for depreciation are dealt with in Chapter 17. The important point to remember is that the adjustments for depreciation are usually made *after* the trial balance has been prepared. Any loss in the value of assets due to depreciation will need to be transferred into a separate Depreciation Account, which will reduce the value of the asset.

Example

If a motor van is purchased during a trading period, the record will be made in a Motor Van Account. At the year end, the trial balance will show the cost price as a debit balance. Depreciation will reduce its value, so the motor van at the end of the year may be worth only £2450. The value of the asset must be reduced and the loss shown as an adjustment.

Trial Balance as at . . .

	£	£
Motor van	2800	
Motor van		350
Depreciation	350	

Since the trial balance and adjustments are used as the basis of the Trading and Profit and Loss Account, you can see that the loss of £350 will be shown in the Profit and Loss Account and the motor van shown in the Balance Sheet at its true value of £2450 (2800 − 350).

Bad debts

As I have already told you, when I finally decide that a debtor will not be paying his debt, the amount owing is written off as a bad debt. This reduces the asset (of debtors) and increases the expenses. Therefore, at the end of a trading period, the Bad Debts Account will show the bad debts actually written off. Consequently the debtors' accounts, if totalled, will give you the asset of debtors to show in the Balance Sheet.

Doubtful debts

At the end of the year I look through the overdue debtors' accounts and try to decide which ones are unlikely to pay me. I take into consideration several factors such as:

1 How long the amount has been overdue
2 Whether the debtor is still in business
3 What replies were given (if any) when I requested payment

I may find *'doubtful debts'* which I think are unlikely to be paid, but which cannot yet be written off as bad debts.

We do not know how many of these doubtful debts will be paid, but since the sales were made during *this current year*, the losses as a result of non-payment should be charged against *this* year's profits and shown in *this* year's Profit and Loss Account.

Provision for bad and doubtful debts

We will find out in due course whether doubtful debts will be paid. But we need to make a provision this year, in case a doubtful debt is later written off as a bad debt. If the loss is subsequently incurred, it does not then 'surprise' us and cause disruption to the business by, for example, leaving us short of working capital.

Definition of a provision
A provision is an amount set aside out of profit for a known future loss, the amount of which cannot be exactly determined.

Purpose of the provision
This is twofold. Firstly, although bad debts may arise in the 'future', the loss sustained is charged to the period in which the transaction arose. Secondly, by making the provision the Balance Sheet figure of debtors is more realistic.

Bookkeeping entries
If we believe that, out of the total debtors at the end of the year of £8975, the amount of £460 will be lost through non-payment, then the Balance Sheet should show only £8515 as the asset. The double entry bookkeeping for this is shown

  Dr Profit and Loss A/c: Cr Provision for Bad Debts A/c

Why does the Provision Account have a credit balance? The provision is created by setting aside some of the profit made (remember that profits appear as credits). If the loss does not arise then the amount set aside is still owed to the owner.

Bad debts and provision for bad debts

Do not confuse the two, they are quite separate.

1 Bad debts are losses which are written off to the Profit and Loss Account. When the loss arises, it is taken out of the debtor's account and put into the Bad Debts Account (irrespective of any provision previously made)
2 The provision for bad debts is an end of year adjustment and therefore (as other adjustments) affects both the Profit and Loss Account and the Balance Sheet. The debtors' accounts are in no way altered.

Example 1

On 31 December 19-6, the debtors totalled £6241, the balance on the Bad Debts Account was £146, and it was considered that £171 should be provided for future possible bad debts.

This is how the accounts will look:

Debtors' Account   F2

Dec 31	Balance	6241.00	

Bad Debts Account   B6

Dec 31	Balance (a)	146.00	Dec 31	Profit and Loss A/c	146.00

Profit and Loss Account (Extract) 19-6

Dec 31	Bad debts	146.00
Dec 31	Provision for bad debts (b)	171.00

Provision for Bad and Doubtful Debts Account

		Dec 31	Profit and Loss A/c	171

Balance Sheet (Extract) 19-6

Asset side	Debtors	6241
	Less Provision for bad debts (c)	171
		6070

Note the following points.

(a) This figure (£6070) is the amount of bad debts written off during the year which has already been taken out of the debtors' account.

(b) The possible future loss of £171 is put into the Profit and Loss Account.

(c) The realistic value of debtors is shown in the Balance Sheet. (See how the provision reduces the debtors, rather than being entered under the liabilities on the Balance Sheet.)

Example 2

In the following year, let us say that £150 of the doubtful debts did become bad debts. These will have been written off in the normal way.

The Provision Account is unaffected by such actual bad debts and will still show a credit balance of £171.

On 31 December 19–7 the bad debts provision is required to be £260. Since a provision already exists of £171, it needs only to be increased by £89. Therefore the entries will be:

Profit and Loss Account (Extract) 19-7

Bad debts written off	150
Increase in provision for bad and doubtful debts	89

Provision for Bad and Doubtful Debts Account

	Dec 31 19–6	Profit and Loss	171
	Dec 31 19-7	Profit and Loss	89

Balance Sheet Extract 19-7

Asset side	Debtors (actual balances)	8672
	Less Provision for bad and doubtful debts	260
		8412

Example 3

In 19–8, the provision required may be only £235. Consequently, since the account already has a credit balance of £260 brought forward from

19-7, some of the profit previously set aside can now be written back into the Profit and Loss Account. The entries will appear as follows.

Profit and Loss Account (Extract) 19-8

	Decrease in provision for bad and doubtful debts	25

Provision for Bad and Doubtful Debts Account

Dec 31 19-8	Profit and Loss		25	Dec 31 19-6	Profit and Loss		171
Dec 31 19-8	Balance	c/d	235	Dec 31 19-7	Profit and Loss		89
			260				260
				Jan 1 19-9	Balance	b/d	235

Balance Sheet (Extract) 19-8

Asset side	Debtors (actual amount)	5968
	Less Provision for bad and doubtful debts	235
		5733

16.01 A trial balance has the following accounts included.

Insurance	£141.00 (Dr)	
Commission		£75.00 (Cr)
Telephones	£293.00 (Dr)	
Carriage	£77.00 (Dr)	

The following adjustments are required in respect of these items.

Insurance is prepaid by £39.00
Commission receivable, due, amounts to £25.00
Telephone bill outstanding £76.00
Carriage expenses outstanding £15.00

Show the ledger account for each item above after the adjustment has been made and the transfer effected to the Profit and Loss Account.

16.02 On 1 January 19-9 the Wages Account had a credit balance brought forward of £87.55. During the year £9174.62 was paid in cash for wages. On 31 December 19-9, £110.76 was outstanding for wages due but unpaid. Show the Wages Account after adjustment.

NA 16.03 Losses are written off to the Profit and Loss Account. How is a future
loss dealt with at the financial year end? Explain the double entry
required.

16.04 When Daniel Martin prepared his final accounts he calculated his net profit
at £8975. However, on more careful inspection of his accounts he found
the following errors. Construct an adjustment of profit statement to show
his true net profit.

(a) A bill for rates of £200 had not been paid
(b) Sales of £28 had not been recorded
(c) Closing stock had been overvalued by £48
(d) Depreciation of £200 had not been provided for
(e) Rent receivable of £50 was outstanding
(f) Sales returns of £22 had not been entered
(g) Rent of £10 recorded in the profit and loss account related to next
     year
(h) A provision for bad debts of £20 should have been created

(PEI Elem)

16.05 After completing a Trading Account for the period ending 31 October 19-4,
the books of S Rix contain the following balances:

	£
Rent Received	155 Credit
Stationery	240 Debit
General Expenses	125 Debit

You are required to take into consideration the following:
(i)   Rix is owed £20 rent
(ii)   There is a stock of unused stationery £55
(iii) An invoice for £25 relating to general expenses remains unpaid

and to show the above mentioned accounts and the Profit and Loss Account
as they would appear after all entries had been made.

(RSA I)

NA 16.06 Tolan's Balance Sheet at 31 March 19-8 included the following
entry:

	£	
Debtors	15 000	
Less Provision for bad debts	300	14 700

At the end of the two following financial years the debtors, before
deducting any provision for bad debts, were:

	19-9	19-0
At 31 March	13 000	16 400

On each of these dates a provision for bad debts was calculated on the same basis as at 31 March 19–8. The actual amounts of bad debts written off were:

	19–9	19–0
During the year to 31 March	940	760

You are required to:

1 Prepare accounts for bad debts and provision for bad debts for the years ending 31 March 19–9, and 31 March 19–0.
2 Show the entries in the Profit and Loss Account for the two years.

NA 16.07 Frederick Layton, a sole trader, extracted the following trial balance from his books as at the close of business on 29 February 19–6.

	Dr £	Cr £
Purchases and Sales	3 190	6 620
Drawings	1 320	
Capital Account 1 March 19–5		2 700
Stock 1 March 19–5	760	
Debtors and creditors	1 450	820
Wages and salaries	1 280	
Bank	860	
Cash	40	
Rent and rates	430	
Office furniture	660	
General office expenses	120	
Discounts	220	190
	£10 330	£10 330

Notes
(a) Stock 29 February 19–6—£830.
(b) Provide for depreciation of office furniture—£60.
(c) Wages and salaries accrued due at 29 February 19–6 amounted to £80.

Required:
Draw up the Trading and Profit and Loss Accounts for the year ending 29 February 19–6 together with a Balance Sheet as at that date.

(LCCI Elem)

16.08 The following particulars relate to the business of P Shaw, a sole trader, on 31 December 19–4.

		£
(a)	Stock in trade 1 January 19–4	1 360
	Purchases of goods for the year	10 820
	Sales	13 850
	Stock in trade 31 December 19–4	1 884

(b)	*Wages and salaries:*	£
	Owing 1 January 19–4	90
	Payments during the year	2 190
	Owing 31 December 19–4	50

	Rates	£
	In advance 1 January 19–4	40
	Payments during the year	260
	In arrears 31 December 19–4	75

Required:
(a) Write up the ledger accounts for Sales, Purchases, Stock, Wages and Salaries and Rates showing, where appropriate, the closure of these accounts, and the relevant transfer to the final accounts.
(b) Prepare the Trading and Profit and Loss Account for the year ending 31 December 19–4 showing clearly the cost of sales, gross profit, and net profit.

(RSA 1)

16.09 Davy Jones owns a small business. At the close of trading on 31 May 19–5 the following balances were extracted from his books:

	£
Stock 1 June 19–4	11 000
Purchases	52 000
Sales	84 000
Carriage inwards	150
Sales returns	650
Purchase returns	400
Insurance	250
Heating and lighting	2 500
Stationery	1 500
Rates	1 200

Motor expenses	1 600
Carriage outwards	100
Discounts allowed	140
Discounts received	110
Wages	4 200
Telephone	180

You are required to take the following into consideration on 31 May 19-5:

(i)	Stock in hand	12 000
(ii)	Insurance paid in advance	50
(iii)	Stock of stationery	100
(iv)	Heat and lighting accrued	150
(v)	Rates prepaid	300

and prepare a Trading Profit and Loss Account for the year ended 31 May 19-5 showing clearly in your trading account the Cost of Goods/Stock sold.
NB   A Balance Sheet is not required.

(RSA 1)

NA 16.10   (i) L George rents his premises at an annual rental of £1200. On 1 June 19-3 George had paid his rent up to the end of July, and during the year ended 31 May 19-4 he made the following payments for rent, by cheque:

August 1	£300
November 5	£300
February 1	£300
June 1	£400

(ii) George sublets part of these premises to S Broke at a rent of £480 per annum, and on 1 June 19-3 Broke's rent was one month in arrears. During the year ended 31 May 19-4 George received the following amounts in cash from Broke:

July 25	£ 40
August 18	£120
December 4	£150
April 9	£ 60

(iii)   On 1 June 19-3 George owed the Electricity Board £74 for electricity supplies up to that date, during the year he made the following payments by cheque:

June 1	£ 74
September 10	£ 82
December 5	£104
April 7	£ 81

On 31 May 19-4 there was a balance outstanding on the electricity account of £96.

You are required:

(a)   To write up George's rent payable account, rent receivable account, and electricity account for the year ended 31 May 19-4 showing clearly the amounts to be transferred to the Profit and Loss Account in each case.

(b)   Show how the balances brought down would appear in the Balance Sheet on 31 May 19-4.

(RSA 1)

NA 16.11 The following trial balance was extracted from the books of Robert Owen on 30 April 19-5:

	£	£
Capital 1 May 19-4		30 640
Furniture and equipment	10 500	
Sales		46 800
Postage and stationery	1 750	
Returns inwards	1 320	
Rates and insurance	1 200	
Wages and salaries	8 440	
Purchases	27 560	
Drawings	6 000	
Trade creditors		2 830
Petty cash	80	
Bank balance		4 600
Sundry expenses	8 570	
Stock 1 May 19-4	6 500	
Loan from Mercantile Bank		5 000
Interest on loan	750	
Freehold premises	15 000	
Trade debtors	2 200	
	£89 870	£89 870

The following additional information is given:

(a)   Stock on 30 April 19-5 was valued at £7640.
(b)   Provide for carriage on purchases owing at 30 April 19-5 £140.
(c)   The annual fire insurance premium of £240 was paid on the due date 1 February 19-5.

Make the necessary adjustment for the unexpired portion at 30 April 19-5.
   You are required to prepare the Trading and Profit and Loss Account for the year ended 30 April 19-5 and a Balance Sheet as at that date.

(RSA 1)

NA 16.12   A decrease in the provision for bad debts will

A   increase the profit for the year
B   decrease the profit for the year
C   increase the cash balance
D   decrease the cash balance

(PEI Elem)

NA 16.13   A bad debt is

A   a large sum of money owing
B   a debt unlikely to be paid
C   a debt owed by one trader to another
D   wages owing to workers

(PEI Elem)

NA 16.14   Which of the following is a current liability?

A   Overpayment of a bill
B   Rates paid in advance
C   A loan to another person
D   Money borrowed from a friend

(PEI Elem)

17. Purchase of Fixed Assets and Depreciation

Fixed assets

So far, I have been hiring a van to bring the carpets to the warehouse. I want to buy a motor van so that I can bring the carpets to the warehouse myself and also deliver carpets.

When a business acquires a motor van, the van is called a *fixed asset*. Fixed assets are those which are acquired and retained in the business and not turned into cash. Such assets are normally used for more than one year.

Other examples of *fixed assets* are:

Plant and machinery
Fixtures and fittings in the shop
Land and buildings

Current assets

You may remember that I once said to you that goods that have been bought to resell, such as carpets, paints and polish are stocks, we turn these into cash by selling them. They are called *current assets*.

Other *current assets* are:

Cash in the till
Cash in the bank
Amounts owed to us by debtors

Capital and revenue expenditure

When I buy a fixed asset, such expenditure is called *capital expenditure*.

Fixed assets are used by the business to help it carry out its activities. Premises are required for offices, factories, shops; lorries are required for deliveries; equipment such as typewriters and computers and furniture are needed for the office. These fixed assets need *revenue expenditure* both to maintain them and operate them. For example machinery needs electric power to drive it and operators to control output.

We can think of many examples of revenue expenditure: wages, gas, telephone, rent and rates, repairs to machinery, and many more.

Joe's Rule No 17
Assets bought for use in the business to earn income represent capital expenditure, *while the expenditure incurred in the daily operating of the business is* revenue expenditure.

You have already learned of the importance of this distinction, but to remind you:

Capital expenditure is recorded in asset accounts, which are shown in the Balance Sheet.

Revenue expenditure is recorded in an expense account—which is then transferred to the Profit and Loss Account at the end of the year.

17.01   Give four examples of (a) capital expenditure and (b) revenue expenditure.

Materiality

I should tell you that quite a number of small value assets are not recorded as assets but are written off directly as an expense when purchased. I do not want you to waste time recording the odd box file, rubbers, pencils, and so on. Any item less than £10 should be written off—otherwise you will spend time at the end of the year calculating the depreciation. Such small items are considered to be immaterial as far as their effect on profit is concerned.

17.02   (a) Ledger accounts are classified as real, nominal, and personal. Distinguish between these types of accounts.
(b) A van was bought for £4400 and mistakenly debited to a nominal account. What effect does this have on the Profit and Loss Account and the Balance Sheet?
(c) Which type of account should be debited?

Depreciation of fixed assets

A fixed asset may have a number of years of useful life. A machine may be used for four years, at the end of which we will sell it or throw it away. During each of the four years, the value of the machine goes down and this decrease in its value is said to be the cost of the use of the machine. Depreciation, therefore, is the permanent reduction in the value of an asset. Depreciation may be due to the following factors.

1 *Wear and tear* Machinery used every day wears out. All fixed assets will lose value because of usage.

2 *Passage of time*   Even if assets are not used, their value will decrease as they rust away!

3 *Obsolescence*   Manual typewriters are 'out of date', they have been replaced by more efficient electronic ones. Other assets become obsolete because spare parts are no longer available.

4 *Depletion*   When a quarry has had all its valuable stone removed the asset no longer exists.

The actual loss does not arise until the asset is sold, destroyed or worn out, but it is one of the principles of accounting that allowances should be made for all possible losses. Since depreciation is a loss, it is transferred at the year end (or on the sale of an asset) to the Profit and Loss Account. In this way we try to show as accurate a profit (or loss) as possible.

To find the precise amount of depreciation of an asset is difficult, if not impossible. The amount of depreciation is determined by the owner of the business or the accountant using one of the main methods in common use.

Straight line method (or fixed instalment method)

This method suggests that we can determine for how long we are going to use the asset. The annual charge is then calculated by dividing the asset cost, *less* any estimated scrap value, by the estimated working life of the asset. For example, if we take a machine for which we have paid £840, and we know it is going to be used for four years at the end of which we can sell it for £40, the depreciation we charge at the end of each year for the use of the machine will be £200. We arrived at £200 by using the following formula.

$$\frac{\text{Cost of the machine less the scrap value}}{\text{Number of years of its useful life}} = \frac{£840 - £40}{4} = £200$$

	Asset value	Depreciation
Year 1	840	200
Year 2	640	200
Year 3	440	200
Year 4	240	200

This method is suitable for plant and machinery and leasehold property.

Reducing balance method (or diminishing balance method)

In this method we do not have to find the number of years the asset will be used.

A fixed percentage of the asset's value is written off annually. However, unlike the straight line method, the annual percentage is based on the reduced asset value.

For example a van cost Joe £7000, and he has decided to write off 10 per cent of the balance at the end of each year as depreciation.

	Asset value	Depreciation	
Year 1	7000	700	
Year 2	6300	630	
Year 3	5670	567	
Year 4	5103	510	(to nearest £)

This method is commonly used by those firms having plant and equipment that may quickly lose value through obsolescence—such as chemical and similar processing plant, and for motor vehicles.

Revaluation method

The asset is revalued annually and any decrease in value is the depreciation for the year. We use this method where the other methods may not be appropriate or practicable. The method is used for livestock, loose tools, and stock in trade.

17.03 Use the straight line method to work out the annual depreciation in these examples.

(a) Plant and machinery, bought in 19–1 for £8000, which will be used for five years and will have no sale value at the end of the five years.
(b) Motor car, cost £12 000, has eight years' useful life and sale value £400.
(c) Fixtures and fittings, cost £2800, have 20 years' useful life and no sale value.
(d) Computer, cost £2500, with five years' useful life, and no sale value.

17.04 Use the reducing balance method to work out the annual provision for depreciation in the following examples for the first two years.

(a) Motor van, cost £2000, depreciation at 15 per cent per annum.
(b) Plant and machinery, cost £8000, depreciation at 20 per cent per annum.

(c) Office machinery, cost £600, depreciation at 10 per cent per annum.

(d) Fixtures, cost £500, depreciation at 8 per cent per annum.

17.05 Use the revaluation method to work out the annual provision for depreciation in the following examples.

(a) Cost of tools on 1 January 19-1 £250, cost of tools on 31 December 19-1 £215.

(b) At the beginning of the year the cost of loose tools was £170; during the year Joe Wynn bought a set of tools for £120; at the end of the year the tools were valued at £250.

(c) Jim Springtime farms in a big way. The value of livestock shown in his books at the beginning of the year was £70 000. During the year there was an outbreak of foot and mouth disease which affected his trade appreciably. He bought some stock costing £25 000 and his net cost of disposals was £35 500. His livestock was valued at £56 000, at the year end.

Bookkeeping entries for depreciation

There are two ways of recording depreciation.

1 The '*simple*' way (after calculating the depreciation for the year) is:

Dr Depreciation Account: Cr Asset Account

Last year, for example, I bought some office machinery which cost £400. I decided to write it off at the rate of 10 per cent per year using the reducing balance method. Using the simple method, the accounts would look like this:

Depreciation Account   D6

19-1 Dec 31	Office machinery	O1	40				

Office Machinery Account   O1

19-1 Jan 1	Bank	CB	400	19-1 Dec 31	Depreciation A/c	D6	40
					Balance	c/d	360
			400				400
19.2 Jan 1	Balance	b/d	360				

2 Unfortunately, this simple bookkeeping procedure is not satisfactory for most firms because:

(a) The cost price of assets cannot be easily seen.
(b) It does not show the total depreciation provided during the life of the asset.

Both of these need to be shown in the accounts of limited companies. Therefore the usual method of recording depreciation is:

Dr Depreciation Account: Cr Provision for Depreciation Account

Using the example above these are how the accounts should look:

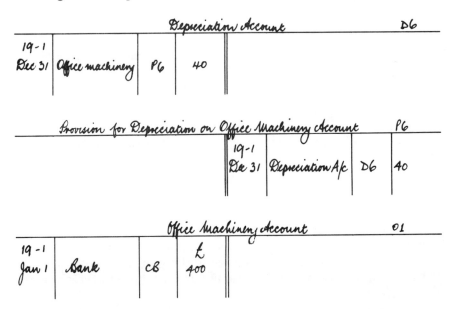

You will notice that the office machinery remains at cost in the ledger account. In the previous illustration it is shown at its written down value (WDV), i.e., £360. The loss of the £40 shown in the Depreciation Account will be transferred to the Profit and Loss Account:

Dr Profit and Loss Account: Cr Depreciation Account

Balance Sheet layout

Fixed asseets are shown as the first item on the asset side of the Balance Sheet. Whatever depreciation method is used, or however the bookkeeping entries are made, it is the written down value of the asset that forms part of the *total assets*.

Using the simple method the Balance Sheet will show:

Balance Sheet (extract) . . .

(Asset side)	£
Fixed assets	
Office machiney (WDV)	360

Using the usual method the Balance Sheet will show

Balance Sheet (extract) . . .

(Asset side)		
Fixed assets	£	£
Office machinery at cost	400	
Depreciation provision	40	360

17.06   What would the Balance Sheet extracts show at the end of the following year using the simple and usual way of recording depreciation?

Purchase and sale of assets

Practices vary when an asset is bought or sold. A business will choose one of the following methods and use it consistently:

1. Depreciation is charged on a time basis—that is from the date of purchase of the asset to the end of the accounting year or to the date of sale. In Joe's case, if the office machinery had been bought on 1 July, a half year's depreciation (of £20) would have been charged.
2. A full year's depreciation is charged in the year of purchase (irrespective of date of purchase), and none in the year of disposal.
3. Depreciation is ignored in the year of purchase, but a full year's charge is made in the year of disposal.

17.07   Thomas Jones, a sole trader, purchases new office furniture for £500. He decides to write off depreciation at 10 per cent per annum but cannot decide whether this would be on the straight line method or diminishing balance method.

Required:
To demonstrate to Jones the difference between the two methods, draw up the Office Furniture Account for the first three years, as it would appear:
(a) for the 'straight line' method, and
(b) for the 'diminishing balance' method.

(LCCI Elem)

(*Author's note*   Use the simple method of recording depreciation.)

Posting the ledger from a book of original entry

You should know the first part of *Joe's Rule No 4* off by heart: *The first record of any transaction must be made in a book of original entry*. Yet in this chapter entries have been made in asset accounts, depreciation accounts and provision accounts, without any mention of being first recorded in a book of original entry.

In fact, depreciation transfers are recorded first in the Journal, as explained later.

NA 17.08 John Jones, a sole trader, purchases a delivery van for £1000. He cannot decide whether to write off depreciation of the van on the straight line method or the diminishing balance method.

Required:
To illustrate how the two methods work, draw up the Delivery Van Account for the first three years as it would appear
(a) for the straight line method, and
(b) for the diminishing balance method.

Note
(i) You must indicate clearly the method used.
(ii) The rate of depreciation in both cases is to be 20 per cent per annum.

(LCCI Elem)

17.09 Allocate the following debits between capital and revenue expenditure, giving reasons.

(a) Purchase of new vehicle
(b) Fuel for vehicles
(c) New tyres for vehicles
(d) Vehicle insurance
(e) Radio equipment fitted to vehicle

(PEI Elem)

NA 17.10 Mr Brown has recently started in business on his own account and is puzzled by the terms 'Capital Expenditure' and 'Revenue Expenditure'.

(a) Explain to him what Capital Expenditure is.

(b) Mr Brown has purchased a new van, the details of the account were as follows:

	£
Van	3000
Seat belts	24
Delivery charges	42
Number plates	15
Road tax	90
Insurance	220
	3391

He has received an account from his local builder, details of which are as follows:

	£
Re-decorate shop front	400
Erect shelves in stock room	90
	490

You are required to list the items from both invoices under their respective headings of Capital and Revenue Expenditure.

(RSA 1)

17.11 On 1 Jan a manufacturing concern purchased from City Traders Ltd a machine valued at £6000. It was decided to depreciate the machine at the rate of 10 per cent per annum on the diminishing balance.

(a) Show the Machinery Account for the next three years.
(b) If the firm had depreciated the machine by 10 per cent per annum on the original value, what difference would this have made to the firm's profits during the three years?

(PEI Elem)

17.12 Reconstruct in good form the following Balance Sheet after taking into account the transactions for December.

Balance Sheet as at 30 November

	£		£
Assets		*Liabilities*	
Cash	500	Capital	3000
Machinery	1000	+ Net profit	1000
Vans	2000		
Debtors	1500		4000
Stock	1000	− Drawings	300
			3700
		Creditors	2300
	£6000		£6000

Dec	1	Received a cheque from debtors £200
	5	Took drawings in cash £150
	10	Sold goods which cost £100 for £300 cash
	15	Purchased goods on credit for £200
	19	Depreciated machinery by £170
	21	Took a loan from the bank to buy machine costing £2000
	31	Paid £25 cash into bank

(PEI Elem)

NA 17.13 G Dixon starts in business at Dock Green on 1 January 19-6, and for his financial years ending 31 December 19-6, 19-7, and 19-8, you are to show:

(a) The Machinery Account.
(b) The Provision for Depreciation Account.
(c) The Balance Sheet extracts for each of the years 19-6, 19-7, 19-8.

The machinery bought was:

Jan 1 19-6   1 machine costing £1000
July 1 19-7   2 machines costing £750 each
Oct 1 19-7   1 machine costing £400
Apr 1 19-8   1 machine costing £200

Depreciation is at the rate of 10 per cent per annum, using the straight line method, machines being depreciated for each proportion of a year.

NA 17.14   Cheryl Steptoe and her son have been in business as rag and bone merchants for many years. They maintain their fixed assets at cost and have Depreciation Provision Accounts, one for each type of asset. The motor van is to be depreciated at the rate of 12½ per cent per annum, and fixtures at the rate of 10 per cent per annum, using the reducing balance method.

The following transactions in assets have taken place in recent years:

Jan 1 19-6   Bought motor van £8400, fixtures £2000
July 1   Bought fixtures £4000
Oct 1 19-7   Bought motor van £7200
Dec 1   Bought fixtures £150.

The financial year end of the business is 31 December.
  Depreciation is to be calculated on assets in existence at the end of each year, giving a full year's depreciation even though the asset was bought part of the way through the year.

Your are to show:

(a) The Motor Van Account.
(b) The Fixtures Account.
(c) The two separate Provision for Depreciation Accounts.
(d) The Fixed Assets section of the Balance Sheet at the end of each year, for the years ended 31 December 19-6 and 19-7.

NA 17.15   A Rogers opened his own business as a newsagent and paid the following:

(a) Wages of shop assistant
(b) The purchase of a new cash register
(c) Repairs to a leaking shop window
(d) Payment of a fire insurance premium
(e) The building of an extension to the rear of the premises to provide more storage space
(f) Purchase of floor cleaning materials for use in the shop
(g) Legal fees paid in connection with the building of the extension
(h) The purchase of stock for resale.

Required:

(i) For each item state whether it is Capital or Revenue expenditure.
(ii) Explain clearly and concisely the difference between these two forms of expenditure.

(RSA 1)

NA 17.16 The following Trial Balance was extracted from the books of William Watson, a sole trader, at the close of business on 31 October 19-9:

	£ DR	£ CR
Debtors and creditors	4 110	2 070
Discounts	530	290
Capital Account 1 November 19-8		5 200
Drawings	2 760	
Bank overdraft		1 090
Bills receivable and payable	550	380
Purchases and sales	9 840	17 630
Sales and purchases returns	720	360
Wages and salaries	3 250	
Office furniture	800	
Delivery van	960	
Van running expenses	420	
Rent and rates	710	
Cash	90	
Stock 1 November 19-8	1 970	
Bad debts written off	270	
Sundry expenses	260	
Provision for bad and doubtful debts		220
	27 240	27 240

Notes
(1) Stock 31 October 19-9—£3040
(2) Increase the provision for bad and doubtful debts by £40 to £260
(3) Wages accrued 31 October 19-9—£70
(4) Rates prepaid 31 October 19-9—£60
(5) Provide for depreciation:
   Office furniture £80
   Delivery van £120

Required:
Prepare the Trading Profit and Loss Accounts for the year ended 31 October 19-9 together with a Balance Sheet as at that date.

(LCCI Elem)

18. Looking at the Results

Measuring success

Most businesses hope to be successful. One measure of success is profit. As Joe says: 'I want to know how much profit I have made (or loss suffered), and this is shown in the Trading and Profit and Loss Account. The gross profit and the net profit, while showing the actual results for the year, do not give me any indication of how well the business is performing in comparison with similar businesses—or whether or not this business is improving in comparison with the previous year.'

You might think that a comparison between profits will quickly show whether or not a business is improving. If, for example, in Year 1 this business made £6000 profit and in Year 2 it made £7000, it appears that Year 2 was the better year. Indeed, Year 2 did make more profit, but if in Year 2:

1 I sold twice as many goods
2 Employed twice as many staff
3 I worked twice as hard

Was Year 2 really a better year than Year 1?

Another point to consider is that of capital invested by the owner. If I invested more capital into the business I would expect more profit. However, unless I knew how much more profit I expected to make, I would not know whether the business was achieving that aim. Measuring success means comparing the actual results of a business

(a)   with its previous results; or
(b)   with other similar businesses; or
(c)   with what you believe it should achieve.

Comparison of results is best done by calculating certain ratios and percentages.

Stock and trading ratios

Let us compare the results of two years' trading.

Trading and Profit and Loss Accounts

	19-7	19-8		19-7	19-8
Opening stock	4 000	6 000	Sales	20 000	30 000
Purchases	18 000	29 000			
	22 000	35 000			
Closing stock	6 000	10 000			
(Cost of goods sold)	16 000	25 000			
Gross profit	4 000	5 000			
	20 000	30 000		20 000	30 000
Admin. expenses	500	1 000	Gross profits	4 000	5 000
Selling expenses	1 000	1 000			
Net profit	2 500	3 000			
	4 000	5 000		4 000	5 000

Gross profit percentages

In terms of gross profit, 19-8 seems the better year. Let us look at some gross profit measures to see if it was.

1 *Mark-up percentage*   This is calculated by dividing the gross profit by the cost of goods sold (made into a percentage by multiplying by 100).

For 19-7 $\dfrac{\text{Gross profit}}{\text{Cost of goods sold}} = \dfrac{4000}{16\,000} \times 100 = 25$ per cent

For 19-8 $\dfrac{\text{Gross profit}}{\text{Cost of goods sold}} = \dfrac{5000}{25\,000} \times 100 = 20$ per cent

Gross profit as a percentage of the cost price of the goods sold is called the *mark-up percentage*. In 19-7 the mark-up was 25 per cent. This means that, on average, for every £1 of goods sold (at cost price), 25p was added for profit. In 19-8 the mark-up was only 20 per cent, i.e., 20p on every £1. Therefore 19-7 was the better year.

2 *Gross margin percentage*   This is calculated by dividing the gross profit by the selling price of the goods sold (i.e., **sales**).

For 19–7 $\dfrac{\text{Gross profit}}{\text{Sales}} = \dfrac{4000}{20\ 000} \times 100 = 20$ per cent

For 19–8 $\dfrac{\text{Gross profit}}{\text{Sales}} = \dfrac{5000}{30\ 000} \times 100 = 16.7$ per cent

This is another way of showing the gross profit as a percentage of the total sales. This measure is called the *gross margin*. It shows, on average, how much of each £1 of sales represents profit. In 19–8, of every £1 of sales 16.7p was profit. In 19–7, the figure was 20p. Therefore (as in (1) above) 19–7 was the better year.

Stock measures

Stock represents an investment of capital. As with other assets it is used to generate profits. You may think it a good idea to have as much stock as possible. From the customer's point of view, more stock means more choice, but from the business point of view, is the extra capital tied up in stock earning its keep?

The business wants maximum sales from minimum stocks. To achieve this the business wants stocks to be bought and sold quickly so that at any one moment the least amount of capital is involved.

Rate of stock turnover

This is the measure of how quickly stocks are bought and sold.

To calculate this figure you must first of all calculate the average value of stock held during the year. With proper stock records it is possible to add together the value of stocks at each month end, divide by 12, and get an accurate average stock value. With only final accounts available for information, the only way to obtain the average stock figure is to add opening stock to closing stock and divide by 2.

Therefore average stock =

For 19–7   Opening stock =   4 000

                  Closing stock +   6 000
                                  _____

                  Average stock = 10 000   ÷ 2 = £5000

For 19-8   Opening stock =   6 000

                Closing stock   + 10 000

                Average stock   = 16 000   ÷ 2 = £8000

Using these average stock figures, *the rate of stock turnover* =

For 19-7 $\dfrac{\text{Value of stock sold (at cost)}}{\text{Average stock}} = \dfrac{16\ 000}{5000} = 3.20$

For 19-8 $\dfrac{\text{Value of stock sold (at cost)}}{\text{Average stock}} = \dfrac{25\ 000}{8000} = 3.12$

The rates show that 19-7 was very slightly better than 19-8, i.e., the stock moved more quickly in 19-7. By the way, rate of stock turnover should not be confused with turnover. Turnover is another word for sales.

Net profit percentage

Since 19-8 had a higher net profit than 19-7, then in that respect it is a better year. Let us look at a measure which will show us whether or not we have been as efficient in 19-8 as in 19-7, in organizing and operating the business.

Net profit percentage of sales

How much of each £ from sales was net profit?

For 19-7 $\dfrac{\text{Net profit}}{\text{Sales}} = \dfrac{2500}{20\ 000} \times 100 = 12.5$ per cent

For 19-8 $\dfrac{\text{Net profit}}{\text{Sales}} = \dfrac{3000}{30\ 000} \times 100 = 10$ per cent

So in 19-8 we made a lot more sales—but the amount of profit on each £ of sales was 2.5p less than in 19-7. Had the gross profit percentage in 19-8 remained the same as 19-7, then this reduction in the net profit percentage would have been a valid measure of decreased efficiency. However, as the gross profit percentage has decreased in 19-8 then a decrease in the net profit percentage is to be expected. Is the decrease better or worse than expected? To measure this we need to look at expense percentages.

Expense percentages

Expenses as a percentage of sales =

For 19–7 $\dfrac{\text{Expenses}}{\text{Sales}} = \dfrac{1500}{20\,000} \times 100 = 7.5$ per cent

For 19–8 $\dfrac{\text{Expenses}}{\text{Sales}} = \dfrac{2000}{30\,000} \times 100 = 6.6$ per cent

This means that 19–8 was more efficient in the use of selling and administrative staff and other resources as the total cost was 6.6 per cent of the sales achieved, while in 19–7 it was 7.5 per cent of the sales.

Put another way:

Between 19–7 and 19–8 expenses increased by 33.3 per cent

(£2000 (19–8) − £1500 (19–7) = £500 which as a percentage = 500 ÷ 1500 = 33.3 per cent)

While at the same time sales increased by 50 per cent

(£30 000 (19–8) − £20 000 (19–7) = £10 000 which as a percentage = 10 000 ÷ 20 000 = 50 per cent)

The expenses can be measured individually to see which have improved or worsened as a percentage of sales. For example administration expenses have doubled between 19–7 and 19–8, while sales have gone up by only half.

Also, selling expenses have not increased at all—yet sales have gone up by 50 per cent. Of course, it may be that because less was spent on selling expenses that the gross profit margins fell in 19–8.

18.01 (i) Calculate the administration expenses as a percentage of sales for 19–7 and 19–8.

(ii) Calculate the selling expenses as a percentage of sales for 19–7 and 19–8.

Overall result

In 19–8 sales were 50 per cent more than in 19–7. Gross profit, however, increased by only 25 per cent. Net profit increased by only 20 per cent.

Stocks increased; expenses increased, but not in the same proportion as sales. Perhaps 19–8 was not so good after all.

Balance Sheet comparisons

In measuring the success or otherwise of a business, some consideration should be given to the capital that the owner has invested in his business.

If Joe could invest his capital in a building society or bank deposit account and earn as much interest as he is earning profit from his business, why bother with the business?

He also ought to compare his profits with what he could earn by working for someone else. Let us first look at his capital position by comparing the balance sheets shown below.

Balance Sheet as at 31 December 19-7			*Balance Sheet as at 31 December 19-8*		
		£			£
Fixed assets		4 500	*Fixed assets*		4 000
Current assets			*Current assets*		
Stock	6 000		Stock	10 000	
Debtors	2 000		Debtors	4 000	
Cash	500		Cash	–	
	8 500			14 000	
Less Current liabilities	4 000		*Less* Current liabilities	8 000	
		4 500			6 000
		9 000			10 000
Financed by:			Financed by:		
Capital 1 Jan 19-7		10 000	Capital 1 Jan 19-8		9 000
Profit for the year	2 500		Profit for the year	3 000	
Drawings	3 500	(1 000)	Drawings	4 000	(1 000)
		9 000			8 000
Loan			Loan		2 000
		9 000			10 000

Owner's investment
Average amount of owner's capital invested:

For 19-7   Opening capital   10 000
            Closing capital   +   9 000

$$19\ 000 \div 2 = £9\ 500$$

For 19-8   Opening capital   9 000

             Closing capital   + 8 000

             _____

                                 17 000   ÷ 2 = £8 500

The owner's investment is decreasing, because he is drawing more money than the profit being made. The profit, even if it remains constant will, when measured as a percentage of his average investment, increase if his investment is going down. It is beneficial to the owner if his investment does go down, since less of his own money is tied up in the business. Clearly, capital will need to be supplied by someone else if the business is to continue. In this illustration, current liabilities have doubled in 19-8 and a bank loan has been received of £2000. The owner's investment is used to calculate his 'return on capital'. If an owner puts his money into a bank he will receive interest and that is his 'return'. If he invests his money in shares he will receive dividends—this will be his 'return'. In a business his profit is his 'return', but is the return good or bad? Is it better than investing in shares or putting the money into a bank? Has it improved over the previous year?

Return on owner's capital

This measures the owner's profit as a percentage of his average investment. The return on owner's capital is:

For 19-7 $$\frac{\text{Profit}}{\text{Average capital invested}} = \frac{2500}{9500} \times 100 = 26 \text{ per cent}$$

For 19-8 $$\frac{\text{Profit}}{\text{Average capital invested}} = \frac{3000}{8500} \times 100 = 35 \text{ per cent}$$

18.02 (i) Is this return better than the owner could expect from a bank deposit account?

(ii) Why would the owner expect to receive a higher return from his business than if he invested his capital in a bank?

In addition to considering the position of the owner, the position of the business itself needs to be measured. Is it using all of the capital employed effectively? (The owner is only one 'supplier' of finance.) Can it pay its debts without causing a shortage of cash? The following measures analyse the Balance Sheet position.

Capital employed

The net capital used by the business in 19-7 was £9000 (all provided by the owner). In 19-8 this had increased to £10 000 (of which the owner provided £8000).

A business uses capital to buy assets and finance its daily activities in order to earn profits. The profits have to be sufficient to 'reward' the suppliers of capital for its use. If, for example, you borrowed money at 10 per cent interest, you need to use the capital to earn at least 10 per cent profits—otherwise it isn't worth borrowing the money. To measure how much the capital being used is earning, the return on capital employed is calculated.

Return on capital employed

The profit measured as a percentage of the total net capital employed is:

For 19-7 $\dfrac{\text{Profit}}{\text{Net capital employed}} = \dfrac{2500}{9000} \times 100 = 27.7$ per cent

For 19-8 $\dfrac{\text{Profit}}{\text{Net capital employed}} = \dfrac{3000}{10\ 000} \times 100 = 30$ per cent

Again this measure shows that 19-8 is the more successful year. Although more 'capital' was being used, it was generating profits at a higher rate.

Working capital

You mustn't think that capital can be divided into working and non-working. The total value of all the assets represents gross capital employed—and this is divided between fixed assets and current assets. All the assets are working for the business (or should be!), but some of the assets remain 'fixed' and do not change over a long period, e.g., land, buildings, machinery, vehicles, etc. Other assets, such as stock, debtors, and cash change every day. It is this latter group of assets which supply the money to repay current liabilities. Creditors have to be paid, tax demands met, bank overdrafts reduced—and if the business does not have sufficient funds to pay these then how can it pay its everyday demands for wages, rent, and all the other expenses. Working capital is the value of assets available to the business over and above current liabilities, to maintain its daily activities. It is measured by the difference between current assets and current liabilities. The working capital figures are:

For 19-7   Current assets   8 500
            Current liabilities   —   4 000

            Working capital   =   4 500

For 19-8   Current assets   14 000
            Current liabilities   —   8 000

            Working capital   =   6 000

Working capital ratio

While the working capital has increased in total in 19-8, the ratio of current assets to current liabilities is:

For 19-7   Current assets   8 500 = 2.1 : 1
            ─────────────
            Current liabilities   4 000

For 19-8   Current assets   14 000 = 1.75 : 1
            ─────────────
            Current liabilities   8 000

This is often referred to as the *current ratio*. What does 2.1 : 1 mean? Remember that we are comparing current assets with current liabilities.

For every £1 of current liabilities in 19-7 there was £2.10 of current assets available to pay them. In 19-8, for every £1 of current liabilities there was only £1.75 of current assets available. The ratio has worsened. The current liabilities take up a greater proportion in 19-8, of those assets which are used to pay them.

If the ratio were to fall 1 : 1 it would mean that the business had no working capital, as all the current assets would be needed to pay the current liabilities.

Acid test ratio

This measure (often referred to as the liquid ratio) is a more critical analysis of the position of the business in relation to its creditors than the working capital ratio. The latter assumes that creditors can be paid out of available cash, money collected from debtors and stock sold. However, if all the creditors wanted immediate payment, only cash and what can be quickly collected from debtors is available.

The ratio is current assets (*less* stock) to current liabilities:

For 19–7   Current assets (*less* stock) $\dfrac{2\ 500}{4\ 000} = 0.625 : 1$

Current liabilities

For 19–8   Current assets (*less* stock) $\dfrac{4\ 000}{8\ 000} = 0.50 : 1$

Current liabilities

What does this mean? In 19–7 the ratio is 62.5p to £1 and in 19–8 it is 50p to £1. It means that for every £1 owed to creditors in 19–7 the business had only 62.5p readily available to pay it. In 19–8 the amount had fallen to 50p. At the end of 19–8 a creditor for a large sum would be unlikely to receive prompt payment because there just isn't enough cash to pay everyone.

Overall result
1 For the owner and other providers of finance 19–8 was the better of the two years. Returns on capital had increased.
2 For creditors of the business the position had deteriorated. Less money was available to pay them and therefore they would have to wait longer for payments to be made to them.

The use of budgets

Earlier on I said that one way of measuring success is to compare actual results with what you believe the business should achieve. In order to do this it is necessary to plan what the business is going to do and convert the plan of activities into a 'financial plan'. If you know how much material is to be purchased, how many people are to be employed, how many goods are going to be sold, it is possible to prepare a budget for the year ahead.

A budget
A budget is a plan expressed in financial terms. It shows all the expected incomes and all the expected expenses and therefore enables a business to see in advance whether the expected results of its activities will be a profit or a loss.

The budget should be carefully prepared if it is to be of any value. A poorly prepared budget that does not represent what the business should achieve will be ignored and is therefore a waste of time.

Budget comparisons

If the annual plan can be determined, so can each month's plan be calculated. It then becomes a routine task of comparing the actual results of each month with the 'planned results' of each month.

Has the budgeted sales income been achieved?
Are the expenses as planned?
Have the actual purchases been as budgeted?

If any of the 'planned' activities have not been achieved then immediately the reason for the difference can be sought. It may be necessary to take some corrective action if the overall plan for the year is to be fulfilled.

Joe's Rule No 18
The results of trading shown in the final accounts and Balance Sheet need to be understood and measured to find out how successful the business is.

Cash flow

Where has all the cash gone?
If you look back at the Balance Sheets on page 191 you will see that at the end of 19-7 there was £500 cash in hand. At the end of 19-8 there was no cash. In fact, the currrent liabilities, when analysed, may show trade creditors £7000, bank overdraft £1000. If the owner wanted to know why this was so, you could draw up a *cash flow statement* as follows, by comparing the two Balance Sheets.

		£
Cash/bank balance 1 Jan 19-8		500
Deduct those items that reduce the cash:		
1 Drawings	4 000	
2 Increase in stock		
(this requires more cash)	4 000	
3 Increase in debtors		
(the business must be providing		
the extra cash to pay for the		
goods)	2 000	−10 000
		− 9 500

Add those items that increase the cash:

4 Profit	3 000	
5 Decrease in fixed assets	500	
6 Increase in creditors	3 000	
7 Loan	2 000	+ 8 500
Bank overdraft		1 000

Notes on cash flow statements

Imagine a simple Balance Sheet.

(a) If stock goes up, then cash goes down (you have had to buy it).
(b) If debtors go down, cash goes up (they have paid you).
(c) If fixed assets go up, cash goes down (you have bought them).
(d) If creditors go up, stock goes up—but when the stock is sold, cash goes up.
(e) If a loan is made to you, the liabilities go up, and cash goes up.
(f) If creditors go down, cash goes down (you have paid them).
(g) The difficult move to work out is that relating to the decrease in fixed assets. The decrease in fixed assets increases cash. The reason may be twofold.

  (i) The asset is actually *sold*, so cash is received.
  (ii) The asset is *depreciated*. Depreciation is an expense that appears in the Profit and Loss Account. Unlike other expenses, cash is not paid to anyone. This expense reduces the profit but does not reduce cash. Profit represents an increase in cash. Therefore the cash increase is made up of net profit *plus* depreciation.

18.03 The Balance Sheets of B Butler on 31 December 19-8 and 19-9 were:

	19-8	19-9		19-8	19-9
Fixed assets	4 050	4 650	Capital 1 Jan	7 000	7 500
Current assets:			Profit	3 000	4 500
Stock	2 840	2 990		10 000	12 000
Debtors	3 265	3 375			
Bank and cash	1 840	30	Drawings	2 500	5 000
				7 500	7 000
			Creditors	4 495	4 045
	11 995	11 045		11 995	11 045

Draw up a statement for Butler, to show how the cash balance has reduced in 19-9.

18.04 A fire in the accounts section of G Illington had destroyed all the records for the year ended 31 May 19-6. However, you are asked to (a) prepare a Trading Account from the information which is available.

Stock in trade: 1 June 19-5, £8500; 31 May 19-6, £7900.
Purchases during year: £29 000.
Gross profit is always 25 per cent of the cost of goods sold.
G Illington's Balance Sheet on 31 May 19-5 showed debtors £3400.
Cash received for credit sales during the year amounted to £36 000.

(b) What should be the figure for debtors in the Balance Sheet on 31 May 19-6?

(RSA 1)

18.05 (a) During the year ended 31 December 19-5, J Wood had a turnover of £72 000. His gross profit was at the rate of 33⅓ per cent on turnover and his net profit 20 per cent on turnover. His rate of stock turnover was 10.

Required:
Insert the missing figures in the account below:

J Wood
Trading and Profit and Loss Account for the year
ended 31 December 19-5

	£		£
Cost of goods sold		Sales	72 000
Gross profit c/d			
	72 000		72 000
		Gross profit b/d	
Expenses			
Net profit			

(b) Calculate the average stock held for the period.

18.06 State the formula for, and explain the usefulness of, each of the following to a sole trader.

(a) Return on capital
(b) Net profit percentage
(c) Working capital
(d) Rate of stock turnover

(PEI Elem)

18.07 Study the following trading account and then answer the questions below.

	£			£
Jan 1 Stock (at cost price)	100	Dec 31	Sales	375
Dec 31 Purchases	200		Stock (at cost price)	75
Gross profit	150			
	450			450

(a) What was the cost of the goods sold?
(b) What percentage is the gross profit on
   (i) cost price?
   (ii) selling price?

(PEI Elem)

NA 18.08 The figures below refer to the trading results of a small retailer for the two years ended 30 April 19-8 and 19-9

	Apr 19-8 £	Apr 19-9 £		Apr 19-8 £	Apr 19-9 £
Stock 1 May	25 000	20 000	Sales	50 000	80 000
Purchases	40 000	120 000	Stock 30 Apr	20 000	70 000
Gross profit	5 000	10 000			
	70 000	150 000		70 000	150 000

You are required to:
(a) State the turnover for the two years.
(b) Calculate for each of the years:
   (1) the average stock;
   (2) the cost of goods sold;
   (3) the gross profit as a percentage of sales;
   (4) the rate of stock turnover.
(c) State which of the two years' trading you think is the more successful. Give your reasons.

NA 18.09 (a) Define turnover.
(b) What is meant by the 'rate of turnover'? Show how it is calculated.
(c) What are the possible reasons for the following rates of stock turnover during the first three years of the business?
Year 1—5
Year 2—4
Year 3—3

NA 18.10 (a) Name three accounting ratios which could be used to judge the efficiency of a business.
(b) The current liabilities of a business exceed its assets. Comment on the financial state of this business.
(c) If a person is able to earn a salary of £5000 a year and has £60 000 invested at 10 per cent interest per annum, what is the lowest figure of profit he could regard as financially satisfactory if he gave up his post and used the £60 000 to start and operate a business?
(d) A business holds an average stock valued at £10 000 cost price. The average mark up is 25 per cent on cost. What must be the rate of turnover if the business is to make a gross profit of £25 000 per annum?
(e) The turnover of a business is £100 000 per annum. Net profit is 5 per cent of sales, while gross profit is 30 per cent of sales.
(i) Calculate the percentage of expenses on turnover.
(ii) Calculate the total expenses.
(iii) Comment on the financial results of the business, making special reference to the level of expenses.

(London 'O')

19. The Accounts of Non-Trading Concerns

So, you have been elected treasurer of your local darts club! I will have to explain how you prepare the end of year accounts.

Charities, clubs, unions, and associations are not established with the intention of carrying on a trade to make a profit—they enable their members to pursue the activity of their choice, be it leisure, politics or sports. In order to carry out the activities some funds are necessary and often fund raising activities play a large part in the financing of a non-trading concern. Members are usually required to pay subscriptions; donations are received; competitions, dances, and outings are organized, and these bring in money as well as causing expenditure. Someone has to look after all these funds and report to members (perhaps monthly) and also prepare the accounts for the Annual General Meeting.

Usually the rules of the club will state that the accounts prepared by the treasurer have to be audited. This means they have to be checked for accuracy by an independent person who is usually elected at the Annual General Meeting of the preceding year. The auditor would usually be someone with experience in accountancy.

Bookkeeping records

Complete double entry set of records
Although 'non-trading', many concerns are big and handle large sums of money, they may own many assets and involve themselves in many activities. The only effective way to record the financial transactions is to maintain a complete set of books and accounts based on the double entry system. This ensures control over assets, debtors, creditors, and stock.

Cash Book only
1 Small clubs do not normally keep a full set of double entry records. Usually the treasurer will record receipts and payment in a Cash Book—analysed so that totals can be easily obtained of the important incomings and outgoings. You do not have to keep an analysed Cash Book, but if you don't then at the end of the year you will have a great deal of analysis to do. The Cash Book would keep both the Cash and Bank Accounts.

2   In addition to the Cash Book, the treasurer (or secretary) would need to keep a separate record of members and their subscriptions paid to the club (to follow up any outstanding subscriptions).

3   Outstanding invoices (yet to be paid) should be kept in a separate file so that at any time members can see what expenses are owing.

4   A separate book should be kept showing the assets purchased, date of purchase, cost and date of disposal. Unless this is kept up to date it is very easy for assets to be lost—particularly as members of voluntary organizations tend to change frequently.

The accounts at the year end

1   *What should happen?*   An account called 'Income and Expenditure Account' should be prepared and presented to members. This is the equivalent of the Trading and Profit and Loss Accounts of a business. A Balance Sheet should also be presented.

2   *What often happens?*   Where treasurers keep only a Cash Book and often have very little knowledge of bookkeeping and accounting, the only account presented is the 'Receipts and Payments Account'. This is not as useful as the Income and Expenditure Account as I will explain.

Receipts and Payments Account

A summary of the Cash Book

For the purpose of this account cash and bank transactions are added together. The account gives a summarized analysis of what appears in the Cash Book, including the opening and closing balances of both cash and bank.

An example of a Receipts and Payments Account is shown opposite.

Disadvantages of the Receipts and Payments Account

1   Members cannot see whether or not the club is paying its way, i.e., do incomes exceed expenses? From the account you might be tempted to say that the club is not paying its way, the cash and bank balances at the year end are lower than at the beginning. However, you will have confused *receipts* with *incomes*, they are not the same. Neither are *payments* the same as *expenses*. For example:

(a)   What expenses are owing at the year end?
(b)   No depreciation is shown on assets owned
(c)   Are there sums prepaid at the year end?

*Receipts and Payments Account of the Wingate Darts Club
for the year ended 31 December 19–8*

	Receipts	£		Payments	£
Jan 1	Cash in hand	26		Subs to national assoc	80
	Cash at bank	232		Donations to charities	160
	Subscriptions	940		Competition expenses	342
	Donations received	365		Bar purchases	869
	Competitions income	249		Disco/dance expenses	635
	Bar sales	1432		Outing expenses	462
	Dance/disco incomes	520		Printing, post,	
	Outings receipts	480		stationery	121
	Misc asset sales	25		Casual wages	1444
	Fund raising events	874		Equipment purchases	616
	Sales of diaries/books	62		Heating and lighting	102
				Hall rent	52
				Treasurer's expenses	13
				Misc expenses	69
			Dec 31	Cash in hand	41
				Cash at bank	199
		5205			5205
Jan 1	Cash in hand	41			
	Cash at bank	199			

2 Payments include the purchase of assets. Assets are not included in any Profit or Loss Account. They do appear in a Balance Sheet, but no Balance Sheet is presented here. What assets are owned?

3 Which activities were profitable? Should any of the casual wages be attributed to the bar?

As this account has so many disadvantages in attempting to present the overall picture to the members, it is necessary to prepare from the Receipts and Payments Account and additional information the Income and Expenditure Account.

Income and Expenditure Account

Preparation

This account is prepared, and laid out in a similar way to a Profit and Loss Account. Using double entry principles, receipts in the Cash Book are posted to the credit side of income accounts.

LAYOUT 1

Wingate Darts Club
Income and Expenditure Account
for the year ended 31 December 19-8

Expenditure		Income	
Bar stocks (Jan 1)	140	Subscriptions	965
National assoc subs	80	Donations received	365
Donations to charities	160	Competition income	249
Competition expenses	342	Bar sales	1432
Bar purchases	902	Disco/dance income	535
Disco/dance expenses	720	Outings income	480
Outings expenses	462	Sale of dart boards	25
PPS	121	Fund raising events	874
Casual wages	1464	Sales of dairies/books	62
Heating and lighting	102	Bar stocks (Dec 31)	165
Hall rent	52		
Treasurer's expenses	13		
Misc expenses	69		
Books/diaries	40		
New bar glasses	58		
Depreciation:			
Sports equipment	250		
Bar fixtures	50		
Surplus of income over expenditure	127		
	5152		**5152**

Therefore, income accounts have credit balances (and expense accounts have debit balances).

Transferred to the Income and Expenditure Account are all the incomes and expenses relevant to the year. This takes into consideration prepayments and amounts owing. Unlike a Profit and Loss Account the excess of income over expenditure results in a *surplus* rather than a *profit*. If expenditure exceeds income, the result is an *excess of expenditure*, rather than *loss*. Let us say that in addition to the information given in the Receipts Payments Account we know that:

1   Bar stocks at 1 Jan 19-8 were valued at £140
    Bar stocks at 31 Dec 19-8 were valued at £165
2   Subscriptions received included £40 for the following year.

3   Subscriptions still owing from this year were £65.
4   Equipment purchases included £58 for new bar glasses (to replace those broken) and £40 for books and diaries.
5   Bills outstanding at the year end were:
      Bar purchases   £33
      Disco hire   £85
      Sports equipment   £79
      Casual wages   £20
6   One-half of the casual wages should be charged to the bar and one-half to cleaning and maintenance.
7   £15 from tickets for the Christmas disco has yet to be received.
8   Depreciation should be provided as follows:
      Sports equipment   £250
      Bar fixtures   £50
9   Replacement bar glasses are treated as revenue expenses.
10 The miscellaneous asset sales were four old dart boards which had been written off in the books.
11 There were no books or diary stocks at the year end.

We can now prepare the Income and Expenditure Account.

Layout
There are several methods of layout:

1 Incomes and Expenses listed in the same manner as the Receipts and Payments Account (but on the opposite sides) as shown opposite.

   While acceptable, this layout does not show the profit or loss on activities. You would have to compare figures appearing on both sides. An alternative layout is shown on page 206.

   Where an activity is intended to be carried out in order to provide a profit for the club, then a separate Trading Account should be prepared (and Profit and Loss Account if expenses can be analysed and charged to the activity).

2 Layout 2 could be refined further by omitting the details of incomes and expenses of activities and showing only the profit or loss. The use of footnotes—or analyses—will enable members to see details if they so wish.

   Furthermore, such analyses can show more detail if required. For example, how many discos and dances were held? One may have made a profit while the others showed a loss. How many outings were held? Did they all show a profit?

LAYOUT 2   *Wingate Darts Club*
                            Income and Expenditure Account
                          for the year ended 31 December 19–8

Expenditure			Income		
Loss on bar		235	Subscriptions		965
National assoc subs		80	Donations received		365
Donations to charities		160	Profit on outings		
Loss on competitions			Incomes	480	
Expenses	342		Expenses	462	18
Income	249	93	Profit on book sales		
Loss on disco/dances			Incomes	62	
Expenses	720		Expenses	40	22
Income	535	185	Sale of dart boards		25
PPS		121	Fund raising events		874
Cleaning & maintenance		732			
Heating and lighting		102			
Hall rent		52			
Treasurer's expenses		13			
Misc expenses		69			
Depreciation:					
Sports equipment		250			
Bar fixtures		50			
Surplus of income over expenditure		127			
		2269			2269

This account will need to be accompanied by a bar Trading and Profit
and Loss Account.

                    Bar Trading and Profit and Loss Account
                      for the year ended 31 December 19–8

Opening stock	140	Sales		1432
Purchases	902			
	1042			
Less Closing stock	165			
	877			
Gross profit	555			
	1432			1432
Wages	732	Gross profit b/d		555
New glasses	58	Net loss to I & E A/c		235
	790			790

For example, the Income and Expenditure Account would show for outings:

'Profit on outings' (Note 1) £18

Note 1 would then show:

Note 1 **Outings**		1. To France		2. To Wisley
		£		£
Income		380		100
Coach/boat fares	372			80
Tips	10	382		–
Profit (or loss)		(2)		20

Balance Sheet

For members to see how the club stands financially at the year end a Balance Sheet needs to be prepared. This is laid out as any other Balance Sheet. Only one term needs to be learned—*Accumulated Fund*.

A club does not have individual owners or shareholders who can lay claim to a portion of the capital. If at any one time the club ceases to exist, its assets would be divided between its (paid-up) members at that time. People who have previously been a member would have no claim to its assets. To distinguish 'investment' by members from 'investment' by owners, such investment is called Accumulated Fund. In effect, this is the same as capital invested by an owner or owners.

Wingate Darts Club
Balance Sheet as at 31 December 19-7

Assets	£
Sports equipment (WDV)	1050
Bar fixtures (WDV)	250
Bar stocks	140
Bank	232
Cash	26
	£1698

Financed by	
Accumulated Fund	£1698

Look at the Balance Sheet for 31 December 19–7 (page 207). From these details and the Income and Expenditure Account on page 206, you can prepare the Balance Sheet as at 31 December 19–8 (opposite). Since any surplus is the equivalent of 'profit' it is added to the Accumulated Fund—thus increasing the members' investment. An excess of expenditure will be deducted from the Accumulated Fund.

In a double entry system the Income and Expenditure Account is closed by transferring the surplus or excess expenditure to the Accumulated Fund Account.

Miscellaneous matters

Subscriptions

The Balance Sheet for 19–8 includes a figure of £65 for subscriptions still owing for the year, this has been added to the subscriptions actually received to show the figure that should have been received for the year. The outstanding amount is then shown in the Balance Sheet as a debtor. Where such unpaid subscriptions appear in an examination question they should be included as shown here, unless otherwise stated.

However, unlike a business where a debtor is usually going to pay, unpaid subscriptions can often represent members who are not going to pay, perhaps having left the club. Therefore it is usual in practice to exclude such unpaid subscriptions in the accounts.

Assets and depreciation

Assets need to be depreciated in accordance with established accounting principles. The Balance Sheet would normally show the cost price *less* depreciation.

Surplus/deficiency

If income exceeds expenses then the difference is referred to as a '*surplus of income over expenditure*'. If the expenditure exceeds income the difference is referred to as an '*excess of expenditure over income*', but this is sometimes referred to as a *deficiency of income*.

Life membership fees/entrance fees

Sometimes a new member has to pay an entrance fee to join the club; sometimes life membership can be obtained by the payment of a suitably large subscription.

There is no reason why such fees from both sources cannot be entered in the Income and Expenditure Account as revenue income for the

Wingate Darts Club
Balance Sheet as at 31 December 19–8

Assets		£
Sports equipment (Note 1)		1397
Bar fixtures (Note 2)		200
Bar stocks		165
Debtors (Note 3)		80
Bank		199
Cash		41
		2082

Financed by		
Accumulated Fund (1 Jan 19–8)		1698
Add Surplus of income over expenditure		127
		1825
Current liabilities:		
Creditors (Note 4)	197	
Accruals and prepayments (Note 5)	60	257
		2082

Balance Sheet Notes £

Note 1	Opening value	1050	
	Add New equipment	597	(616 + 79 − (58 + 40))
		1647	
	Less Depreciation	250	
		1397	

Note 2	Opening value	250
	Less Depreciation	50
		200

Note 3	Subscriptions owing	65
	Christmas tickets	15
		80

Note 4	Bar purchases outstanding	33
	Disco hire outstanding	85
	Sports equip outstanding	79
		197

Note 5	Casual wages outstanding	20
	Subs received in advance	40
		60

year—shown as Entrance fees or Life membership subscriptions respectively. This would no doubt distort the annual income in comparison with previous years and it could be argued that both types of fee relate to a series of succeeding years.

An alternative to entering the whole amounts in the year of receipt is to enter fees/subscriptions in an Entrance Fees Account and a Life Subscription Account. Both accounts would then have an amount transferred annually to the Income and Expenditure Account. The amount would depend on the number of years that the club decides should be the basis of the transfer. The (credit) balance on these two accounts at each year end (until totally transferred) would then appear in the Balance Sheet under each respective heading, beneath the Accumulated Fund.

Joe's Rule No 19
Club members do not usually understand the accounts you present. Keep them as simple as possible.

19.01 On 1 January 19–6 the Scott Youth Club had subscriptions owing from the previous year of £25. During 19–6 subscriptions actually received totalled £490. This sum included the £25 outstanding from the preceding year and £15 in advance for 19–7.

Show the Subscription Account at 31 December 19–6 and the amount transferred to the Income and Expenditure Account.

19.02 Show the Subscription Account at **19.01** above if at 31 December 19–6 subscriptions outstanding totalled £30.

19.03 Show the Subscription Account at **19.01** above if of the £490 received at 31 December 19–6 only £15 of the outstanding subscriptions at 1 January 19–6 was included and the remainder was written off as a bad debt.

19.04 The Forest Golf Club elected ten new members during 19–6 who each paid £300 entrance fees.

The club rules state that such fees should be spread evenly over five years.

Show the Entrance Fees Account for the first three years assuming that the year ends on 31 December.

19.05 From the following details which relate to the Village Social Club, prepare the Club's receipts and payments and income and expenditure accounts.

		£ p
1 Jan	Balance of cash in hand	15.12
Jan to June	Subscriptions received	30.00
	Expenses paid	31.23
30 June	Subscriptions owing	2.00
	Expenses unpaid	3.27
		(PEI Elem)

19.06 From the following receipts and payments account and notes prepare the income and expenditure account, showing clearly within it the profit or loss on the bar and disco. Receipts and Payments Account for the year ended 31 Dec 198–

	£		£
Bar sales	5000	Furniture	265
Sale of disco tickets	100	Loss on raffle	40
Subscriptions	2350	Hire of disco equipment	400
		Rent	100
		Rates	625
		Purchases of bar stock	3000
		Secretary's expenses	20
		Bar staff wages	2000
		Balance	1000
	£7450		£7450

Subscriptions due amounted to £45
Rent paid in advance was £25
Bar stock remaining was valued at £250
Depreciate furniture by 20 per cent
Rates due amounted to £15

(PEI Elem)

NA 19.07 (a) Prepare the Receipts and Payments Account for the Happy Old 'Uns Social Club from the following information:

		£
1 January 19-5	Cash in hand	£45
31 December 19-5	Total subs received	£196
	Collections towards expenses	£49
	Jumble sales receipts	£64
	Expenses paid	£78
	Outings expenses paid	£192
	Christmas party expenses	£81

(b) Using the information above and the following details, prepare an Income and Expenditure Account for the Happy Old 'Uns Social Club for the year ended 31 December 19-5.

Subs outstanding at 31 Dec 19-5	£18
Christmas party expenses owing	£22
Deposit for coach trip booked in advance	£20

NA 19.08 At 31 December 19-4 the records of the Uptown Sports and Social Club showed the following:

	£
Club premises	5000
Creditors (bar supplies)	238
Bar stock	61
Subscriptions received for 19-4	837
Bank overdraft	28
Cash in hand	10
Deficit for 19-4	59
Sports equipment	149
Rates paid (including prepayment £25 for 19-5)	225
Fixtures and fittings	180
Travel expenses owed to members	18

You are required to:
(a) Calculate the Accumulated Fund at 1 January 19-4.
(b) Prepare the Balance Sheet of the Club as at 31 December 19-4.

(RSA I)

NA 19.09 The following Trial Balance was extracted from the books of the ABC Social Club as at 31 October 19-3:

	DR £	CR £
Creditors for refreshment supplies		990
Refreshment stocks 1 November 19-2	1 760	
Subscriptions received		1 970
Accumulated Fund 1 November 19-2		5 090
Freehold premises	5 500	
Income from social events		470
Rates and insurance	610	
Wages and salaries	3 790	
Furniture and fittings	860	
Refreshment purchases	8 640	
Cash	60	
Income from special events		2 460
Repairs	160	
Refreshment sales		10 180
Sundry expenses	470	
Discount received		130
Bank overdraft		560
	21 850	21 850

Notes
1 Refreshment stocks 31 October 19-3—£1920.
2 £600 of wages and salaries should be debited to the Refreshment Trading Account.
3 Rates prepaid 31 October 19-3—£70.
4 Subscriptions due but unpaid at 31 October 19-3—£110.
5 Provide for depreciation of furniture and fittings—£80.

Required:
Draw up the Refreshment Trading Account and General Income and Expenditure Account for the year ended 31 October 19-3 together with a Balance Sheet as at that date.

(LCCI Elem)

20. The Journal

A book of original entry

This book has been mentioned before but not yet explained. It is a book used to record, first, those transactions which do not have their own book of original entry. Credit sales, for example, are recorded in the Sales Day Book. Bank transactions are recorded in the Cash Book. But where are the following recorded?

1 Credit purchases and sales of assets.
2 Details of bad debts written off.
3 The correction of errors by entries or transfers.
4 The introduction of assets into the business by the owner.
5 Transfers at the year end—e.g., depreciation.
6 Opening entries upon purchase of a business (including goodwill) or at the commencement of a trading period.

The Journal proper (to distinguish it from the Sales Journal, Purchases Journal, and Returns Journal) is a very useful book, since it can be used for recording all transactions that are not entered in the other books of original entry. You should note that the Sales Journal is another name for the Sales Day Book; similarly the Purchases Journal is another name for the Bought Day Book (or Purchases Day Book); the term *journal* is used because the pages in the Journal are the same as the day books.

The Journal provides a written record of the details of the transaction and enables an explanation to be noted. It acts as an instruction to the ledger clerk to make entries in the ledgers.

While the pages are the same as other books of original entry, the layout of entries is different as shown:

Journal

Page 6

Date	Details	Folio Ref	£ p	£ p
	Account to be debited Dr Account to be credited Narration (explanation of the entries made)			

The Journal is very often completed by the accountant, who, dealing with the unusual and difficult items, can show the ledger clerk exactly what entries are required in the ledgers. Remember that this book is *not* an account. It is a memorandum book; it shows the accounts that are to be entered. When the ledger clerk has made the ledger entries, then the folio reference of the ledger accounts will be entered in the Folio column of the Journal. The ledger accounts show the Journal folio number. As the folio references are shown below, the entries will have been made in the ledger accounts.

Journal   Page 7

	Date	Details		Folio Ref	£ p	£ p
(a)	Sept 3	Motor Vehicles A/c	Dr	NLM6	12 850	
		Handytruck Ltd		BLH8		12 850
		Purchase of truck no 1234 per Invoice number HT/142 dated 3/9/19-7				
(b)	Sept 4	S C Rapman	Dr	SLR8	135	
		Furniture and Equipt A/c		NLF3		135
		Sale of typewriters nos 131 and 142 per Invoice no C1831 dated 4/9/19-7				
(c)	Sept 5	Machinery A/c	Dr	NLM7	6 800	
		Machine Tool Supp. Ltd		BLM9		6 800
		Purchase of machine no 925 per Invoice no MTS/47 dated 5/9/19-7				
(d)	Sept 5	Machine Tool Supp. Ltd	Dr	BLM9	100	
		Machine Disposal A/c		NLD5		100
		Part exchange value of machine no 97, per agreement and Invoice MTS/47 dated 5/9/19-7				
(e)	Sept 5	Machine Disposal A/c	Dr	NLD5	150	
		Machinery A/c		NLM7		150
		Written down value of machine part-exchanged transferred to Disposal A/c				
(f)	Sept 5	Profit and Loss A/c	Dr	PLP1	50	
		Machine Disposal A/c		NLD5		50
		Loss on part-exchange of machine no 97 (under depreciation)				

Narration

The narration is most important: it explains the ledger entries, and reference should always be made to the document authorizing the entry. It may be the invoice from the supplier, or the schedule of bad debts prepared by the accountant. No entries should be made in the Journal without the narration.

1   Purchases and sales of assets on credit (see page 215)

(a)   Handytruck Ltd supplies a forklift truck on credit, at a cost of £12 850, on 3 September.

(b)   Two old electric typewriters are sold on credit to S C Rapman for £135, on 4 September.

(c)–(f) On 5 September a milling machine, standing in the books at £150, was traded in on a part-exchange deal with Machine Tool Supplies Ltd for a new machine costing £6800. £100 was allowed for the old machine.

2   Bad debts written off and provisions created

(a)   Syd Jones owes the business £45, but, having gone bankrupt, pays us only £15. The balance is to be written off (18 May).

(b)   At the year end, the provision for bad debts is required to be increased by £88.

		Journal				8
(a)	May 18	Bad Debts A/c Dr Syd Jones's A/c Balance of account being written off per court notice of bankruptcy dated 30/11/19–7		NLB7 SLJ4	30	 30
(b)	Dec 31	Profit and Loss A/c Dr Provision for bad debts Increase required per schedule dated 31/12/19–7		PLP1 NLP5	88	 88

3 Correction of errors

Errors should always be corrected by making an adjusting entry. It may seem simpler to cross out the incorrect item and enter the correct item. This is unsatisfactory. Since entries should always be in ink, crossings out are unsightly, and often become indecipherable.

Errors should be corrected when discovered. This may be during the course of a year or when the trial balance is taken out (prepared) at the year end. Some errors may remain undetected until a later trading period and correcting such errors may involve the alteration of final accounts for previous years.

Dealing with errors arising this year

Look at the entries which have been made and decide what entries should have been made. Your adjusting entry will now have to cancel out the incorrect entry and put in what should be the correct entry. This may involve two 'adjusting' entries (a debit and a credit) or only one entry.

Examples

(i) If the Wages Account has been debited with £936, instead of £963, then it has been debited with £27 less than the correct figure. The Journal entry to correct this will be:

		Journal			11
(i)	Aug 14	Wages Account Dr	NLW6	27	
		——	——		27
		Correction of error in posting £963 to the Wages Account as £936			

Note that only one entry has been made in the ledger but £27 has been entered in the Credit column of the Journal. This is to enable the Journal columns themselves to be totalled. The Wages Account will now be as follows:

		Wages Account			W6
27 July	Bank	cB 33	936		
14 Aug	Correction	J 11	27		

The following examples were all corrected on 15 August.

(ii)   Salaries of £266 were incorrectly debited to the Factory Wages Account.

(iii) A payment by cheque of £145 to A Evans was wrongly posted to A Evans's account in the Sales Ledger.

(iv) The total of the Sales Day Book for July was incorrectly totalled, and posted to the ledger as £3846. The correct total was £3956.

J11

(ii)	Aug 15	Salaries Dr Factory wages Correction of the error of posting salaries to the Wages Account	NLS5 NLW6	266		266
(iii)	Aug 15	A Evans's A/c (Bought Ledger) Dr A Evans's A/c (Sales Ledger) Transfer of payment by cheque from the Sales Ledger Account	BLE3 SLE2	145		145
(iv)	Aug 15	———— Dr Sales A/c Correction for the incorrect totalling of the Sales Day Book for July	— NLS3	110		110

Dealing with errors arising in a previous year

Adjusting entries necessary to deal with this type of error depends upon whether or not the error affected the trial balance at the end of the relevant year. Also, the effect of any correction on the profit or loss of the previous period.

Adjusting entries

If the error did not affect the trial balance, it means that any correction will involve both a debit and a credit entry. Look at example (iii) above. This error could well be discovered after the end of the year, when all the accounts have been prepared—nevertheless, the correcting entries are the same as illustrated. Although the correcting entries do not affect the profit of the previous year, the error did affect the personal accounts of a debtor and a creditor. Therefore these errors have to be corrected.

Example (ii) may also be discovered after the year end; it did not affect the profit, or any personal or private accounts, so no correcting entries will be made.

Examples (i) and (iv) affect the trial balance. If these errors had not been found at the date of the trial balance, the trial balance would not have balanced.

Imagine for a moment that these two errors had not happened—the trial balance would show:

	£	£
Wages	963	
Sales		3 956
	18 462	18 462

Because the errors have been made the trial balance actually shows:

	£	£
Wages	936	
Sales		3 846
	18 435	18 352

. . . and it doesn't balance!

The final accounts should not be prepared until the books balance, but perhaps the errors cannot be traced despite considerable investigation. Consequently, in order that the accounts can be prepared it is possible to 'make the books balance' by adding in the difference. This means opening an account called the Suspense Account, and entering the amount required to balance the trial balance. The Suspense Account is 'holding' the errors until discovered.

The trial balance now becomes:

	£	£
Wages	936	
Sales		3 846
Suspense Account		83
	18 435	18 435

and the Suspense Account is opened as follows:

Suspense Account				S8	
		31 Dec	Difference in books per trial balance	83	

All the errors have now been transferred to a Suspense Account and the figure is the net result of all the errors added together. This balance is a 'liability' and should appear in the Balance Sheet under Current liabilities.

Now we can consider the action to be taken when, in the following year, the errors are found. In the case of wages:

Dr Wages Account: Cr Suspense Account

In the case of the incorrect totalling of the Sales Day Book:

Dr Suspense Account: Cr Sales Account

The Journal entries are:

	Journal				12
Aug 14	Wages Account Dr			27	
	Suspense Account				27
	Correction of error in posting £963 as £936 in November 19-7				
Aug 14	Suspense Account Dr			110	
	Sales Account				110
	Correction of error in Sales Day Book for November 19-7				

The Suspense Account now looks as follows:

Suspense Account								S8
Aug 14	Sales	J 12	110	31 Dec	Difference in books per trial balance			83
				14 Aug	Wages	J 12		27
			110					110

Corrections to profits

Look again at the corrections above to the Wages Account and the Sales Account. In both cases there has been an additional amount posted to them. These amounts are in respect of a previous year, and therefore the profit (or loss) of the previous year needs correcting as follows:

Statement of Corrected Profit for the year ending . . .

			£
Profit per accounts	(say)		9840
Add Additional sales			110
			9950
Less Additional wages			27
Corrected profit			£9923

4 Introduction (and withdrawal) of assets by owner

If the owner introduces cash, the first entry is in the Cash Book. It is then posted to the Owner's Capital Account. However, should the owner introduce other assets, such as stock, vehicles, plant and machinery, tools, etc., then some entry must be made to record what has happened. Equally, should the owner take assets other than cash, it is necessary to make a Journal entry.

Example

(a) The owner brings into the business the following assets on 15 August: stock £845, fixtures and fittings £195.

(b) On 19 September the owner of the business takes for his own use stock valued at £75, and a machine that is standing in the books at a written down value of £130.

(a)	Aug 15	Stock A/c	Dr	NLS8	845	
		Fixtures and Fittings A/c		NLF3	195	
		Capital A/c		PLC1		1040
		Assets brought into the business by the owner				
(b)	Sept 19	Drawings A/c		PLD1	205	
		Purchases A/c		NLP4		75
		Machinery A/c		NLM7		130
		Items taken by the owner				

5 Year end transfers (and closing entries)

At the end of a trading period, certain adjustments have to be made in the accounts to allow for depreciation, interest due on loans, amounts to be set aside to provisions, and many others. You will remember that to provide for depreciation the two entries in the accounts are:

Dr Depreciation Account: Cr Provision for Depreciation Account (or the asset account)

Example

(a) Depreciation on motor lorries is to be provided at £5200 (20 per cent of cost).
(b) Interest on loan from Fast Funds Ltd is due at the year end, amounting to £80.
(c) An amount of £2500 is to be set aside out of profits as a provision for possible stock losses.

(a)	Dec 31	Depreciation A/c Dr Provision for depreciation on 　motor lorries Year end provision calculated as 　20 per cent on cost	NLD8 NLP7	5200	 5200
(b)	Dec 31	Profit and Loss A/c Dr 　Loan Interest A/c Amount due to Fast Fund Ltd. 　at year end	PLP1 NLL4	80	 80
(c)	Dec 31	Profit and Loss A/c Dr 　Provision for stock losses Amount estimated at the year end 　of possible losses due to lower 　sales prices	PLP1 NLP10	2500	 2500

At the year end, the income and expense accounts are transferred to the Trading and Profit and Loss Account. These transfers should be made through the Journal, but this is rarely done in practice.

6 Purchase of a business

When a business is bought, not only does the purchaser obtain actual physical assets, such as stock, buildings, vehicles, and so on, he also purchases an existing 'trade'. Customers exist, and the value of their trade is measured by the term *goodwill*. This goodwill, in financial terms, is the amount paid for the business in excess of the current value of the physical assets taken over. Imagine Joe was going to buy the business of a competitor in a near-by town.

If I bought the business of Jarvis Carpets what would I be getting?

Carpet stocks valued at	£14 800
Warehouse and showroom valued at	28 400
Fixtures, fittings, display stands, etc., valued at	6 850
Total	£50 050

I would expect to pay at least £50 050 because this is what I would have to pay if I bought all the items separately. Now, Jarvis Carpets obviously hopes to receive as much as possible—and certainly in excess of this sum. I would look at the latest set of accounts to see how much profit the business is making. If it was making £10 000 profit a year—that is what I am buying. Jarvis Carpets may believe the goodwill to be worth £30 000 (three times profit) or £40 000 (four times profit), while I may be willing to give only £20 000. Jarvis Carpets would want to sell the business to the highest bidder. If I bid £72 000 and it was accepted, this is how I would journalize the transaction.

Date				
	Stock	Dr	14 800	
	Warehouse and showroom	Dr	28 400	
	Fixtures, fittings, etc.	Dr	6 850	
	Goodwill		21 950	
	Capital A/c—Joe Wynn			72 000
	Assets acquired from Jarvis Carpets			

Since I have paid £21 950 more than the tangible (i.e., physical) assets acquired are worth, I have bought another asset, called *goodwill*. This is known as an *intangible asset*. It exists, but you can't see it.

7 Opening entries

This does not happen very often in practice—only when a business is transferred to a partnership (or a limited company) and a new set of books and accounts are started. The opening assets and liabilities of the new business need to be entered in the Journal for posting to ledger accounts. Examinations often ask for the opening debit and credit balances to be journalized and posted to the appropriate accounts in the ledgers. Frequently, these balances are not equal, and the difference is usually the owner's capital at that date—which you will need to enter.

Example (a)

T Browne acquired the business of J William on 18 December and paid £28 500 as the purchase price. The assets and liabilities acquired were valued as follows:

Leasehold premises	£10 500	
Stock	8 750	
Debtors	6 500	£30 000
Fixtures, fittings, etc.	4 250	
Creditors	3 700	

In journalizing the opening entries, it will be possible to calculate the value of goodwill:

Goodwill = Purchase price of business *less* Net asset value taken over
= £28 500 − £(30 000 − 3700)

Dec 18	Leasehold premises	Dr		10 500	
	Stock	Dr		8 750	
	Debtors	Dr		6 500	
	Fixtures	Dr		4 250	
	Goodwill	Dr		2 200	
	Creditors				3 700
	Capital—T Browne				28 500
	Being assets and liabilities acquired per agreement dated 18/12/19-7			32 200	32 200

Example (b)

On 1 January the assets and liabilities of E Evans were:

	£	
Cash	150	⎫
Stock	970	⎬
Leasehold shop	1000	£2855
Debtors	550	⎬
Fixtures	185	⎭
Bank overdraft	640	
Creditors	430	

Enter these balances in the Journal and calculate E Evans's capital
Show the books to which the entries will be posted.

Jan 1	Cash	Dr	CB		150	
	Stock	Dr	NL		970	
	Leasehold shop	Dr	NL		1000	
	Debtors	Dr	SL		550	
	Fixtures	Dr	NL		185	
	Bank overdraft		CB			640
	Creditors		BL			430
	Capital		PL			1785
					2855	2855
	Being opening balances on Jan 1					

Note the following points.

1 The accounts in the ledger are posted from the Journal—as shown by the folio number.
2 The capital is the balancing figure (£2855 − 1070) = £1785.
3 Strictly speaking, the entry for cash should not appear in the Journal, since that entry will be in the Cash Book—itself a book of original entry. In examinations you will be told whether or not to journalize cash.

Joe's Rule No 20

Journalize all transactions that cannot be recorded in any other book of original entry.

20.01 Show, by means of Journal entries, how the following items should be entered in the books of B Waltham.

(a) Purchase of office equipment on credit from B Kirkland & Co £75

(b) The Safeway Insurance Co agreed a claim for £750, being the loss incurred on a motor vehicle due to an accident

(c) Interest on the bank deposit account had been credited to that account by the bank £23

(d) Discount allowed to P Carter of £4.50 now disallowed on the receipt of his cheque returned by the bank marked 'R/D—No Funds'

(e) B Waltham took stock for his own use valued at £18.50

20.02 (a) A suspense account had been opened because the trial balance failed to agree. Indicate which correction should be made if a cash discount of £75 to K Adams was entered in the discount allowed account but omitted from K Adams's account:

A credit suspense account £75, debit discount allowed account £75

B credit suspense account £75, debit K Adams's account £75

C debit suspense account £75, credit K Adams's account £75

D debit suspense account £75, credit discount allowed account £75

(b) Which one of the following is entered in the journal proper? Purchase of:

A fixed assets for cash

B fixed assets for credit

C stock on credit

D stock for cash

(PEI Elem)

20.03 On 1 June 19–4 T Jones had the following assets and liabilities:

Freehold premises, £25 000; Mortgage on premises, £12 500; Motor vehicle, £2700; Amount owing on motor vehicle, £1400; Fixtures and fittings, £2000; Stock, £2750; Debtors, £1580; Bank overdraft, £920; Unpaid electricity bill, £72.

On 1 April 19–4 Jones had paid rates £180 for the half-year ending 30 September 19–4 and on 1 February 19–4 had paid one year's insurance premium £60. You are required to prepare an Opening Journal Entry as at 1 June 19–4 showing clearly the Capital of Jones at that date.

(RSA 1)

20.04 Prepare the Journal entries and brief narrations in the books of C Shell, a boat builder, to correct the following errors.

(a) £560 had been included in the Wages Account and £240 in the Materials Account, which amounts represented expenditure on C Shell's private sailing yacht.

(b) A cheque payment of £84 to A H Clark had been debited to H Clarkson's account.

(c) The purchase of a calculating machine for the office, value £300, had been posted to the Purchases Account.

(RSA 1)

NA 20.05 (a) On 1 May 19-5 J Drake had the following assets and liabilities:

Assets: Freehold land and buildings £25 000, Fixtures and fittings £1250, Vehicle £2000, Stock £2600. Cash at bank and in hand £1580, Debtors £1500.
Liabilities: Long-term loan £1200, Trade creditors £1300, Electricity account outstanding £30.

You are required to prepare an opening journal entry for Drake showing his capital as at that date.

(b) During the month of May, the following transactions took place:

May 7 Drake purchased a new van costing £4750 from Better Motors paying £1000 and being given credit for the remainder

14 Drake sold on credit to A Baker fixtures and fittings which the business no longer required, at their book value of £250

18 Notification was received by Drake that J Smith, a debtor for £100, had been declared bankrupt. It was decided to write off this account as a bad debt

21 It was discovered that a purchase of goods on credit from T Murphy value £25 had been debited to Murphy's account and credited to sales.

You are required to show the Journal entries necessary to correct the error discovered on 21 May and giving effect to the other transactions.

(RSA 1)

20.06 William Smithson, a sole trader, had the following transactions during the month of May 19-4:

(1) During the month Smithson paid wages amounting to £128 – wages account having been debited. It has now been discovered that the work carried out by the workmen was in respect of fixtures and fittings in Smithson's office.

(2) Smithson purchased a safe which cost £545 from Jackson Bros Ltd. The safe was installed by Thomas Franks Ltd, at a cost of £93. Payment in respect of these items has not yet been made.

(3) During 19-2 Smithson wrote off as a bad debt the sum of £84 due from Arthur Shiply. During May 19-4 he received from Shiply the sum of £39 in full settlement.

(4) Smithson purchased a new delivery van at a cost of £1650. In part exchange Smithson traded in his old van at an agreed price of £490. The old van appears in his ledger at a figure of £530. He issued a cheque in payment of the amount due and he also issued separate cheques for £176 (insurance) and £70 (taxation).

Required:
Draw up the Journal entries to record (2), (3) and (4), and to correct the error in (1).

Note Cash entries should be journalized.

(LCCI Elem)

NA 20.07 William Jones, a sole trader, had the following transactions during May 19-6.

(a) Jones purchased on credit new office furniture costing £96 from Office Suppliers Ltd.
(b) Goods £46 were sold on credit to Alfred Shipley. The entries made in both the Sales Day Book and the personal account in the ledger gave the figure as £64.
(c) Jones purchased a new delivery van for £1160. In payment for this he trades in his old van at an agreed figure of £420 and issues a cheque for £740. The book value of the old van was £460.
(d) Jones received cash £71 from a debtor named Richard Jackson. This was correctly entered in the Cash Book but in the ledger the entry was made in the account of Robert Jackson.

Required
Draw up Journal entries to record transactions (a) and (c), and to correct the original entries for (b) and (d).

Note You should journalize the cash entries.

(LCCI Elem)

NA 20.08 On 1 June 19-7 T Brown's Balance Sheet was as follows.

	£			£
Fixed assets			Capital	6 290
Motor van	1 000			
Fixtures	700	1 700	*Current liabilities*	
Current assets			Bank overdraft	1 010	
Stock	4 950		Creditors	2 750	3 760
Debtors	3 400	8 350		
		10 050		10 050

On this date he sold the business for £8300 to J Parker, who took over
the motor van at an agreed valuation of £850 and debtors subject to a
provision for bad debts of £150. Brown agreed to pay off the bank overdraft. The rest of the assets and liabilities were taken over at the Balance
Sheet values.

On 1 June Parker paid £8750 into a business bank account and paid
Brown a cheque in settlement of the business purchase.

(a) Show the Journal entries, including cash, in the books of
J Parker.

(b) Show Parker's Balance Sheet at the commencement of the
business.

NA 20.09 To correct errors entries should be put through the Journal because

A   it is easier to do
B   it saves entering it in the ledger
C   this provides a record explaining the entries made in the ledger
D   this completes the double entry

(PEI Elem)

NA 20.10 The Trial Balance of a business did not balance and a Suspense Account
was opened. It was later found that a payment representing the cost of
improvements to freehold premises, correctly entered in the Cash Book,
had been debited to the Repairs Account. This should be corrected
by

A   crediting Premises Account, debiting Repairs Account
B   debiting Premises Account, crediting Repairs Account
C   debiting Suspense Account, crediting Cash Book
D   crediting Suspense Account, debiting Cash Book

(PEI Elem)

NA 20.11 Which one of the following is not a book of original entry?

A   The Cash Book
B   The ledger
C   The Journal
D   The Sales Day Book

(PEI Elem)

21. The Bank Reconciliation Statement/Credit Cards

As the owner of a business I need to know at all times the balance on our business Bank (Current) Account. Cash is needed to keep the business going—to pay wages, expenses, creditors, to repay loans, to pay taxes, and so on.

If insufficient cash is available at particular times, I may need to see the bank manager to obtain either overdraft facilities or to arrange a loan. The business Cash Book should give an up-to-date picture of the position regarding cash in hand and at the bank. The cash balance is checked by the physical counting and the balance at the bank is checked by looking at the bank statement that is prepared by the bank and sent to its clients.

Bank statement

You will remember that this shows the account of our business in the books of the bank; the statement is a copy of the account entries made by the bank. However, our Bank Account in our Cash Book is not going to look exactly the same as our account in the bank's books. One reason for a difference is that if we have money in our Bank Account the bank is a 'debtor' to us. In the bank's books we are a 'creditor' since the bank owes us the money. Therefore, debits in the business Cash Book are shown as credits on the bank statement. Payments made by us are shown as debits by the bank. Another reason why the two accounts look different is because the bank keeps our account in 'columnar' form. The statement, being a copy of the account, is also in columnar form. For example, our Bank Account in our Cash Book:

Bank Account

May 1	Balance b/d		192	May 2	Rates			92
May 1	A Bailey Ltd		486	May 12	Salaries			346
				May 20	Road Tax			55
				May 31	Balance		c/d	185
			678					678
June 1	Balance	b/d	185					

Our Bank Account in the bank's books (as we would expect to see it):

J Wynn's Account

May 3	Debit		92	May 1	Balance			192
May 14	Debit		346	May 3	Credit			486
May 28	Debit		55					
	Balance	c/d	185					
			678					678
				May 31	Balance	b/d		185

In fact it is in columnar form

	J Wynn	Debit	Credit	Balance
May 1	Balance b/fwd			192
May 3	Credit		486	678
May 3	Cheque no 3456	92		586
May 14	Cheque no 3457	346		240
May 28	Cheque no 3458	55		185

Paying amounts into the bank

Paying-In slip

Every time an amount is paid into our Bank Account we have to complete a paying-in slip (see page 232). This is required by the bank to identify the account and record the amount received by it. The paying-in slip enables us to record the value of the coins, notes, and cheques paid in.

For example, say we had

the following to pay in: The paying-in slip would show:

	Notes: £50		
Two notes of £20 each	£20	40	00
	£10		
	£5		
115 £1 coins	£1	115	00
Four (£10) bags of	50p	40	00
50p coins	20p		
Eight (£5) bags of silver	Silver	40	00
Nine (£1) bags of bronze	Bronze	9	00
	TOTAL CASH	244	00
	Cheques, etc	426	17
	(see over)		
	TOTAL CREDIT	670	17

The reverse side shows:

CHEQUES, ETC		
A Brown	182	67
T Jones	243	50
Total c/o	426	17

Cheque for £182.67
Cheque for £243.50

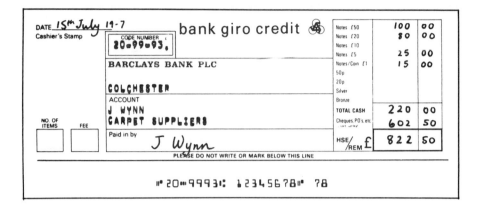

A specimen completed paying-in slip (both sides)

The counterfoil

So that we can keep an exact record of what is paid into the bank, we enter the paying-in slip counterfoil in exactly the same way as the paying-in slip itself. The counterfoil is either a carbon copy of the paying-in slip or a tear off portion.

Drawing amounts from the bank

The principal method of drawing money from the bank is by means of a cheque. In the same way as a paying-in slip, a cheque has a counterfoil. When paying by cheque the counterfoil is completed showing the date, person to whom it is paid, and the amount. The counterfoil is then used as the source of entry in the Cash Book.

Some banks have counterfoils in cheque books that enable us to keep a running balance total of the account. This is illustrated on the specimen cheque shown on page 16.

Differences in the two balances

Unless very few entries appear in the Cash Book, it is unlikely that the balance shown in the Cash Book agrees with the balance shown on the bank statement. There are several reasons why differences arise.

1 Cheques paid and entered in our Cash Book have not yet been presented to the bank for payment.
2 Payments made by the bank on our behalf under standing orders may not be entered in our Cash Book.
3 Receipts by the bank of dividends, interest, and credit transfer payments will be shown on the statement but will not yet be entered into our Cash Book.
4 Charges made by the bank (debited to our account) will be shown on the bank statement but are not yet entered into our Cash Book.
5 Amounts paid into our Bank Account may not yet be credited on the statement.

In addition, errors that may have arisen in making entries in the Cash Book will be discovered, since, when adjustments have been made for the differences above, the balances in the Cash Book and the statement should agree.

Example

Cash Book (Bank A/c)

Aug 1	Balance		72	Aug 10	Rent (2)		15
Aug 14	Sales		196<	Aug 12	Cash		25<
Aug 30	Sales (1)		100	Aug 14	A Taylor		39<
				Aug 15	British Telecom		22<
				Aug 31	Balance	c/d	267
			368				368
Aug 31	Balance	b/d	267				

Bank Statement

		Debit	Credit	Balance
Aug 1	Balance			72
Aug 12	Cash chq no 106341	25<		47
Aug 16	Credit		196<	243
Aug 24	Cheque no 106342	39<		204
Aug 25	Cheque no 106343	22<		207
Aug 30	Charges	5		182
Aug 30	Credit trans W Wood		44	221

Which balance in the example above is correct? The £267 or the £221? The following procedure will give the answer.

Verifying the bank balance

Step 1   Mark those items that appear in both the Cash Book and the bank statement. Those items not marked cause the differences in the two totals. (Note that the < sign is used in the example to denote items that agree.)

Step 2   All those unmarked items on the statement should now be entered in the Cash Book. These items should then be marked with a < sign.

The Cash Book will now appear as follows:

Cash Book (Bank A/c)

Aug 1	Balance		72	Aug 10	Rent (2)		15
Aug 14	Sales		196<	Aug 12	Cash		25<
Aug 30	Sales (1)		100	Aug 14	A Taylor		39<
				Aug 15	British Telecom		22<
				Aug 31	Balance	c/d	267
			368				368
Aug 31	Balance	b/d	267	Aug 31	Bank charges		5<
Aug 31	W Wood		44<	Aug 31	Balance	c/d	306
			311				311
Sept 1	Balance	b/d	306				

All the items on the statement should now be marked. The difference between the £306 Cash Book and the £221 statement balances is caused by the unmarked items in the Cash Book.

Step 3 Prepare the Bank Reconciliation Statement as follows:

Bank Reconciliation Statement as at 31 August 19–6

		£
Balance per bank statement		221.00
Add Item not credited (1)		+ 100.00
		321.00
Less Cheques unpresented (2)		− 15.00
Corrected Cash Book balance		306.00

The Bank Reconciliation Statement can also be prepared by starting with the 'corrected' Cash Book balance, as shown below:

Bank Reconciliation Statement as at 31 August 19–6

		£
Balance per Cash Book		306.00
Add Cheques unpresented (2)		15.00
		321.00
Less Item not credited (1)		100.00
Balance per bank statement		221.00

Balance Sheet item

The bank balance shown in the Balance Sheet must be correct. The amount to be shown, therefore, as an asset in the trial balance and the Balance Sheet is £306. This is the figure disclosed after 'correcting' the Cash Book. 'Correcting' means the entering of those additional items required to bring the Bank Account balance in the Cash Book to the correct figure.

Joe's Rule No 21
In practice always 'correct' the Cash Book before preparing the Bank Reconciliation Statement.

Examination notes

Examination questions should specify what is required. Sometimes the Cash Book balance does not need to be corrected before reconciliation. Using the example above the Reconciliation Statement would be:

Bank Reconciliation Statement as at 31 Aug 19–6

			£
Balance per statement			221
Add Debits not in Cash Book		5	
Credits not on statement		100	105
			326
Less Credits not in Cash Book		44	
Debits not on statement		15	59
Balance per Cash Book			267

Customer payments by credit card

Use of credit cards

Many customers in the shop pay for their carpets using a credit card. These cards are issued by an organization which provides the individual with a 'credit facility', i.e., it lends the individual money which is paid back at an agreed monthly rate. Most of the organizations providing such a source are banks and this method of providing personal finance is an alternative to allowing customers to overdraw on current accounts or granting them a loan. A card holder is given a 'credit rating' by the credit card company. We do not know what that rating is but if we telephone the credit card company to obtain authorization for the payment to be accepted, the company will tell us if the customer can or cannot proceed with that payment method.

Recording the sale

To complete the transaction using a credit card the customer has to sign a sales voucher which we prepare using an imprinter. The top copy is given to the customer and the remaining copies are for our use. One copy is handed in to the bank and we retain the others in case of queries. A completed voucher is to us the same as a cheque. It is added in with cheques and cash received to obtain the total daily sales.

Bookkeeping entries for the sales value

The daily sales total from 'Recording the sale' above is debited in the

Cash Book (cash column) and credited to the Sales Account. When the sales vouchers are paid into the bank the following procedure is followed:

1 All the vouchers to be paid in are recorded on a summary sheet (provided by the credit card company) showing all the vouchers and the total value and number of vouchers.
2 The summary sheet and vouchers are placed in an envelope (again provided by the credit card company).
3 The value of the summary sheet is then entered on the bank paying-in slip as a cheque and the envelope at (2) is handed in with other cheques/cash.
4 The bank paying-in slip copy is then used to credit Cash Account and debit Bank Account

Bookkeeping entries for credit card services

The credit card company makes a charge to us for the service it provides.

We receive from it a statement (usually monthly) showing the total amount paid into our bank (which we 'reconcile' with our bank paying-in slips) and also the charges (plus VAT) that will be made to us. The charges will be debited to our Bank Account *by the bank*. Such charges will appear on our bank statement and will have to be entered in our books as follows

Credit Bank Account:*Debit* Card Services Account.

21.01 From the following Cash Book and bank statement draw up a statement reconciling the two balances.

Cash Book (bank columns only)

April	1	Balance b/f	600.00	April 8	Rates	110.00
	6	Cash paid in	75.20	15	Wages	40.00
	12	Cheque from A	64.80	15	Electricity	60.42
	18	Cheque from B	72.40	15	Paid X	72.15
	28	Cash paid in	85.00	26	Rent	30.00
	30	Cheque from C	54.62	26	Wages	40.00
				27	Paid Y	64.10
				30	Paid Z	24.10
				30	Balance c/f	511.25
			952.02			952.02
May	1	Balance b/f	511.25			

Bank Statement

		Debit	Credit	Balance
April 1	Balance			600.00
6	Cash		75.20	675.20
12	A		64.80	740.00
12	Rates	110.00		630.00
15	Wages	40.00		590.00
18	B		72.40	662.40
19	Electricity	60.42		601.98
20	X	72.15		529.83
26	Wages	40.00		489.83
28	Cash		85.00	574.83

(PEI Elem)

21.02 The following extract is from the bank columns of the Cash Book of J Coral.

19-6			£	19-6			£
Apr 26	Balance	b/f	260	Apr 27	M Turner		53
27	L Brown		84	30	K Jones		21
29	Cash		100	30	S Cooper		42
30	H Cane		62		Balance	c/f	390
			£506				£506

On 30 April, he received the following bank statement from the bank.

19-6		Payments £	Receipts £	Balance £
Apr 26	Balance (credit)			260
28	Brown		84	
28	Credit transfer—S King		48	392
29	Cash		100	492
30	Turner	53		
30	Charges	25		414

You are required to:
(a) Bring the Cash Book up to date, and carry down the new balance at 30 April 19-6.
(b) Prepare a statement under its proper title to reconcile the difference between the revised balance in the Cash Book and the balance in the bank statement on 30 April 19-6.

(RSA 1)

NA 21.03 (a) Smith receives his bank statement showing a balance in bank of £1340 on 31 May 19-6. Cheques totalling £130 paid to creditors have not yet been presented for payment, and a sum of £75 credit transfer received by the bank has not been entered in his Cash Book. Calculate the balance which Smith's Cash Book should show before any corrections are made.

(b) Smith receives a statement of account from one of his suppliers. It shows a balance due of £180. The account in Smith's ledger indicates that the amount due is only £50. Explain how this difference could arise without any mistakes being made.

(RSA 1)

21.04 On the 30 June 19-6, B Back's Cash Book showed a balance of £40.00 overdrawn on his Bank Account. After checking his Cash Book with his bank statement, Back located the following errors and omissions.

(a) Cheques drawn and entered in the Cash Book on 29 June for £35.00 in favour of C White and £25 in favour of J Green had not been passed through the bank for payment.

(b) Interest charges of £15 shown in the bank statement had not been entered in the Cash Book.

(c) £80 cash banked by B Back on the 30 June was not credited by the bank until 1 July although it had been entered in the Cash Book.

You are required to:
(a) Make the necessary entries to amend the Cash Book balance.
(b) Prepare a Bank Reconciliation between the bank statement balance of £75 (overdrawn) and the revised Cash Book balance.
(c) Briefly describe the reason for preparing a Bank Reconciliation Statement.

(RSA 1)

NA 21.05 Explain briefly the difference between:

(a) Bank statement and Bank Reconciliation Statement.
(b) Fixed assets and current assets.
(c) Trade discount and cash discount.
(d) Personal and impersonal accounts.

Note You should give examples in (b) and (d).

(LCCI Elem)

21.06 At the close of business on 29 February 19-4, the balance of cash at bank as shown in the Cash Book of Joseph Williams, a sole trader, did not agree with his bank statement. On comparing the two, Williams discovered that the following matters accounted for the difference:

(1) During February the bank had allowed Williams bank interest amounting to £27. This had not yet appeared in the Cash Book.

(2) The following cheques issued by Williams during February had not yet been presented for payment:

£38; £42; £17.

(3) During February the bank had paid, under a banker's standing order, rent of Williams' shop amounting to £65, which did not appear in his Cash Book.

(4) On 29 February Williams paid into his bank cash amounting to £74. The item had been entered in Williams' Cash Book but had not yet appeared on his bank statement.

(5) The Cash Book balance at 29 February 19-4 showed cash at bank £634.

Required:

(i) Draw up the bank column of the Cash Book of Williams for the end of February 19-4, commencing with the figure of £634 given in (5) above. Enter the omitted items, and carry down the balance.

(ii) Prepare the Reconciliation Statement as at 29 February 19-4. This should commence with the final bank balance as in (i) and end with the balance as shown on the bank statement.

(LCCI Elem)

NA 21.07 Prepare a Bank Reconciliation Statement from the following particulars.

	£
Balance overdrawn per bank statement 31 March 19-8	572
Cheques received and paid into the bank but not yet entered on the bank statement	996
Cheques drawn and entered in the Cash Book but not presented to the bank for payment	314
Bank charges made by the bank but not entered in the Cash Book	28
Balance at bank per Cash Book 31 March 19-8	138

21.08 From the extracts below prepare the Reconciliation Account after correcting the Cash Book.

Cash Book

Dec				Dec				
1	Balance	146.00		10	Rent			25.00
2	T Tolley	98.00		14	B Brown & Co			193.00
3	F Formby	226.00		21	Wages			432.50
14	Cash sales	948.00		23	Petty cash			40.00
18	Cash sales	321.00		31	Telephones			96.25
22	J Symons	94.00		31	Customs and Excise			148.25
30	Cash sales	435.00		31	Balance	c/d	1371.75
31	P Paul	38.75						
		2306.75						2306.75

Bank Statement

			Dr	Cr	Balance
Dec	1	Balance			169.20
	3	Credits		324.00	493.20
	15	012	25.00		468.20
	15	Credits		948.00	1416.20
	16	011	23.20		1393.00
	18	013	193.00		1200.00
	18	Credits		321.00	1521.00
	22	014	432.50		1088.50
	23	Credits		94.00	1182.50
	24	015	40.00		1142.50
	31	Chgs	8.50		1134.00

Note the following information:

The Bank Reconciliation Statement 30 Nov 19...

Balance as per bank statement	169.20
Less Cheques unpresented	23.20
Balance as per Cash Book	£146.00

22. Control Accounts

Joe wants to know:

1 How much is owed to us by debtors.
2 How much we owe to creditors for goods supplied to us.

To obtain these figures you will have to balance the accounts in both ledgers and then total up these balances. If there are many debtors (and creditors) a regular calculation of the balance is a time-consuming job.

Joe has decided that as his business has expanded and the number of both customers and suppliers has increased it is necessary to start using a method of recording debtors and creditors. This will help to speed up the job of calculating the total balances and at the same time act as a check on the accuracy of the double entry.

Sales Ledger Control Account

Joe explains.

I want to open an account that will record the totals of our transactions with customers. These are credit sales, receipts from debtors, the returns made, and the discounts we have allowed. This information is already available in our books as monthly figures.

22.01   (a)   Where is the total of the monthly credit sales?
　　　　　(b)   Where is the total of receipts from debtors?
　　　　　(c)   Where is the discount allowed?

I want you to open a *summary* account for debtors. I call this the *Sales Ledger Control Account*. (Other names for this account are Debtors' Control Account, Total Debtors' Account, and the Debtors' Total Account.)

It is entered in exactly the same way as a debtors' account but with totals rather than individual amounts.

Memorandum account

The Sales Ledger Control Account is kept in the Nominal Ledger, but it is a memorandum account. It is an extra *summary* account which uses the existing books and records to enable it to be entered. It is *not* a part of the double entry system.

22.02   The term 'memorandum item' is used to describe certain records. List these records and outline their role in the double entry system.

Look at this example, say that today we sell goods on credit to

> Able for £150
> Barry for £62
> Coe for £197

The accounts for Able, Barry, and Coe would be debited and the total £409 would also be debited to the Sales Ledger Control Account (1).

				Sales Ledger Control Account			
(1)	Total		409	(2)	Cash		347
					Bal	c/d	62
			409				409
(3)	Bal	b/d	62				

If tomorrow both Able and Coe paid their bills, then their accounts would be credited and the total received (£347) would also be credited to the Sales Ledger Control Account (2), when the balance would then be £62 (3)—showing how much is still owed to us.

In other words, this Control Account summarizes the position regarding debtors.

Let us look now at our own books.

1 *The Sales Day Book*   The credit sales for each month are totalled and posted to the Sales Account (as a credit). This total represents the total of all the individual amounts that have been entered in the Sales Ledger Accounts. I have given you an illustration of this before so refer to page 44. You will see that the Total Sales in the Sales Day Book for March are £924.90. This has been debited by individual amounts to customers' accounts and credited to the Sales Account. Therefore, this figure will now be entered in the Sales Ledger Control Account as a debit.

2 *The analysed Cash Book*   Look at page 263. One of the analysis columns is headed Receipts from debtors. The total is used to post to the Sales Ledger Control Account (on the credit side). Remember that individual accounts have already been credited in the Sales Ledger— so the total being credited in the Sales Ledger Control Account is really an extra entry.

What else has to be entered in the Sales Ledger Control Account? Anything that is entered in a debtor's account. For example:

(a) Cash discount is posted to a debtor's account (as a credit). The monthly total for discount is in the memorandum column in the Cash Book. The total is posted to the Discount Allowed Account (as a debit) and to the Sales Ledger Control Account (as a credit).

(b) Returns from and allowances given to customers are shown in the Sales Returns Book. Once again the total can be used to post to the Sales Ledger Control Account (as a debit).

Also some entries arise from Journal entries:

(a) In writing off bad debts, I will enter in the Journal:

Journal

May 15	Bad Debts A/c TWE customer Being debt w/o on notice of bankruptcy	148	148
May 15	— Sales Ledger Control A/c Being entry for bad debt w/o on May 15 (TWE customer)	—	148

Notice that a third entry has been made. Because the debt is being written off (w/o) it is credited in the debtors' account. Therefore, this must be entered in the Sales Ledger Control Account.

(b) Offsetting accounts, where a customer of ours is also a creditor, then one balance can be used to offset the other. The Journal entry will be:

Journal

	B Woodward (Bought Ledger A/c) B Woodward (Sales Ledger A/c) Offsetting accounts due to us against a liability	160	160

At the same time a second Journal entry is made:

Journal

	Purchase Ledger Control A/c	160	
	Sales Ledger Control A/c		160
	Being offset on accounts of		
	B Woodward		

(c)   Where adjustments are made for cheques dishonoured or discounts disallowed.

A customer's cheque that is dishonoured is entered in the Cash Book on the credit side (to cancel the receipt on the debit side) and debited in the Sales Ledger Account. As we do not have a column in the Cash Book for recording 'dishonoured' cheques it will be necessary to make an entry in the Journal as follows:

Journal

May 17	Sales Ledger Control A/c	95	—
	—		
	Being entry for dishonour of		
	customer's cheque—Cash Book		
	page 20 on 10 May		

Looking at the example below:

Sales Ledger Control Account

Dec 1	Bal	b/d	86 920	Dec 31	Total receipts	cb	27 560
Dec 18	Dish chqs	J	420		Total disc allow	cb	540
Dec 18	Disc cancelled	J	10		Total sales ret	SR B	850
Dec 31	Total sales	SDB	24 000		Accts offset	J	160
					Bad debts w/o	J	148
Dec 31	Bal	c/d	80	—	Bal	c/d	82 172
			111 430				111 430
Jan 1	Bal	b/d	82 172	Jan 1	Bal	b/d	80

Note 1   The folio references show the source of the entries.
Note 2   Both a debit balance and a credit balance have been brought down.

Year end action

Although it is not a part of the double entry system, this account acts as a summary for all the debtors' accounts. It is kept in the Nominal Ledger and the total is shown in the trial balance at the year end. At this time (and monthly if desired), the Sales Ledger balances should be totalled and checked against the Sales Ledger Control Account balance. The two figures should agree. The total for debtors appears in the Balance Sheet as an asset and this must be accurate. If the two balances do not agree then an error has been made in either the Sales Ledger Control Account or the Sales Ledger. To find the error:

1 Check the arithmetical accuracy of the Sales Ledger Control Account.
2 Check the arithmetical accuracy of the total of the debtors' balances taken from the Sales Ledger.
3 Check the accuracy of each debtor's account—that the balance is correct and brought down on the correct side of the account.

If the error has still not been found then either one (or more) posting has been omitted or made incorrectly—by either transposing figures or entering an item on the wrong side of an account. Detailed checking of all entries must then be made.

It may be that due to returns and other allowances one of the debtor's accounts has (temporarily) a credit balance. At that point it is a liability and must be shown as such. It has to be entered therefore in the Sales Ledger Control Account and carried down as a credit balance (see illustration page 245).

Notes regarding illustration opposite
When a posting is made from a book of original entry to the Sales Ledger Control Account the detail and folio reference is entered to indicate the posting has been made.
Note 1   The double entry for the credit sales in the Sales Account.
Note 2   The total of the Sales Returns Book is posted to the Sales Returns Account in the ledger.
Note 3   The Discount Allowed Account in the Nominal Ledger is debited with the £20.75 total.

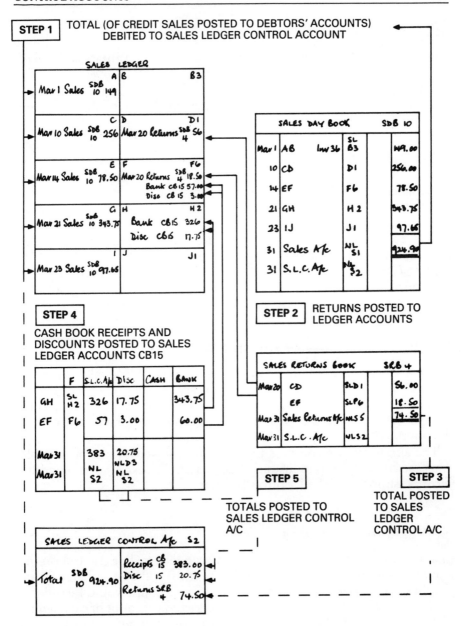

SOURCE OF ENTRIES TO THE
SALES LEDGER CONTROL ACCOUNT

Bought Ledger Control Account

This is also kept in the Nominal Ledger and acts as a summary account of creditors for goods and materials supplied.

It is entered in the same way as the Sales Ledger Control Account—from books of original entry in which totals have already been calculated. These are:

1. *Bought Day Book*   The monthly total posted to the Purchases Account is also posted in the Bought Ledger Control Account.
2. *Purchases Returns Book*   The monthly total posted to the Purchases Returns Account is also posted to the Bought Ledger Control Account.
3. *Cash Book*   The monthly payments are totalled and entered in the Bought Ledger Control Account.
4. *Journal*   Sometimes an entry is required in the Bought Ledger Control Account, this is an additional third entry where, for example, accounts are offset or discounts are disallowed.

An alternative view of Control Accounts

There are two ways of looking at Control Accounts. Joe takes the view that a Control Account is an extra, summary account of a set of ledger accounts, debtors or creditors (although any 'set' of accounts, e.g., Stock Ledger, Asset Ledger, Nominal Ledger, could have a Control Account).

The alternative viewpoint is that the Control Account is the 'double entry' account and the individual accounts are the extra, memorandum records, supporting the Control Account.

Self-balancing ledgers

If a 'Control' Account was included in each ledger, but entered on the opposite side to the individual account entries, then the ledger itself would be self-balancing. In this case, such an account would be called a *total account*. If a business has many ledgers a total account in each ledger enables errors to be located more quickly. Unfortunately a great deal of extra analysis work is required in the books of original entry to operate this system.

Joe's Rule No 22
By providing a summary of all the accounts in a ledger, the control account can give

an 'instant' total (of debtors, creditors, stock, plant and machinery), and provide a check on the accuracy of the ledgers.

22.03 The following figures are supplied by a business:

	£
Bank payments for period to suppliers	3620
Returns outwards for period	95
Purchases for period	4936
Creditors at start of period	3890

The total creditors at the end of the period shown by the purchases control account are:

A £3715
B £3890
C £4025
D £5111

(AEB 'O' Nov 1984)

22.04 The final balance on a correctly compiled purchase ledger control account represents the

A value of unsold purchases
B total creditors of the business
C profit on goods bought and resold
D amount owing to suppliers whose accounts are in that ledger

(AEB 'O' June 1984)

NA 22.05 R Pettit's purchase ledger contains the accounts of two creditors with the following balances:

19-2			£	
Aug	1	S Nicholls	260	credit
		G Price	310	credit

During August the following transactions took place.

Aug	4	Bought goods from S Nicholls on credit £624
	5	Purchases from G Price on credit £414
	10	Returned damaged goods to S Nicholls £24
	14	Sent S Nicholls a cheque in settlement of his account at 1 August, less 10 per cent cash discount
	19	Received a credit note from G Price for £8 in respect of an overcharge on 5 August
	28	S Nicholls complained that the discount on 14 August should have been 5 per cent. Correct this error

Aug 31   G Price also bought some goods from Pettit. The debit balance of £16 on Price's account in the sales ledger was transferred to his account in the bought ledger

Pettit had many customers to whom he sold goods on credit. Such debtors totalled £700 on 1 August 19–2 and during that month transactions with them were:

	£
Sales	· 5300
Returns inward	29
Cheques received	5356
Discounts allowed	281
Bad debts	35

In addition the transfer of the balance on the account of G Price (see 31 August above) was carried out.

Required:
(a) The accounts of Nicholls and Price as they would appear in Pettit's purchase ledger for the month of August 19–2.
(b) The Sales Ledger Control Account for the month of August 19–2.
(c) A comment on the purpose of control accounts.

(AEB 'O' Nov 1982)

NA 22.06 (a) Briefly explain the role of the total account as part of the double entry bookkeeping system.
(b) Describe the methods by which a trader using total debtors' and creditors' accounts as an integral part of the double entry system, may keep account of his debtors and creditors.

(RSA 1)

22.07 A Purchases Ledger Control Account draws on information obtained from several different sources.
You are required to:

(1) Explain the purpose of a Purchases Ledger Control Account.
(2) State the sources of the following totals:

(i)   The opening balances.
(ii)   The total credit purchases.
(iii) The total purchases returns.
(iv)   The total discount received.
(v)   The total amount paid to creditors.

(RSA 1)

NA 22.08   The following figures relate to the sales and purchases of a business for the month of May 19–4.

		£
May 1	Total debtors	1 270
	Total creditors	650

Month ended

May 31	19–4	£
	Sales	34 760
	Purchases	22 176
	Payments received	31 800
	Discount allowed	175
	Sales returns	1 830
	Payments made	20 080
	Purchases returns	2 140
	Bad debts written off	125

(a) Write up the sales ledger and the purchases ledger control accounts for the month of May 19–4 and ascertain the total of debtors and creditors on 31 May.

(b) The actual total of all the personal accounts in the debtors' ledger was £100 less than the balance shown on the control account and the total of the personal accounts in the creditors' ledger was also £100 less than shown on the control account.

On the assumption that all the figures given are correct, suggest an item which may have been omitted from the control accounts.

(London 'O')

23. Analysed Books

The Petty Cash Book

Purpose

So far you have been keeping the record of cash payments and receipts in a three-column Cash Book. Joe is now going to give you some more responsibility. You are going to have to keep the Petty Cash Book and also keep the petty cash box in order to pay out sums of money to those employees who have incurred expenses. This means that you will no longer keep a detailed record of cash payments in the Cash Book. (Look at the Cash Book shown on page 75 and see how *all* cash payments are shown.) Now you will have:

1 The Cash Book for recording bank payments by cheque and receipts into bank.
2 The Petty Cash Book for recording *every* detail of cash payments.

The system is simple. Joe is going to give you a sum of cash, called the float. He has got to take this out of the Bank Account so when he draws the cheque it will appear in the Cash Book, on the credit side, as follows.

Cash Book					38
	Oct 4	*Petty Cash*	PCB 1	25.00	

The folio reference is PCB 1. What does this mean?

The corresponding debit entry is in the Petty Cash Account, which is kept in . . . which book? Yes, of course: the Petty Cash Book. Joe has already got a suitably ruled Petty Cash Book (see opposite) and you can see how he has made the entry into the Petty Cash Account.

From now on you are going to keep the Petty Cash Book and the petty cash box containing the £25. You can pay money out to the following people only, and no more than £5 at any one time: to Joe himself; to Tom Brown, the warehouse foreman; to Ben Fury, the senior salesman; to Robin Coalman, the delivery driver; and to yourself.

Petty Cash Book Ruling

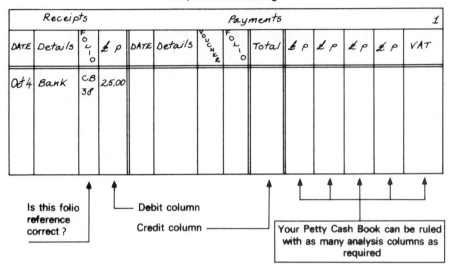

Remember that this book is a record of the Petty Cash Account.

Petty cash vouchers

When you pay out, *you must obtain a receipt from each person* and also *make sure that the person signs a petty cash voucher*—like the one below.

Petty Cash Voucher	001	
Date		
Details	£	p
Signature		

This is your proof that the expense is a real one. If you do not obtain the signature, how does Joe know that it is a genuine expense?

Example

During the next three days you pay out the following sums.

Oct	4	To Robin Coalman	Parking £2.50	voucher no 1
	4	To Robin Coalman	Spares £1.25	voucher no 2
	5	To Ben Fury	Postage £0.38	voucher no 3
	5	To Ben Fury	Travelling £3.20	
	5	To Tom Brown	Tea £1.20	voucher no 4
	5	To the milkman	Milk £1.68	voucher no 5
	6	To the office cleaner	Cleaning £1.00	voucher no 6
	6	To James Brown	A creditor £2.50	voucher no 7
	6	To Ben Fury	Travelling £1.15	voucher no 8
	6	To Ben Fury	Stationery £0.85	

You did remember to sign voucher nos 5 and 6 yourself? You drew out the money to pay these expenses and should have signed the vouchers yourself. Joe now explains how you should record these in the Petty Cash Book.

Petty Cash Book

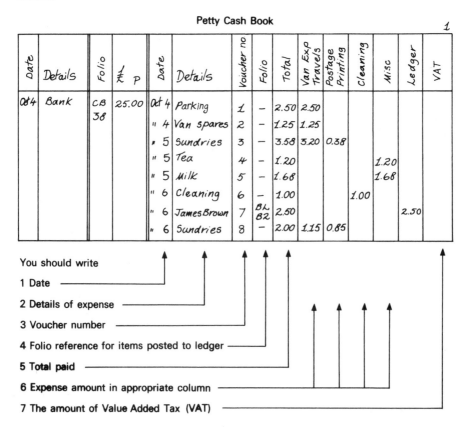

You should write
1 Date
2 Details of expense
3 Voucher number
4 Folio reference for items posted to ledger
5 Total paid
6 Expense amount in appropriate column
7 The amount of Value Added Tax (VAT)

Note   No entries have been made in this chapter for VAT. Entries which should be made are explained in Chapter 24.

Voucher nos 3 and 8 each have two different items.

Joe asks you to total up the payments and work out the amount left. Do that now. The answer should correspond to what you have in the petty cash box. If it does not—beware of trouble. You may or may not spend all of the £25 within the week—as Joe explains in laying down the following rule.

Imprest system

Bring your vouchers to me every Friday morning and I will reimburse you with the amount you have spent. I call this the *imprest system* of Petty Cash Recording. The effect is that you will always have your 'float' made up to the agreed figure at the end of every week. So this means that you now receive £15.71 and should record this in the Petty Cash Book.

Posting to the ledger

The only thing that Joe now needs to explain is how to post the items of expense to the ledger accounts (see illustration overleaf).

Remembering the rule that every debit has a credit, you have not so far entered any debits in the ledger for the credits (payments) in the Petty Cash Book.

You will notice that the Petty Cash Book has a column headed 'Ledger'. That column will be used to record payments made to persons to whom we owe small amounts of money, and whose accounts appear in the Bought Ledger. (These suppliers would normally be paid by cheque but they may visit your business and expect cash payment.) When the payment is made, the Petty Cash Account will be credited and the corresponding debit entry made in the personal account in the Bought Ledger.

When the posting is made, the ledger folio reference is entered in the Folio column. Having now made the double entry you must remember that when the Petty Cash Book is totalled, the column headed 'Ledger' will not need to be posted again.

Look how Joe rules off the Petty Cash Book and the references he has written in order to show that the expenses and payments have been posted.

The Bank Cash Book

Because all cash transactions are now recorded in the Petty Cash Book, the Cash Book proper reverts to being purely a Bank Book, recording the

Cash Book

| | | | | | Oct 4 | Petty Cash | PCB1 | 25.00 |
| | | | | | Oct 11 | Petty Cash | PCB1 | 15.71 |

Petty Cash Book

Date	Details	Folio	£ p	Date	Details	Voucher no	Folio	Total payments	Van expenses and travels	Postage and printing	Cleaning	Miscellaneous	Ledger	VAT
Oct 4	Bank	CB 38	25.00	Oct 4	Parking	1	–	2.50	2.50					
				4	Van spares	2	–	1.25	1.25					
				5	Sundries	3	–	3.58	3.20	0.38				
				5	Tea	4	–	1.20				1.20		
				5	Milk	5	–	1.68				1.68		
Oct 11	Bank	CB 42	15.71	6	Cleaning	6	–	1.00			1.00			
				6	James Brown	7	BL B2	2.50					2.50	
				6	Sundries	8	–	2.00	1.15	0.85				
					Balance c/d			15.71	8.10	1.23	1.00	2.88	2.50	
								25.00						
			40.71					40.71	NLV1	NLP4	NLC3	NLMS	–	
Oct 11	Balance b/d		25.00											

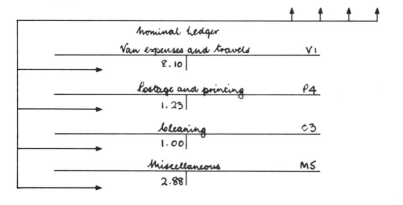

Nominal Ledger

Van expenses and travels	V1
8.10	

Postage and printing	P4
1.23	

Cleaning	C3
1.00	

Miscellaneous	MS
2.88	

transactions on the bank Current Account. When this occurs it may be called the *Bank Cash Book*.

Analysis columns in the Bank Cash Book are useful in providing details of individual amounts banked and the breakdown of payments where one cheque is used to draw money for several purposes. This use arises from the fact that, when a business examines its bank statement, the bank shows only the total of a payment into the account, although that payment may consist of cash and several cheques received from customers. The Bank Cash Book is entered from bank paying-in counterfoils, cheque counterfoils, and bank statements, in the same way as the normal Cash Book. It can be used in any Cash Book, with any Cash Book ruling.

Example

On 24 May, a payment into the bank consisted of five cheques. The paying-in slip counterfoil showed the total to be £187.25, but also recorded the individual cheque values enabling the cashier to record the amounts.

Also on 24 May, the owner drew a cheque value £96.43—this was for reimbursement of petty cash £30.43, and Drawings £66.

The individual accounts are posted in the usual way, but the amount actually banked, £187.25, and the cheque drawn, £96.43, will appear on the bank statement.

Bank Cash Book

May 24	P Harwood	92.15		May 24	Petty Cash	30.43	
	R T Corker	16.45			Drawings	66.00	96.43
	Maypole Ltd	25.65					
	K P Walters	18.70					
	Niger Containers	34.30	187.25				

23.01   Write up a trader's Bank Cash Book from the following information.

(a)   His balance at the bank at the close of business on 26 May according to his Cash Book was £983.77.

(b)   The counterfoils of his paying-in book give the following details:

May 29   Total paid in £197.16, consisting of cash from sales £49.66, a cheque from J Izzard for £50, and a cheque from L Waterlow for £97.50. Waterlow's cheque was accepted in full settlement of £100 owed by him

May	30	Total paid in £48.46, consisting entirely of cash from sales
	31	Total paid in £75.48, consisting of cash from sales £39.50 and a cheque from H Benskin for £35.98

(c) The counterfoils of his cheque book show the following details:

			£
May	29	J Ormerod and Co Ltd	£327.67
	30	Ivens and Co	195.00
	31	Petty cash	29.92
		Self	100.00
		Ashton's Garage	18.34

The cheque to Ivens and Co was accepted in full settlement of £200 owing to them.

The cheque to Ashton's Garage was for petrol, oil, repairs, etc., for the previous month, and no previous record of this transaction had gone through the books.

The Particulars column of the Cash Book should indicate clearly which ledger account should be debited or credited in respect of each Cash Book entry. Rule off and balance the Cash Book at the close of business on 31 May.

(RSA 1)

(*Authors note*   Particulars column = Details column.)

Bought Day Book

What is the advantage of having analysis columns in the Petty Cash Book? Posting column totals saves time. This advantage can also be obtained if similar analysis columns are used in all the books of original entry except the Journal. I hope you can remember the books of original entry—the Bought Day Book is one and there are five others.

The reason why Joe is now explaining the use of analysis columns in the Bought Day Book is because his business is expanding and in addition to selling carpets, he is going to sell furniture. Let Joe explain.

I shall be receiving invoices from suppliers of furniture and I shall want to know how much I am buying so that I can work out whether or not I am making a profit on selling the furniture.

I have got a new Bought Day Book (see opposite) which is bigger than the one you have been using so far, because it has a lot of analysis columns which are used in the same way as the analysis columns in the Petty Cash Book. I have already entered the invoices received today and you can see how the invoice total is entered in the Total column and also written in the proper analysis column. Look at the invoice from ABC Ltd. The total is £175.00 but it is made up of carpets priced at £75.00 and

Bought Day Book (With Analysis Columns)

Date	Supplier	Invoice no	Bought Ledger Folio	INVOICE TOTAL	CARPETS	FURNITURE				VAT
May 2	TKM Ltd	92 A	T1	148.00	148.00					
4	SHILLERS Ltd	0641	S2	79.00		79.00				
5	MICKER Ltd	9132	M3	91.00		91.00				
14	SKP & Co	849	S5	493.00	493.00					
18	ABC Ltd	71834	A4	175.00	75.00	100.00				
23	CEEDY Ltd	S921	C9	147.00	147.00					
28	S&K Ltd	498	S3	88.00		88.00				
				1221.00	863.00	358.00				
				NLP7	NLP1	NLP2				

Date (on invoice)
Supplier's invoice number

Creditor's account number
(folio reference)
to which invoice total
is posted

Analysis columns

Credit to Bought
Ledger Control Account
(memo only)

furniture priced at £100.00. This needs the use of both analysis columns. Look at page one of the new book. I have also totalled the three columns being used and you can see that the two analysis columns added together equal the Invoice Total column.

$$\text{Carpet} + \text{Furniture} = \text{Total}$$
$$£863.00 + £358.00 = £1221.00$$

Look at the reference number written under the totals.
   NL P1 means what?
   NL P2 means what?

It means that now we are going to open two Purchases Accounts. P1 is for purchases of carpets and P2 is for purchases of furniture, and as you already know, NL means the Nominal Ledger, in which the nominal (general) accounts are kept.

   The creditors' accounts are entered in the normal way. In the illustration above, the posting has already been done, as shown by the folio entries.

Illustration of the Double Entry Posting
From the BOUGHT DAY BOOK – To **CREDITORS' ACCOUNTS**
– To PURCHASES ACCOUNT

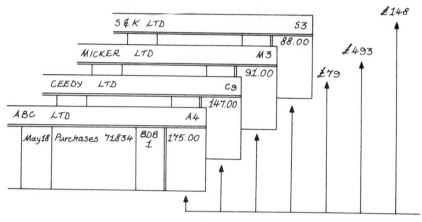

TOTAL CREDITS OF £1221

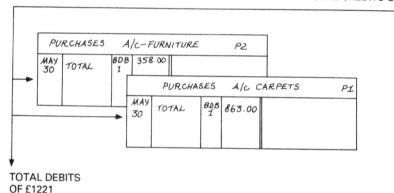

TOTAL DEBITS
OF £1221

Sales Day Book

If we are *buying* furniture as well as carpets, then obviously we are also
selling furniture. So you will also need an analysed Sales Day Book.
Having learned how to enter the Bought Day Book, this new, analysed,
Sales Day Book is easily understood, as Joe explains.

The ruling is the same as the Bought Day Book. It is entered from our
copy invoices. The customer's account is debited in the usual way—the
only difference is that *two* Sales Accounts are opened in the Nominal
Ledger and the totals posted from the analysis columns. So all the debit
entries in the debtors' accounts are represented by two credit entries in
the Sales Accounts. Here is my illustration to explain the entries.

Note   An analysed Sales Returns Book could be ruled in the same
way.

Entering and Posting the Analysed Sales Day Book

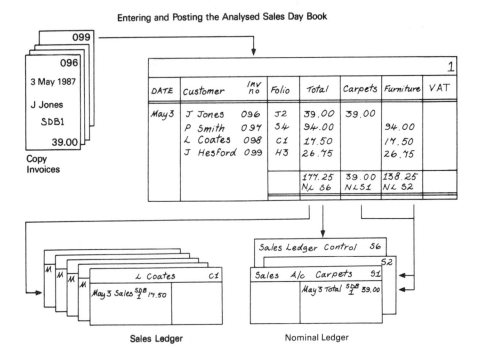

Miscellaneous credit sales

Although not shown in the illustration, additional analysis columns can be provided if required for regular recurring income arising from the sale of scrap and waste, the disposal of assets, the charging of rents for office or factory space sublet—all of which will require the raising of a sales invoice.

Extended Bought Day Book

Joe receives telephone bills, stationery bills, electricity bills, and so on. So far he has put all the bills he has received in his file and taken them out only when he has paid them; when he has paid we have entered them in his Cash Book (as a payment) and made the double entry in his Nominal Ledger, in the appropriate expense account. Now that he has decided to use an analysed Bought Day Book, we can begin to enter all invoices and bills received in this book.

As Joe says: this means that the Bought Ledger will now contain accounts for every person or business that is owed money by us (remember that a *creditor* is *someone who is owed money*). So the Electricity Board will have an account opened when we receive the electricity bill. The local authority will have an account when we receive the rates bill. British Telecom will have an account when we receive our telephone bill.

Extended Bought Day Book (with Analysis Columns for Goods and Services)

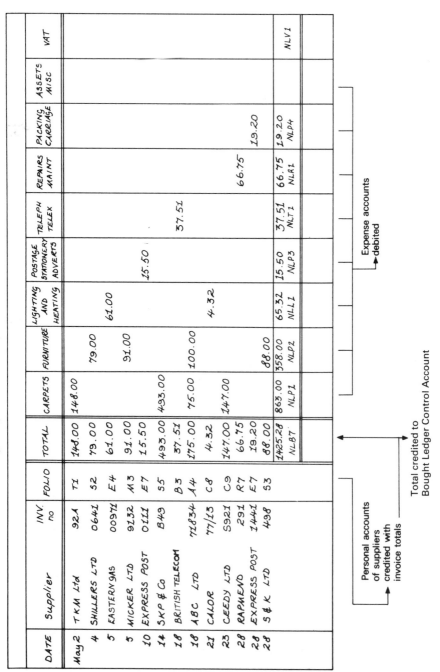

DATE	Supplier	INV no	FOLIO	TOTAL	CARPETS	FURNITURE	LIGHTING AND HEATING	POSTAGE STATIONERY ADVERTS	TELEPH TELEX	REPAIRS MAINT	PACKING CARRIAGE	ASSETS MISC	VAT
May 2	TKM Ltd	921	T1	148.00	148.00								
4	SHILLERS LTD	0641	52	79.00		79.00							
5	EASTERN GAS	00971	E4	61.00			61.00						
5	MICKER LTD	9132	M3	91.00		91.00							
10	EXPRESS POST	0111	E7	15.50				15.50					
14	SKP & Co	B49	55	493.00	493.00								
18	BRITISH TELECOM		B3	37.51					37.51				
18	ABC LTD	71834	A4	175.00	75.00	100.00							
21	CALOR	77/13	C8	4.32			4.32						
23	CEEDY LTD	5921	C9	147.00	147.00								
28	RAPMEND	291	R7	66.75						66.75			
28	EXPRESS POST	1441	E7	19.20							19.20		
28	S & K LTD	498	53	88.00		88.00							
				1425.28 NLB7	865.00 NLP1	358.00 NLP2	65.32 NLL1	15.50 NLP3	37.51 NLT1	66.75 NLR1	19.20 NLP4		NLV1

Personal accounts of suppliers credited with invoice totals

Total credited to Bought Ledger Control Account

Expense accounts debited

These creditors are no different from those from whom we have purchased carpets and furniture—they will all have an account in the Bought Ledger. Posting the invoice or bill total and entering the folio reference is just the same as for creditors for goods. Look at the example of the Bought Day Book opposite. The analysis columns are used in the same way as the analysis columns in the Petty Cash Book; the total of the expense is posted to the ledger account. In this way it saves posting each individual invoice to the expense account in the Nominal Ledger. Remember that the individual invoice is still posted to the creditor's account.

Assets purchased on credit

Invoices received can be entered in the book and shown in either a separate column or a Miscellaneous column. Either way, the posting should be made to the appropriate asset account from the column total. Even with a separate column, the total may need analysing if different assets have been purchased.

Analysed Cash Book

Analysis columns can be used for any number of purposes, but the main object is to enable totals of similar transactions to be obtained, such that the posting of a total saves the posting of numerous individual entries. This is the same principle that is applied in the Petty Cash Book; the analysis extends not only to payments but also to receipts. The layout below illustrates the Bank Cash Book that could be used in the situation outlined in Question 23.01.

Bank Cash Book (Receipts Side Only)

Date	Details	F O L I O	Misc	Discount allowed	Receipts From Debtors	Cash sales	VAT	Bank
May 29	Sales	—				49.66		—
	J Izzard	SLI2		2.50	50.00			—
	L Waterlow	SLW1			97.50			197.16
30	Sales	—				48.46		48.46
31	Sales	—				39.50		—
	H Benskin	SL B2			35.98			75.48
				2.50	183.48	137.62		321.10
				NLD1	NLC4	NLS1		

Note that debtors accounts are posted directly

Discounts allowed are posted in total

Cash sales are posted in total

Note that the column for receipts from debtors is totalled and posted to the credit of the control account (memo only). Should the business have a number of sales ledgers (A–G; H–M; N–R; S–Z) then the Receipts from Debtors column would need to be extended to four columns to allow control account totals for each ledger to be collected. The Folio column entries indicate the individual postings.

Daily Cash Receipts Book

If daily cash sales were to be entered directly into the Cash Book, particularly if some form of analysis is required, the Cash Book might become congested by so many entries. This can be eased by the use of a Cash Receipts Book, whose sole purpose is to record and analyse cash receipts, and provide a book of original entry from which debtors' accounts are posted.

Firms that sell goods by mail order will receive cheques, postal orders, and even cash every day through the post. It is important that such orders (and payments received) are recorded immediately. A responsible employee is in charge of opening the mail and all monies received are recorded in a Daily Cash Receipts Book. The total daily receipts are banked and therefore the entries in the Cash Book would correspond to the daily totals in the Daily Cash Receipts Book.

Again using 23.01:

Daily Cash Receipts Book

6

Date	Details	Folio	Total	Disc	Debtors' receipts	Cash Sales	VAT
May 29	Sales	-	49.66			49.66	
	J Izzard	SLI2	50.00		50.00		
	L Waterlow	SLW1	97.50	2.50*	97.50		
29	Cash Book	CB4 1	197.16	2.50	147.50	49.66	
30	Sales	-	48.46			48.46	
30	Cash Book	CB41	48.46			48.46	
31	Sales	-	39.50			39.50	
	H Benskin	SLB2	35.98		35.98		
31	Cash Book	CB 41	75.48		35.98	39.50	

*Discount is not received and therefore is not added in cross-casting the column.

Cash Book (Receipts side)

Date	Details	Folio	Misc	Disc	Receipts from debtors	Cash Sales	VAT	Bank
May 29	Cash receipts	CRB 6		2.50	147.50	49.66		197.16
30	„	CRB 6		-	-	48.46		48.46
31	„	CRB 6			35.98	39.50		75.48
				2.50	183.48	137.62		321.10
				NLD1	NLC4	NLS1		

Again, the totals of the columns are the amounts to post to the various ledger accounts, the total of the Receipts from debtors column being used to credit the Sales Ledger Control Account.

The analysed (multicolumn) Cash Book

For a small business that pays cash (or cheque) for most items it buys, a Cash Book with analysed columns is often the most useful type of Cash Book to use. The analysis columns operate in exactly the same way as those in the Petty Cash Book. When the payment is made, the credit entry in either the Cash or Bank column is also made in the appropriate analysis column. A Bought Ledger column is used to record payments to creditors, a Sales Ledger column is used for receipts from debtors, and a *Contra* column on either side of the book records *contra* transfers. The columns themselves can be totalled and cross-cast to verify the accuracy of the arithmetic. If insufficient analysis columns are available, a Miscellaneous or Sundries column can be used, but these items should be posted direct to the appropriate Nominal Ledger Account.

In the illustration overleaf, telephone bills, electricity bills, and other expenses for which a column was not available would need to be recorded in the Miscellaneous column.

Joe's Rule No 23
Analysis columns enable the posting to be made of the total of similar transactions (at a period end) thereby saving time and effort in posting the individual transactions.

Analysed Cash Book (Credit Side Only)

Date	Detail	FOLIO	RENT	WAGES	MOTOR EXP'S	CASH PURCHASES	BOUGHT LEDGER	CONTRA	MISC.	VAT	CASH	BANK
July 1	Rent	✓	20.00									20.00
4	Wages	✓		89.45							89.45	
6	Bank	C						109.00			109.00	
8	Rent	✓ BL	20.00									20.00
8	R. Taylor & Co	74					42.50					42.50
11	Wages	✓		97.66							97.66	
12	Petrol	✓			10.00						10.00	
15	Rent	✓	20.00									20.00
18	Wages	✓		94.73							94.73	
22	Bank	C						285.75			285.75	
22	Rent	✓	20.00									20.00
25	Wages	✓		110.40							110.40	
	T T (Spares) Ltd	✓				96.80						96.80
	Stationery	NL 53							5.45		5.45	
31	Balance	c/d							1752.61		94.98	1667.63
			80.00 NL R3	392.24 NL W1	10.00 NL M1	96.80 NL P1	42.50 NL B2	394.75	1758.06		897.42	1876.95

Notes

1 Folio column entries represent items posted directly to the Nominal Ledger, for miscellaneous items, and the Bought Ledger, to creditors' accounts.

2 Analysis column totals are posted to the Nominal Ledger. The Bought Ledger column is posted to the Bought Ledger Control Account (memo only).

3 The total balance carried down is entered in the Miscellaneous column so that the cross-casting of the totals can be carried out at the month end. Total Cash + Total Bank = Other column totals added together.

23.02   A firm maintains a Petty Cash Book using the imprest system; the amount of the imprest is £30. On 1 March the balance of Petty Cash in hand was £8.50, and during the following week these transactions occurred:

March   1   Cheque received from cashier to refund previous week's expenditure
2   Purchased postage stamps £1.40
3   Repaid travelling expenses £3.15
4   Purchased stationery £6.00, postage stamps £1.15
5   Paid for milk for office teas £1.40, telemessage £1.15
6   Paid window cleaner £2.00
7   Cheque received to restore imprest

Enter the above details into the Petty Cash Book, using the following headings:
Postage and telemessages, Travel expenses, Stationery, Miscellaneous.

(PEI Elem)

23.03   Walter Holmes is a sole trader who keeps his Petty Cash on the imprest system—the imprest amount being £40. For the month of December 19-3 his petty cash transactions were as follows:

Dec   1   Petty cash in hand £3.47
1   Petty cash restored to the imprest amount
4   Stamps purchased £3.96
8   Envelopes purchased £4.15
10   Paid wages £6.30
14   Paid to Alfred Jackson, a creditor, £5.60
20   Stamps purchased £4.29
21   Typing paper purchased £3.70
24   Paid wages £7.10
31   Stamps purchased £2.00

Required:
(i)   Draw up the Petty Cash Book of Walter Holmes and enter the above transactions in it.
(ii)   Balance the Petty Cash Book as at the close of business on 31 December 19-3 and carry down the balance.
(iii)   Give the entry necessary on 1 January 19-4 to restore the Petty Cash to the imprest amount.

Note   Your analysis columns should be postages, stationery, wages, and ledger.

(LCCI Elem)

23.04   Joe starts his financial year on 1 January. He had received the following receipts by 31 January. Enter these receipts in the analysed Cash Book and total each column for January.

Jan   5   Received cheque from J Brown Ltd (a debtor) for £606.20 for carpets supplied

Jan   6   Rent received (from subletting) £125.00 (cheque)
      7   £155.80 cash paid by customer buying floor tiles
   10   Cash received for taking up and relaying carpets £210.65
   10   Cheque received for £1000.00 from Greens Co, a debtor
   17   Cheque received from a 'Cash On Delivery' supply of industrial flooring £1422.30
   20   Rent received £125.00 cheque
   24   Cash sales £189.35

Note   Cheques received are immediately banked.

23.05   S Makie has a wholesale business selling goods for cash and on credit. He keeps an analysed Cash Book and a Sales Day Book as well as other normal books. During May the following transactions occurred.
Draw up only the payments side of the analysed Cash Book for May.

May   2   Drew two cheques £50.00 for Drawings and £18.72 for petrol
     4   Invoices received from creditors and paid by cheque:
         T T Textiles £146.46
         M Edwards £73.10
         Cash payments of £4.40 for stamps and £42.65 for a new van tyre
     5   Cash sales totalling £642.00 were banked on the same paying-in slip as cheque for £95.20 from P Billings
     8   Sales on credit made to P White £138.50 and K Williams £264.22
   12   Drew cheques as follows:
         £128.00 for wages
         £100.00 for Drawings
         £ 10.50 for stationery
   15   Cash sales banked £539.39, together with cheques value £144.00 from J White and £64.00 from K Williams
   18   Paid invoices by cheque:
         M King £59.59
         F Stanley £924.81
   21   Drew cheques to pay £119.40 general repairs, and £30.40 for van service
         Paid cash for £20.50 petrol, £2.60 stamps (stationery), £1.22 light bulb (misc)

23.06   (a) Write up the Petty Cash Book of J Stone from the following information.

      (i)   The book is to be kept on the imprest system.
      (ii)   The 'float' amounts to £20.
      (iii) You are to provide analysis columns to record (a) postage, (b) travelling expenses, (c) stationery, (d) miscellaneous items.
      (iv) Record the following transactions for the two-week period.

Sept	1	Balance of imprest	£ 6.20
		Payment received from the main cashier to make up imprest	
	4	Travelling expenses paid	3.00
	5	Parcel	0.75
	6	Bus fares	0.65
	7	Sundries for office	1.35
	8	Postage stamps	3.00
	8	Carbon paper and paper clips	0.95
	12	Packet of pencils	0.96
	13	Parcel	1.55
	14	Travelling expenses	4.00
	15	Received payment from main cashier to make up imprest float.	

(b) Explain how the Petty Cash Book is 'posted' to the ledger.

23.07 T Woods Ltd operates a garage which sells petrol, oil, some spares, and also repairs and services motor cars. The following invoices were received by T Woods Ltd during the first week of November. Enter in the Bought Day Book with three analysis columns, post to the ledger, and post the totals of the analysis columns to the Nominal Ledger.

Date	Invoice no	Supplier	Goods/services	Prices
2 Nov	IP 321	Transworld Tyres	12 tyres	£10 each less 25% trade discount
2 Nov	N43	S.O. Oils	2000 litres petrol	£210 net
3 Nov	6738	Repair-Speed	Assorted spare parts	£55 net
4 Nov	9321846	Battery Builders	12 batteries (super)	£15 each less 33⅓% trade discount
4 Nov	78574	Conoco Company	20 litres oil	68p per litre net
4 Nov	N48	S.O. Oils	2000 litres petrol	£210 net
5 Nov	A/342	Parkins Motors	Panel beating	£88 net
5 Nov	22532/M	Larkswood Tyres	Car towing	£15 net
5 Nov	6941	Repair-Speed	16 Sparking plugs	90p each less 25% trade discount

23.08 Rule up a Purchases Day Book with eight analysis columns and enter the following invoices. Total all the columns and check your arithmetic.

May	1	Smith & Co 24 pocket calculators at £5 each. Stationery £61 net. Invoice no S 114
	4	B M Carpets Ltd: assorted carpets £149.00; 10 rolls of hand-woven Indian carpets at £85 each. Invoice no BX 176
	8	Whitewood Furniture Ltd 10 bookcases at £24.15 each; 6 chairs at £5 each, and 1 set of coffee tables for £36. Invoice no Y 007
	16	F T Hardwares: 50 tins of 5 litre gloss paint at £4.60 per tin; 2 boxes of nails at £10.50 per box. Invoice no 114
	17	Jones & Jones Ltd: 1000 metres curtain materials at 75p per metre; 650 metres lining materials at 30p per metre. Invoice no J 0751

May   20   S T C Ltd: 10 Sankey saws at £15 each; 18 hammers at £2.50 each; 20 screw drivers at £1.25 each. Invoice no 74 X

      28   Smith & Co: 10 pocket calculators at £5 each. Invoice no S 128

      30   F T Hardwares: 25 tins paint at £2.50 per tin. Invoice No 2104

NA 23.09   D Logan is a trader whose Sales Ledger showed the following amounts owing to him on 30 June 19-8: G Horden £210; B Norris £240; T Quilter £160; M Taylor £170. His Sales Day Book for the month of July 19-8 was as follows:

Sales Day Book

			Total	Leather	Pottery	Plants
			£	£	£	£
July	7	G Horden	148	12	20	116
	9	T Quilter	210	–	–	210
	17	M Taylor	280	160	–	120
	18	B Norris	300	–	300	–
	26	S Ireland	200	40	132	28
			1138	212	452	474

Also during the month of July 19-8 the following occurred.

July   10   G Horden returned goods valued at £18

      14   Cheques were received from G Horden and T Quilter in settlement of the amounts owing by them at that date less 5 per cent cash discount

You are required to:
Open the accounts in the Sales Ledger and record the transactions for the month of July 19-8 in these accounts. Balance accounts on 31 July 19-8. Also make the postings from the Sales Day Book to the Nominal Ledger.

NA 23.10   Tammy Makeaste has a wholesale business selling goods for cash and credit. She keeps a Petty Cash Book, a Bank Cash Book and a daily cash sales record, as well as the other normal books. On 1 May her accounts contained the following balances: Petty cash £27; Bank £849; Stock £3840; Creditors—XY Manufacturers Ltd £895, T T Textiles Ltd £634; Debtors—Jon White £144, P Billings £97; Fixtures and fittings £775.

(a)   Calculate Tammy Makeaste's capital and open the accounts in her ledger. During May the following transactions occurred.

May   2   Drew a cheque for £58; £8 for petty cash and £50 Drawings

        4   Invoices received from T T Textiles £146 and Mary Edwards & Co £73. Petty cash payments of £1.40 for stamps and 65p travelling

        5   Cash sales totalling £642 were banked on the same paying-in slip as a cheque for £95 received from P Billings

        8   Sales on credit made to Jon White £38 and Kenny Williams £64

     10   Cash sales of £491 banked. Petty cash payments of £3.45 for stationery and 72p for groceries.

     12   Drew a cheque for £38 as follows: £28 for wages, £10 Drawings. Petty cash expenses of £1.48 were paid for stationery

     15   Cash sales banked £536, together with cheques value £144 from Jon White and Kenny Williams £64

     18   Invoices received from M L King £59 and F S Stanley £193

     21   Drew a cheque £49 to pay £19 repairs to the office, £26 part-time wages, and £4 parking

     24   Cash sales banked £299

     27   Sent cheque value £895 to XY Manufacturers Ltd, and £634 to T T Textiles Ltd

     28   Paid rent by quarterly cheque £400
Cash sales banked £588, plus cheque received of £38 from Jon White

     31   Drew one cheque for Drawings £25, wages £36 and to reimburse petty cash to the float of £35

         (b) Enter these transactions in the books of original entry, post to the ledger, and take out a trial balance.

NA 23.11   Using the details in Question **23.10** assume that Tammy Makeaste uses an analysed Cash Book instead of separate Petty Cash and Bank Cash Books. Draw up her Cash Book for May.

          You will need at least nine analysis columns on the payments side, which together with Cash and Bank gives eleven columns. On the debit side you will need at least five columns altogether.

23.12   The information required to make the entries into the business books will come from documents received or prepared by the business. Give the name of the documents used for each of the following books.

     (a) Analysed Purchases Book
     (b) Petty Cash Book
     (c) Analysed Cash Book
     (d) Cash Received Book
     (e) Sales Returns Book

24. Value Added Tax (VAT)

Value added tax, referred to as VAT, is a tax payable on goods and services supplied by a registered trader. VAT began on 1 April 1973. There are two rates of tax: the standard rate of 15 per cent and the zero rate. Both the numbers of rates and the percentage rates themselves are subject to change. There are also some exemptions. We do not intend to give you all the detailed information about VAT, as this is beyond the scope of this book. In this chapter we shall concern ourselves with the calculation of VAT, the preparation of the VAT invoice, and recording in the accounts. If you wish to know more about VAT you should read the *VAT Guide* issued by HM Customs and Excise.

Registration

Everyone carrying on a business whose value of taxable supplies is above a certain limit (given by the VAT provisions) must complete Form VAT 1, and send it to Customs and Excise in order to be registered. As Joe says 'My business falls into this category'. Since we supply taxable goods and services, we are taxable persons. Besides sending off Form VAT 1, we must do the following.

1 Record our outputs (sales) and the VAT added to them (called *output tax*).
2 Issue tax invoices showing the VAT charged on the sales to customers.
3 Record inputs (purchases) and the VAT paid on them (called *input tax*).
4 Work out, for each tax period, the difference between output tax and input tax, in order to complete the VAT return.
5 Keep records and accounts.
6 Keep a VAT account.

How VAT works

VAT is collected at each stage of the process of producing and distributing goods and services. The consumer pays the final tax. Let Joe explain how it works.

At each stage, the taxable person is charged VAT by his suppliers on the goods and services they supply to him for his business. These goods and services are called his *inputs*, and the tax on them is his *input tax*. When we in turn supply carpets, or any of the goods we sell to our customers, we charge the customers VAT. The goods and services we supply are called our *outputs*, and the tax we charge is our *output tax*. At intervals, when we have to make a return to Customs and Excise, we add up all our output tax and all our input tax and deduct the smaller amount from the larger; the difference is the amount we have to pay to Customs and Excise or which will be repaid to us.

Zero-rating and exemptions

On supplies that are zero-rated and those that are exempt no output tax is chargeable. But there are the following important differences.

1 Zero-rated supplies are technically taxable (though the rate of tax is nil), and the VAT charged on inputs relating to them can be reclaimed by a registered trader, together with all other input tax. Exempt supplies, on the other hand, are outside VAT and input tax cannot be reclaimed in respect of the activities of the business. Activities that fall into these categories include insurance, lettings and property leases, education, and medical care.
2 A person who makes zero-rated supplies will generally be registered with Customs and Excise and make VAT returns. A person who makes only exempt supplies does not have to register or make returns.

Recording output and input tax

When we sell goods to our customers, the VAT charged is based on the value of the goods.

Example 1
Joe Wynn sells carpets at a price of £100 plus VAT to John Winters. John Winters will buy the goods at £115, made up as follows.

The value of the supply	= £100
The tax chargeable at 15 per cent	= 15
Total payable by J Winters	= £115

The output tax is £15.

Example 2

Supposing Joe Wynn buys £50 worth of goods during this same period and pays 15 per cent tax on the value, the total cost to Joe Wynn will be £57.50 made up as follows.

The value of the goods bought	=	£50.00
The tax chargeable at 15 per cent	=	7.50
Total payable by Joe Wynn	=	£57.50

The input tax is £7.50.

Tax periods

At the end of a tax period (the usual tax period is three months, but it can be one month) Joe Wynn will send a return to the Customs and Excise, showing the net amount of VAT payable by him or repayable to him. Suppose in a tax period the only transactions made by Joe were those recorded in Examples 1 and 2 above; his net amount will be worked out as follows.

Total output tax	=	£15.00
Total input tax	=	7.50
Net amount of VAT payable by J Wynn	=	£ 7.50

Sometimes goods and services are supplied at a cost which already includes the VAT. For example, entrance fees charged at football matches are inclusive of VAT, and goods and services supplied in retail shops are priced with the VAT included if they are standard rated. The amount of VAT due is found by using the following fraction.

$$\frac{\text{Rate of tax}}{100 + \text{Rate of tax}} \times \text{Price paid for goods or services} = \text{VAT}$$

Example 3

Joe Wynn sells carpets, rugs, and paint to Edward Rockbottom. The total value of the goods, including VAT at 15 per cent, is £460. The tax to be accounted for as output tax is:

$$\frac{15}{100 + 15} \times 460 = \frac{15}{115} \times 460 = £60$$

Therefore

$$
\begin{array}{lr}
\text{Value of goods without the VAT} = & £400 \\
\text{VAT at 15 per cent} & 60 \\
\hline
\text{Amount paid by Rockbottom} & £460 \\
\hline
\end{array}
$$

Tax invoices

Examples of tax invoices and a VAT Account are shown below. A tax invoice must show clearly the following:

1 Identifying number.
2 Time of supply (the tax point).
3 Supplier's name, address, and VAT registration number.
4 Customer's name (or trading name) and address.

VAT Invoice

Blackmore Wholesale 123 The Broadway ③ Dock Green RA1 4AA			① Invoice no **4654** Date: **24 June 19-7**	
VAT Registration No 423 4567 89				
To: ④	J Wynn (Carpet Suppliers) 20, Amy Street Colchester Essex.			
Delivery note no **XP 10**	Tax point: ② 24 June		⑨ Terms: Strictly Net	
⑦ Quantity	⑥ Description		£ Cost	⑧ Total
2	Pressure guns at £45.00		90.00	
1	Stapler (Floor) at £18.00		18.00	
25	Doormats at £4.00		100.00	
50	1m Gripper rods at £1.00		50.00	
	Delivery charges		5.00	
	Total goods		263.00	
⑩+⑦	VAT at 15 per cent		39.45	
⑤	SALE TOTAL			302.45

5 Type of supply (sale; hire purchase; sale or return; loan; exchange, etc.).
6 Description sufficient to identify the goods or services supplied.
7 For each description, the quantity of the goods or the extent of the services, the rate of tax, and the amount of tax payable.
8 Total amount payable (excluding VAT).
9 Rate of any cash discount offered.
10 The total amount of tax chargeable.

VAT Account

This account is part of the double entry system and is posted from the analysis columns in the books of original entry.

VAT Account

	INPUT TAX					OUTPUT TAX		
Apr 30	Total	PcB	49.10		Apr 30	Total	SDB	632.00
"	Total	BDB	183.00		May 31	Total	SDB	848.00
May 31	Total	PcB	39.42		June 30	Total	SDB	527.00
"	Total	BDB	200.10					
June 30	Total	PcB	28.16					
"	Total	BDB	148.93					
June 30	Balance	c/d	1358.29					
			2007.00					2007.00
					July 1	Balance	b/d	1358.29

The sum owing of £1358.29 is required to be paid to Customs and Excise within one month of the VAT period.

Should a business be owed VAT then this will be repaid to the business by Customs and Excise.

Discounts

Cash discount

If a supplier allows a customer a discount on condition that payment is made immediately or within a specified time, he must calculate the VAT on the discounted amount, whether or not the customer takes advantage of the discount.

Example 4

Joe Wynn sells a quantity of carpets to Sunspot Hotels as follows:

Gross value of goods £700. VAT at 15 per cent.
Terms: 5 per cent for seven days' settlement, otherwise strictly net.
The VAT invoice for Sunspot Hotels will show the following details:

	Cash discount	Normal price
Value of goods	700.00	700.00
Less Cash discount	35.00	—
	665.00	700.00
VAT at 15 per cent (calculated on £665)	99.75	99.75
Sales total	764.75	799.75

Trade discount

Where a trade discount is allowed tax must be calculated on the discounted amount.

Bookkeeping procedures for VAT

Having already dealt with analysed books, the procedures for recording VAT are straightforward. Essentially, all that is required is an additional column in the books of original entry.

Bought Day Book

Bought Day Book

Date	Details	Folio		Purchases	VAT	Invoice Total
4 Jan	A B Carter & Co	BLC6	Further	150.00	22.50	172.50
"	C Taylor Ltd	BLT4	analysis	92.00	13.80	105.80
10 Jan	Roger Knight & Co Ltd	BLK1	columns as required	76.00	11.40	87.40
				318.00 NL P1	47.70 NL V1	365.70 NL B7
		(d)		(a)	(b)	(c)

Notes

(a)   Total is debited to Purchases Account.
(b)   Total is debited to the VAT Account (this is the input tax).
(c)   Control account total, memo only, credited to the Bought Ledger Control Account.
(d)   Individual purchases are credited to creditor's personal account in the Bought Ledger. The *invoice total* is credited, since that is the sum due to the supplier.

Sales Day Book

This is ruled in exactly the same way as the Bought Day Book. The total of the output VAT is credited to the VAT Account.

Cash Book

Payments made to creditors are entered in the Cash Book, the total amount being shown in the Creditors' Ledger column. The fact that a certain portion of the payment may be for VAT is immaterial, since the VAT was recorded in the Bought Day Book upon receiving the supplier's invoice. The VAT column in the Cash Book on the credit side will be used only in circumstances where bills, with VAT included, are paid without having been passed through the Bought Day Book. The column for VAT on the debit side will be used where cash sales arise to which VAT has been added.

Payments received from debtors are recorded in full in the Sales Ledger column, since the output tax on credit sales was recorded in the Sales Day Book.

Cash Book (Credit Side Only)

Date	Details	Folio	Misc	Expenses	Bought Ledger	VAT	Bank
17 Jan	A B barter + Co (a)	BLC b			162.00		162.00
18 Jan	Petrol (b)	NLM 3		8.00		1.20	9.20
21 Jan	Stationery (c)	NLP 2		6.00		0.90	6.90
				14.00	162.00	2.10	178.10
				^	NLB 7	NLVI	^
					(d)	(e)	

Notes

(a) Posted to A B Carter & Co £162.00.
(b) and (c) Motor expenses debited £8 and stationery debited £6.
(d) Bought Ledger Control Account, memo only, debited £162.00.
(e) VAT debited £2.10.

The net effect of these entries:
Bank is credited with   £178.10
The debit total:

	VAT	2.10
Motor expenses		8.00
Stationery		6.00
Creditors		162.00	£178.10

Cash Book (Debit Side Only)

Date	Details	Folio	Cash Sales	Misc	Receipts from debtors	VAT	Bank
13 Jan	Sales	^	200.00			30.00	230.00
14 Jan	Commission received (a)	NLC8		10.00		1.50	11.50
19 Jan	P Sharp (b)	SLS 8			49.00		49.00
			200.00	10.00	49.00	31.50	290.50
			NLS 1	^	NLC4	NLVI	^
			(c)	(d)	(e)	(f)	(g)

Notes
(a) Commission Received Account credited with £10.00.
(b) P Sharp (debtor) credited with £49.00.
(c) Total of cash sales credited to Sales Account.
(d) Total not posted since individual entries have been posted as arising.
(e) Total credited to Sales Ledger Control Account, memo only.
(f) Total credited to VAT Account.
(g) Total of cash banked, used to cross-check arithmetic.

The net effect of these
entries:

Bank is debited with   £290.50

The credits total:

	VAT	31.50	
	Sales	200.00	
	Commission	10.00	
	Debtors	49.00	£290.50

Petty Cash Book

All payments should be checked to see if VAT has been paid. If so, the bill needs to be analysed between the expense and the VAT. An additional column is required to record the sums of VAT paid. When the Petty Cash Book is balanced and the individual analysis columns totalled, the VAT column is posted to the debit side of the VAT Account. Chapter 23 contains an illustration of a Petty Cash Book with a VAT column.

Journal

If VAT arises on a transaction that is recorded in the Journal (such as the purchase or sale of assets if an analysed Purchases Book is not kept), the entries necessary are as follows.

Suppose that an asset costing £966.00 is purchased from Machine Supply Ltd. The price consists of Cost £840 + VAT £126.00.

	Journal			10
July 7	Machinery Account VAT Account 　　Machinery Supply Ltd Credit purchase of machinery re Invoice no 874 dated 4/7/19–7		840.00 126.00	 966.00

Joe's Rule No 24
Since a business must pay for the collection and payment of VAT, the records should be simple to understand and easy to operate.

24.01 Sue Woodpecker, a furniture manufacturer, is a registered taxable person for VAT purposes. She made the following transactions.

(a) She sold furniture for £700 less settlement discount of 5 per cent to A Wholesaler, who did not take advantage of the discount.

(b) She sold furniture for £300 to S Rockbottom, who was later declared bankrupt. The trustee in bankruptcy will pay a dividend of 20p in a £.

(c) She hired a disco to play at a staff party at a cost of £60.

(d) She bought petrol for the delivery van, £16.10 including VAT.

(e) She paid her solicitor legal charges of £30.

All items exclude any addition of VAT (except (d)) and the standard rate is to be taken as 15 per cent.

Work out, in respect of each item, the amount of VAT chargeable and state who would be responsible for accounting for it to the Customs and Excise.

24.02 On 1 March 19-6, A Bembridge & Son, Maldon Way, Swansea, sold the following goods on credit to James Foster, 26 Broad Street, Birmingham 4: order no 162.

10 000 coils sealing tape @ £4.46 per 1000 coils
20 000 sheets Bank A5 @ £4.50 per 1000 sheets
12 000 sheets Bank A4 @ £4.20 per 1000 sheets

All goods are subject to VAT at 15 per cent.

(a) Prepare the sales invoice to be sent to James Foster.

(b) Show the entries in the personal ledgers of James Foster, and A Bembridge & Son.

(RSA 1)

NA 24.03 Explain (a) zero rate, and (b) exemption, and show their differences.

NA 24.04 The following is a summary of purchases and sales and the relevant figures for VAT for three months ended 31 March 19-4.

	Purchases		VAT
19-4	January	20 000	2000
	February	21 000	2100
	March	22 000	2200
	Sales		
	January	21 000	2100
	February	20 000	2000
	March	15 000	1500

Required:
(a) Write up and balance the VAT account for the three months to 31 March 19-4.
(b) Explain briefly the significance of the balance and how it will be cleared.

(RSA 1)

NA 24.05 You are required to complete the following paragraph using words from the list below.

The document a supplier sends to his customer setting out full details of a credit sale transaction is an (i)_____ . In order to encourage bulk purchases he may have offered his customer (ii) ____ ____ . VAT will be added to the total of the account (iii)_____ deduction of this amount. At the end of the trading period the supplier will send a (iv)_____ to his customer summarizing the transactions which have taken place. If the customer returns goods he will issue a (v)____ ____ to the supplier and the supplier will acknowledge receipt of these goods by the issue of a (vi) ____ ____ .

List of words:
advice note, goods received note, before, after, receipt, statement, invoice, delivery note, credit note, debit note, trade discount, cash discount.

NB *Do not* copy out the paragraph. Simply list the words against the appropriate number.

(RSA 1)

24.06 (a) Enter the following transactions in the appropriate accounts in the Sales and Purchases ledgers. Balance the accounts at the end of May 19-6.

		List price £	VAT %
19-6			
May 1	Bought goods from P Ellison (20 per cent trade discount is allowed)	150	10
3	Sold goods to G Brandon	300	10
	Sold good to R Strong	200	10
7	Returned goods to P Ellison	50	10
8	G Brandon returned goods	40	10
10	Settled P Ellison's account less 2½ per cent cash discount		
	Sold goods to R Strong	200	10

18	Sold goods to G Brandon	300	10
24	G Brandon settled his account		
28	Received information that R Strong's premises had been completely destroyed by fire. The premises were not insured and R Strong had disappeared		
29	Bought goods from P Ellison (this transaction subject to 25 per cent trade discount)	200	10

(b) Write up the VAT Account in the General Ledger. (*Note* Ten per cent may not be the rate ruling at the present time, but it is selected for its convenience in calculations.)

(RSA 1)

24.07 The Leafy Service station has two separate sections selling car tyres and exhaust systems.

Credit purchases for the month of February 19–5 were:

Feb 4 Ace Tyres Ltd. Invoice no AT 1714
     40 tyres size 145 × 10 list price £15 each, *less* trade discount 25 per cent
     30 tyres size 155 × 13 list price £20 each, *less* trade discount 33⅓ per cent

   14 Fast Exhausts Ltd. Invoice no FE 762
     5 exhausts type MIN list price £20 each
     10 exhausts type CAV list price £40 each
     6 exhausts type DAT list price £50 each
     All exhausts less trade discount 40 per cent

   25 Ace Tyres Ltd. Invoice no AT 1783
     50 tyres size 165 × 13 list price £24 each, *less* trade discount 25 per cent

All transactions are subject to Value Added Tax at 10 per cent.
The suppliers do not allow any cash discount.

You are required to:
(a) Prepare a purchases day book with four columns, headed as follows: (1) Totals; (2) Tyres; (3) Exhausts; (4) Value Added Tax.
(b) Write up the day book for the month of February. It is the firm's policy to make entries in the book as and when each invoice is received, and to record there full details of the items bought and the total of each invoice.
(c) Post the items to the personal and nominal accounts in the ledger.

(RSA 1)

NA 24.08   The following relate to M Clover's business for the month of May.

Credit purchases

			£	
May	2	R Wilkins	250	less 20 per cent trade discount
	8	T Edwards	410	net
	14	W Bondman	300	less 10 per cent trade discount

Credit sales

			£	
May	1	L Batchelor	420	net
	3	R Copeman	210	net
	9	T Dorman	450	net
	12	L Batchelor	120	net
	13	T Dorman	160	net

Returns inwards

			£	
May	4	L Batchelor	40	net
	12	T Dorman	30	net

Returns outwards

			£	
May	8	R Wilkins	100	List Price

(from goods purchased on 2 May)

Assume VAT is payable on all transactions at the rate of 10 per cent.

(a) Write up day books in three column form to show in each case the amount of the goods, the amount paid for VAT and the total to be posted to the appropriate personal and nominal accounts.

(b) Write up the VAT account as it would appear in M Clover's ledger.

(London 'O')

25. Partnerships

The reasons for a partnership

Joe has told you of his intention of amalgamating his business with that of an old friend who has a similar business in a nearby town.

As Joe says 'Two heads are better than one', and by expanding in this way it saves me having to find more capital. Our new bigger business will mean we should be able to obtain better discount from suppliers and so provide a better service. The legal term to describe the new arrangement is a partnership.

Amalgamating two sole trader businesses

Partners are always co-owners although they may agree to share profits other than equally and each partner may contribute a different amount of capital.

The present position

Let us look at the business of my friend and compare it with mine. To do this we need a Balance Sheet of each business drawn up to the date of amalgamation (see pages 286 and 287).

These balance sheets show that I have capital in my business of £146 500, and George has £84 200.

The agreement

Before we agree to join our two businesses together we need to decide a number of matters.

1 Are we going to use the Balance Sheet figures as the basis of our agreement? If so, are we going to be 'equal' partners—particularly as I would have more capital than George. If not, how do we come to an agreement on the figures?
2 If George or I were to each sell our own business rather than joining into partnership how much would we get? After all neither George nor I wish to be worse off after forming the partnership than we would be if we each sold our own business.
3 If the new business borrows money from one of the partners (rather than from the bank) how does that affect the partnership?
4 What happens if George decides to leave the business?
5 What happens if I die?

George Boon

Balance Sheet as at 31/3/-8

Fixed assets	£ Cost	£ Depn	£ WDV
Premises	45 000	–	45 000
Fittings and equip	8 000	4 000	4 000
Motors	6 000	1 500	4 500
	59 000	5 500	53 500

Current assets			
Debtors		9 000	
Stock		48 000	
Bank and cash		3 500	
		60 500	

Less Current liabilities			
Creditors	16 000		
VAT	1 800		
Inland Revenue	2 000	19 800	40 700
			£94 200

Financed by			
Capital G Boon		84 200	
Bank loan		10 000	£94 200

You can see that quite a lot of problems need to be ironed out. However, these are not your concern at the moment. All I want to explain are a few of the important decisions we will make to enable you to enter the new books of the partnership. If you carry on your training and become an accountant you will need to know all the legal aspects of a partnership, as contained in the Partnership Acts of 1890 and 1916.

Let me answer the first question. Neither of us will accept all the Balance Sheet figures as the basis of our new joint business because:

1 Some of the assets, such as premises are probably undervalued.
2 If we were each to sell our own business as a 'going' concern, we would expect to receive more than our capital invested.
3 Each of us may wish to keep some of the assets.

In fact, I have agreed with George the figures shown on page 288.

J Wynn

Balance Sheet as at 31/3-8

Fixed assets	£ Cost	£ Depn	£ WDV
Premises	75 000	–	75 000
Fittings and equip	9 000	3 000	6 000
Motors	10 000	6 000	4 000
	94 000	9 000	85 000
Current assets			
Debtors		16 000	
Stock		58 000	
Bank and cash		5 000	
		79 000	
Less Current liabilities			
Creditors	12 000		
VAT	2 400		
Inland Revenue	3 100	17 500	61 500
			£146 500
Financed by			
Capital J Wynn			£146 500

Goodwill

In discussing the Journal (page 223) I explained how goodwill arose. Now if George and I were to sell our own businesses to someone else we would hope to receive £220 000 and £250 000 respectively (see page 288). The difference between the net assets taken over and the sales value of the business represents the additional amount a buyer is prepared to pay to obtain an existing business; one that is trading and making profits from existing customers.

Goodwill is the value attaching to an existing business with a reputation and a set of established customers. Our new partnership is really the 'buyer' of the two existing businesses, including the goodwill.

The new partnership

The Balance Sheet on the formation of the partnership is on page 289.

For G Boon's Business

	£	Notes
Premises	150 000	(i)
Fittings, etc.	6 000	(ii)
Motors	2 250	(iii)
Debtors	8 000	(iv)
Stock	48 000	
	214 250	
Less Current liabilities	19 800	
	194 450	
Plus Goodwill	25 550	
Sales value of business	220 000	

For J Wynn's Business

	£
Premises	140 000
Fittings, etc.	5 000
Motors	1 000
Debtors	16 000
Stock	58 000
Bank	4 000
	224 000
Less Current liabilities	17 500
	206 500
Plus Goodwill	43 500
Sales value of business	250 000

Notes

(i) This would be the cost of buying these premises now.

(ii) George had over-depreciated his fittings.

(iii) George intends to keep a car worth £2250 for himself.

(iv) One of the debtors has owed £1000 for a long time and therefore we agreed that this should be excluded.

You will see that the Bank loan isn't shown—George is paying that off himself.

Therefore the net assets to be put into the partnership are £194 450 before adding goodwill.

(i) As with George.

(ii) We agreed that the fittings are worth only £5000.

(iii) I am keeping a car worth £3000, so £1000 is left in the business.

(iv) I am leaving £4000 in the bank.

Therefore my net assets before goodwill are £206 500.

25.01 Can you make the opening Journal entries in the books of the new partnership? (This was explained in learning about the Journal.)

Share of ownership

George and I intend to be equal partners, sharing profits and losses equally. After all, if the business is successful we each wish to share the

Joe Wynn & George Boon
Balance Sheet as at 31/3/-8

Fixed assets	£	£	£	From GB £	From JW £
Goodwill			69 050	25 550	43 500
Premises			290 000	150 000	140 000
Fittings and equip			11 000	6 000	5 000
Motors			3 250	2 250	1 000
			373 300		
Currents assets					
Debtors		24 000		8 000	16 000
Stock		106 000		48 000	58 000
Bank and cash		4 000		–	4 000
		134 000			
Less Current liabilities					
Creditors	28 000			16 000	12 000
VAT	4 200			1 800	2 400
Inland Revenue	5 100	37 300	196 700	2 000	3 100
			470 000		
Financed by					
Capital			£470 000	220 000	250 000

profits, but if it makes a loss we must share the loss as well. Because I have put more capital into the business than George we have agreed that once the annual profit of the new business is known it will be shared as follows:

	GB £	JW £	Total
Interest on capital at 6%	13 200	15 000	28 200
Agreed salaries	10 000	12 000	+22 000
Remainder of profit	50%	50%	50 200

Now, let us say for example that during the first year the net profit is £63 000. Interest and salaries will total £50 200 and the remainder,

£12 800, is split equally. Altogether we receive:

	GB £	JW £
Interest on capital at 6%	13 200	15 000
Agreed salaries	10 000	12 000
Remainder of profit	6 400	6 400
Total	29 600	33 400 = £63 000

We agreed on this basis of sharing profits because:

1 If we put our capital in the bank, building society or other investment we would receive interest.
2 If we didn't run the business but went out to work we would each receive a salary, according to our ability and experience.

Having taken out of the profit those amounts necessary to reward us for our 'investment' and our 'work', what is left is the true profit or risk profit. This is the extra reward for the risk of operating the business—it can be shared equally.

Deed of Partnership

If partners haven't agreed on matters relating to their partnership (either expressly or by implication) then the law gives a ruling on what should happen. The most important points are:

1 Partners equally share profits and losses.
2 Partners are not entitled to a salary.
3 Interest on capital is not payable.
4 Interest on Drawings is not chargeable.
5 If a partner puts more money into the business than his agreed capital, he is to receive interest at 5 per cent per annum on that extra amount.

Bookkeeping entries

The books, accounts, and entries in partnership records are the same as those of a sole trader, but you will need to learn:

Partner's Current Account (one for each partner)
Appropriation Account
The Balance Sheet layout

Current Accounts

Each partner will have a Capital Account and a Drawings Account. It is possible for the Capital Account to be used in the same way as in a sole trader business, i.e., share of profits credited and Drawings debited. In this case the Capital Accounts are known as *Fluctuating Capital Accounts*.

It is preferable for each partner's capital to remain unaltered, showing only the agreed capital contributed to the business—and agreed alterations to that capital. The reason for keeping *Fixed Capital*

G Boon Capital Account

			1/4/19-8	Opening capital		220 000

J Wynn Capital Account

			1/4/19-8	Opening capital		250 000

G Boon Current Account

31/3/19-9	Drawings		15 000	31/3/19-9	Interest on capital		13 200
"	Bal	c/d	14 600	"	Salary		10 000
			29 600	"	Profit		6 400
							29 600
				1/4/19-9	Bal	b/d	14 600

J Wynn Current Account

31/3/19-9	Drawings		34 000	31/3/19-9	Interest on capital		15 000
				"	Salary		12 000
				"	Profit		6 400
					Bal	c/d	600
			34 000				34 000
1/4/19-9	Bal	b/d	600				

Accounts is that the agreed original amount contributed is used as the basis of calculating interest on capital and possibly other calculations.

Where such Fixed Capital Accounts are used it becomes necessary for each partner's position regarding share of profits and Drawings to be recorded in a *Partner's Current Account*.

As Joe says: George and I will need to record what we draw out of the business so we keep a Drawings Account for each partner. At the end of the year when profits have been decided, each partner will be credited with his share. Using my example of the share of profits explained earlier (on page 289) let me show you the way of recording the end of year position, using Fixed Capital Accounts (see page 291).

Drawings Accounts are closed by transfer to Current Accounts. Assuming that I had drawn out £34 000 you can see that I would have 'overdrawn' and owed £600 to the business. Because I would be taking out more than my entitlement to profits I could be charged 'interest' on this excess amount. This would involve complicated calculations as the profit has already been calculated. So different ways of charging interest on drawings are used.

Two methods are possible:

1 Interest is charged on the total Drawings made by each partner during the year.
2 Interest is charged on the Drawings made in excess of the agreed amount of Drawings.

In fact George and I have agreed that we should be charged 5 per cent on the total Drawings we make. Assuming the Drawings above, the result would be:

J Wynn Drawings Account

31/3/19-9	Int on Drawings	1700			

G Boon Drawings Account

31/3/19-9	Int on Drawings	750			

Interest on Drawings Account

			31/3/19-9	J Wynn Drawings A/c	1700
				G Boon Drawings A/c	750

What happens to the Interest on Drawings Account, which is an income account? It is transferred to the appropriation section of the Profit and Loss Account usually referred to as the *Appropriation Account*. As an additional income has been 'received' so the profits will be altered from those shown in the Current Account on page 291.

Appropriation Account

This account shows the distribution of profit between partners.

The net profit having been calculated, it is brought down from the Profit and Loss Account. The profit is now divided between, or 'appropriated' by, the partners in accordance with the Partnership Deed.

Using the figures assumed so far the Appropriation Account will appear as follows.

J Wynn & G Boon
Appropriation Account for the year ended 31/3/19-9

Interest on capital			Net profit		b/d	63 000
J Wynn	15 000		Interest on Drawings			
G Boon	13 200	28 200	J Wynn	1 700		
			G Boon	750		2 450
Salaries						
J Wynn	12 000					
G Boon	10 000	22 000				
Share of profits						
J Wynn	7 625					
G Boon	7 625	15 250				
		65 450				65 450

25.02 Draw up the Current Accounts for George Boon and Joe Wynn based on this Appropriation Account. *Remember* Drawings for the year are G Boon £15 000, J Wynn £34 000.

Balance Sheet layout

The Balance Sheet layout for partnerships follows the same pattern as a sole trader except that full details of the share of profits and Drawings of each partner are shown.

*Extracts from the Balance Sheet of G Boon and J Wynn
as at 31.3.19–9*

Liabilities side		£		£
Capital	G Boon	220 000		
	J Wynn	250 000		470 000

Current Accounts (3)		*G Boon*		*J Wynn*	
Balance 1/4/19–8 (1)		—		—	
Interest on capital		13 200		15 000	
Salary		10 000		12 000	
Profit		7 625		7 625	
		30 825		34 625	
Less Drawings	15 000		34 000		
Int on drawings	750	15 750	1 700	35 700	
(2)		15 075		(1 075)*	15 075

Assets side
Current assets
J Wynn
  Current Account   1 075

---

*This figure (being a debit) is the amount by which Joe has 'overdrawn' his available profits. As he owes this sum to the partnership business he appears as a debtor under Current assets.

Note 1   No opening balances as the partnership commenced on that date.
Note 2   Closing balances become next year's opening balances.
Note 3   If Current Accounts are not used then all the details of profits and Drawings should be shown under the heading Capital Accounts.

Joe's Rule No 25
Profits in a partnership are divided between partners in accordance with the Partnership Deed—which can be changed if the partners agree.

Examination points

Joe wishes to give you some examination advice. If the question does not give precise details of the partnership agreement you should apply the five points mentioned on page 290 regarding the Partnership Acts. For example, if salaries are not mentioned, then they are not payable; if the share of profits and losses is not mentioned, then such are shared equally; unless interest on capital is stated, no interest is payable.

25.03 Boyd and Girled decide to amalgamate their business as from 1 January 19-8.

The net assets as at 31 December 19-7 are:

Boyd £17 400
Girled £18 900

All assets and liabilities are to be taken over and the agreed net asset valuations are:

Boyd £20 000
Girled £19 500

Draw up the opening Balance Sheet of the new partnership.

25.04 From the following Appropriation Account, and notes, draw up the Current Accounts of the partners as shown in the books at the close of business on 30 September 19-7.

Appropriation Account

Interest on capital G	350		Net profit				20 610
H	400		Interest				
I	120	870	on Drawings				
					G	60	
Salaries	G	5000			H	80	
	I	6000	11 000		I	420	560
Share of profit G ⅓ 3100							
H ⅓ 3100							
I ⅓ 3100	9 300						
		21 170					21 170

Notes

1 Current Account balances on 1 October 19-6 were:
G £250 credit
H £650 credit
I £480 debit

2 Drawings Account balances on 30 September 19-7 were:
G £6 200
H £3 600
I £10 400

3 Drawings Accounts do not include interest charged.

NA 25.05 From the following details draw up the Appropriation Account of A Branch and T Twigg for the year ended 30 October 19-8 together with a Balance Sheet as at that date.

	£	£
Net profit		14 800
Debtors and creditors	6 000	4 000
Premises (WDV)	22 000	
Motor vehicles (WDV)	8 000	
Stock 31/10/19-8	12 500	
Current Accounts - B	850	
(1/11/19-7) T		2 100
Capital Accounts - B		25 000
(1/11/19-7) T		20 000
Drawings Account - B	7 950	
T	8 840	
Prepaid expenses	580	
Accrued expenses		820
	66 720	66 720

Notes
1 Branch and Twigg share profits in the ratio of 3:2.
2 Salaries are paid to partners:
   Branch £4000
   Twigg £6000

25.06 F Moore and C Potter are in partnership sharing profits and losses on the basis of 2:1. The following Trial Balance was extracted from their books at the close of business on 31 May 19-4:

		DR £	CR £
Capital Accounts 1 June 19-3	Moore		4 000
	Potter		3 000
Current Accounts 31 May 19-4	Moore	1 270	
	Potter	1 140	
Debtors and creditors		2 110	1 040
Purchases and sales		11 620	19 860
Bank		4 210	
Cash		60	
Bad debts written off		190	
Rent and rates		600	
Wages and salaries		2 170	
Discounts		570	290
Stock 1 June 19-3		1 480	
Fixtures and fittings		850	
Delivery van		1 200	
Sales returns		540	
Sundry expenses		180	
		28 190	28 190

Notes
1 Stock 31 May 19-4—£1380
2 Wages accrued 31 May 19-4—£70
3 Rates prepaid 31 May 19-4—£40
4 Provide for depreciation—fittings £50; van £100
5 There are no purchases returns
6 Drawings have already been debited to the Current Accounts
7 Allow 5 per cent interest per annum on the partners' Capital Accounts
8 Potter is entitled to a partnership salary of £650
9 Partners' Capital Accounts are to remain *fixed* at the figures shown in the Trial Balance Sheet

Required:
Prepare Trading and Profit and Loss Accounts for the year ended 31 May 19-4 together with a Balance Sheet as at that date.

(LCCI Elem)

NA 25.07   Alfred Gardner and George Williams are two sole traders who decide to form a partnership as from 1 April 19–5. Their respective Balance Sheets as at the close of business on 31 March 19–5 are as follows:

Alfred Gardner

	£		£
Freehold premises	4400	Capital Account	4900
Office furniture	770	Creditors	910
Stock	1340	Bank overdraft	1950
Debtors	1250		
	£7760		£7760

George Williams

Delivery van	1740	Capital Account	5500
Office furniture	860	Creditors	1170
Stock	1580		
Debtors	1720		
Bank	770		
	£6670		£6670

The new partnership does not take over Gardner's Bank Overdraft but all the assets and other liabilities are taken over at the above figures *except* for the following:

Gardner	Premises valued at £5000; Office furniture £700; Goodwill valued at £1000.
Williams	Delivery van valued at £1600; Office furniture £800. Goodwill valued at £500. Of the Debtors £80 are considered to be Bad Debts and are therefore *not* taken over by the partnership.

Required:
(i) Calculate the opening Capital of each partner.
     Note Calculations must be shown.
(ii) Draw up the opening Balance Sheet of the new partnership.

                                                          (LCCI Elem)

NA 25.08 Adams, Brown, and Carter are in partnership sharing profits and losses on the basis of 2:1:1. Their Net Profit for the year ended 29 February 19–4 is £9530, before taking into consideration the following matters.

The Capital Accounts of the partners have been fixed for the past year at the following figures:

Adams	£10 000
Brown	£6 000
Carter	£4 000

The partners are entitled to interest on their Capital Accounts at the rate of 8 per cent per annum. In addition, partnership salaries are due as follows:

Brown	£1500;	Carter	£1100

The partners' total drawings for the year ended 29 February 19–4 have been as follows:

Adams	£2000
Brown	£1800
Carter	£1600

Since the drawings have been made at various times during the year, it is agreed that the partners should be charged interest at the fixed rate of 5 per cent on their total drawings.

Required:
Prepare the Appropriation Account of the partnership for the year ended 29 February 19–4.

(LCCI Elem)

26. Recording Wages and Salaries – PAYE

Employer's responsibilities

Employing staff
One of the results of increasing the size of my business is that more staff are employed and therefore more time will have to be spent on calculating and paying wages and salaries due, and meeting the legal requirements relating to employees.

Legal requirements
The law puts many obligations on an employer. In the case of wages and salaries the employer must:

1 Keep records of employees (names, addresses, and National Insurance numbers).
2 Notify the Inland Revenue when an employee joins or leaves the business.
3 Keep records of wages and salaries paid.
4 Deduct income tax and National Insurance Contributions from employees—and keep records of these amounts.
5 Pay to the Inland Revenue the sums deducted from employees.
6 Pay an additional amount to the Inland Revenue called 'Employer's National Insurance Contribution' based on the amount earned by each employee.
7 Give proper records of wages earned to employees.
8 Make statutory sick payments to employees who are ill.

Importance of accuracy
Everybody is interested in pay, particularly employees, so you need to make sure all calculations are correct!

Preparing the payroll

Gross wages and employer's National Insurance Contributions
So far, I have given you the wages and salaries amount shown in the accounts: this comprises the gross amount payable to our employees

(before stoppages for tax, etc.) together with the employer's proportion of National Insurance Contributions (NIC).

Now, let us look at the payroll for the two warehouse employees.

Payroll Sheet Week 22	Gross Salary	Employer's NIC
A Brown	139.92	14.60
B Carruthers	151.64	15.86
	£291.56	£30.46

The Journal entries will be:

6 Sept	Wages Account (see Note)	Dr	322.02	
	Bank			291.56
	Inland Revenue			30.46
	Being wages and employer's NIC for Week 22			

Note This is the total labour cost to Joe Wynn.

Income tax and employee's NIC

If everything were as simple as the example above then the operation of a wages system would be very easy. Unfortunately, further complications arise, since we must deduct from employees' wages those amounts due for taxation and also the employees' proportion of NIC. To do this we need a more detailed payroll sheet as follows.

	(a)	(b)	(c)	(d)	(e)	(f)
Payroll sheet Wk 22 *Employees*	Gross salary	Tax deducted	NIC deducted	Total deduction	Net pay	Employer's NIC
1 A Brown	£139.92	15.60	12.58	28.18	111.74	14.60
2 B Carruthers	£151.64	25.80	13.66	39.46	112.18	15.86
	£291.56	41.40	26.24	67.64	223.92	30.46

Always check arithmetic: (b) + (c) = (d)

(a) − (d) = (e)

The Journal entries (summarizing the position) will be:

Wages Dr		322.02	
Bank (Note 1)			223.92
Inland Revenue (Note 2)			98.10
Being wages and employer's NIC			
for Week 22			

Notes

1 The employees do not receive all their wages and therefore it is only necessary to draw from the bank the net wages payable (£223.92).
2 Both tax and National Insurance Contributions are paid to the Inland Revenue. Since the amount is always required to be paid about four weeks in arrears, the Inland Revenue Account is credited at this point. When the cheque is sent for payment, the entry will be:

Dr Inland Revenue Account: Cr Bank Account

Bookkeeping entries

The payroll sheet becomes the source document and is used to make the Journal entries.

Calculation of gross pay

This calculation depends upon the wage agreement. Salaried staff usually receive a fixed weekly or monthly sum—so no calculation is required unless they work overtime. For weekly paid employees who can earn a bonus, depending upon output, and can also earn overtime payments, it is necessary to have a detailed wages sheet. The total hours worked need to be recorded for the wages clerk in the payroll department to be able to enter them on the wages sheet.

Wages Sheet Week 22
Hours Worked

Name	Sat	Sun	Mon	Tue	Wed	Thu	Fri	Total	Rate of pay	Basic earnings	Bonus	Gross pay
A Brown	–	–	8	8	8	8	8	40	3.15	126.00	13.92	139.92
B Carruthers	4	–	8	8	8	8	8	44	3.10	136.40	15.24	151.64
												291.56

Either the foreman or departmental manager has to record the daily attendance hours or an employee will clock on using a time card (large firms usually use the time card system).

When the time card is inserted into the 'clock' the date and time are automatically recorded on the card (see illustration below).

TIME CARD					
Name: B Carruthers		Pay no 2		Wk no: 22 Ending: 6 Sept 19-6	
	ON	OFF	ON	OFF	Total hours
SAT	0800	1300			4
SUN					
MON	0758	1300	1358	1700	8
TUES	0755	1300	1342	1701	8
WED	0756	1300	1344	1700	8
THURS	0802	1300	1352	1700	8
FRI	0801	1301	1349	1700	8
Hours entered by: AW B Checked by: J Wynn					44

At the end of the week the cards are collected, and the wages clerk calculates the hours of attendance which he enters on the wages sheet. Because of the time it takes to calculate the gross pay and net pay, most large organizations work a 'week in hand'. This means that the wages received at the end of the week are those earned for the previous week.

It is not possible to illustrate every type of wages sheet that exists. Wages systems vary from firm to firm. Sometimes employees earn additional rates for working overtime, or night work, or special shifts. This extra pay is usually shown on the wages sheet and payslip. Whatever system is operated, it is usual to calculate the gross pay and then transfer this figure to a payroll sheet.

Payroll sheet

Having calculated the gross pay, we need to calculate the deductions for each employee. These are recorded on the payroll sheet. In addition, those required by law:

> Net pay
> Income tax
> National Insurance Contributions

are recorded on a special Deductions Working Sheet provided by the Inland Revenue. It is important to keep a record of employees' wages and deductions. The payroll sheets, bound together, provide a permanent record. Alternatively, we could use a Wages Book, which normally contains the equivalent of 53 payroll sheets bound together (53 because in some tax years the employee will receive 53 pay cheques). When we start using our computer for the payroll calculations we can devise our own Deductions Working Sheet.

Payslip (or wage packet)

We give each employee a payslip which shows the same detail as on our payroll sheet. Other firms print these details on to a wage packet.

Joe Wynn (Carpet Suppliers)	NAME B Carruthers		TAX CODE 338		WEEK 22	DATE 6/9/19-6
		DEDUCTIONS				
GROSS PAY	TAX	NIC	OTHER	TOTAL		NET PAY
£151. 64	25. 80	13. 66	–	39. 46		£112 . 18

Coin and note analysis for cash payments

Having calculated the net pay of each employee we now have to prepare the wage packets for employees being paid cash. Before doing this we need to work out the number of notes and coins required so that the correct numbers can be drawn from the bank. We use a separate coin and note analysis sheet, although many firms extend the payroll sheet to accommodate this requirement.

Starting with the net pay of each employee we calculate the number of notes and coins required to make up that sum. To be consistent, we use the highest denomination of notes/coins available, otherwise we would be unable to make up all the pay packets correctly.

Take the example above of A Brown with net pay of £111.74 Which of the two make-ups should be used?

		£
(a)	£20 note × 5	100.00
	£1 coin × 11	11.00
	20p coin × 3	.60
	10p coin × 1	.10
	1p coin × 4	.04
		111.74

		£
(b)	£50 note × 2	100.00
	£10 note × 1	10.00
	£1 coin × 1	1.00
	50p coin × 1	.50
	20p coin × 1	.20
	2p coin × 2	.04
		111.74

Coin analysis (b) is correct.

However, we have made a policy decision to use £20 notes as the largest note, because employees find £50 notes difficult to change.

For the two warehouse employees, our coin and note analaysis will be:

Coin and Note Analysis Sheet

PAY no	NAME	NET PAY £ p	£50	£20	£10	£5	£1	50p	20p	10p	5p	2p	1p
1	a Brown	111. 74	5	1			1	1	1			2	
2	b Carruthers	112. 18	5	1			2			1	1	1	1
	TOTAL	223. 92	10	2			3	1	1	1	1	3	1

The withdrawal request to the bank will show

	£
£20 × 10	200.00
£10 × 2	20.00
£1 × 3	3.00
50p × 1	.50
20p × 1	.20
10p × 1	.10
5p × 1	.05
2p × 3	.06
1p × 1	.01
	223.92

Credit transfers/cheque payments

I would prefer to pay staff by cheque or credit transfer as it reduces the risks associated with handling cash.

1 *Credit transfer*   I would need to tell the bank every week (or month) each employee's net pay. The bank would then transfer this amount into the bank account of our employees (for large firms this is the most commonly used method).

2 *Cheque payment*   This is even easier for me as all I have to do is sign the cheques drawn up by the wages clerk.

The operation of PAYE (pay as you earn)

PAYE is a system operated by the Inland Revenue to collect income tax from an employee when he is paid.

Code numbers

An employee will be given a code number based on his annual tax return. This represents the total allowance to which he is entitled in that year. He can earn up to his allowance before he starts paying income tax. In order to pay tax 'as you earn' the allowance is divided by 52 for weekly paid employees (and 12 for monthly paid employees).

Consequently an employee who earns in one week more than his 'weekly' allowance will have to pay tax. The code number is made up of the total allowances without the last digit. For example a single man with only his personal allowance of £2335 (1986/87) is given the code 233.

Tax tables

Each employer is supplied with a printed set of tax tables which come in two parts:

1 *Free Pay Table*   This is used to calculate the total allowance or 'free pay', which the employee is entitled to up to that week. The free pay deducted from the total pay will give the taxable pay.
2 *Taxable Pay Table*   We calculate income tax to be paid on the 'taxable pay' from this table.

We need to keep a weekly record of calculations (on the Inland Revenue's Deductions Working Sheet) of income tax and National Insurance deducted, together with the employer's National Insurance Contribution. At the year end we have to make several returns to the Inland Revenue showing, among other things:

1 All our employees during the year—and their gross pay.
2 The income tax and National Insurance Contributions deducted.

Documents

1 *Deductions Working Sheet*   Mention has already been made of a Deductions Working Sheet being kept for each employee.
2 *P.45 Leaving Certificate (three copies)*   This is a form which must be completed when an employee leaves. The employee receives two copies which he will give to his new employer, this allows the new employer to continue to deduct tax at the proper rate of allowance.
  Both the old employer and the new employer send one copy to the Inland Revenue. In this way the tax authorities can keep a check on where people are working.
3 *P.46 Starting Certificate*   If a new employee joins our business and has no P.45 (for example a school leaver, or a housewife returning to work) then the employer must send a P.46 to the Inland Revenue. This enables the Inland Revenue to issue a Coding Notice.
4 *Coding Notice*   The employee's code number is notified to both the employer and the employee.
5 *P.60 Certificate of Pay, Tax Deducted and National Insurance Contributions*   A certificate must be completed at the end of the tax year for all employees for whom a Deductions Working Sheet has been used. One copy is given to the employee and two other copies are sent to the Inland Revenue.
6 *Payslip booklet*   A set of preprinted payslips is given to each employer to accompany payments made for tax and National Insurance Contributions.

Joe's Rule No 26

Of all the bookkeeping procedures, wages is the one where results have an immediate effect. Both employees and your employer expect wages to be calculated correctly, prepared for payment when due, and recorded accurately.

26.01 The following is an extract from the payroll of a self-service store employing four shop assistants.

Payroll for week ending 3 May 19–5

Name	Net pay
	£
A Anson	58.66
B Cole	68.90
C Davis	59.42
T Evans	74.85

You are required to:
Compute the number and denomination of notes and coins required for the making up of each employee's pay packet. Total and cross-cast your analysis to prove your figures. Notes of £5, £10, £20, and coins of 1p, 2p, 5p, 10p, 50p, and £1 are available.

(RSA 1 Amended)

26.02 (a) Make a list of the deductions which an employer is required by law to make from his employees' wages.
(b) Write down three deductions which an employer will make at the employee's request.
(c) What is the importance of an employee's code number

(RSA 1)

26.03 Telly Vission has four employees: Sharples, Regan, Rippon, and Watts, each of whom works a 40-hour week. Time worked in excess of this is paid at 'time and a half'. The hourly rate for Sharples and Regan is £5.50, for Rippon £4.40, and for Watts £4.60. During the week ending 14 May 19–5 the following hours were worked:

Sharples	35
Regan	50
Rippon	40
Watts	45

You calculate the following.

	Tax	Employee NIC	Employer NIC	Other deductions
Sharples	39.75	17.35	20.14	2.50
Regan	61.50	23.85	28.73	–
Rippon	36.30	15.86	18.42	1.40
Watts	42.60	18.65	21.66	–

(a) Draft a payroll sheet for the week recording the above details and showing for each employee gross wages, deductions, and net wages.

(b) Total your columns to cross-check your arithmetic.

NA 26.04 From the payroll sheet prepared in answer to **26.03** journalize *all* the bookkeeping entries required.

NA 26.05 Peter Price is paid a basic wage of £2.40 per hour for a basic 35-hour week: the first five hours in excess of this are paid at time and a quarter and any further hours are paid at time and a half.

During the week ending 15 June 19–5, he worked a total of 42½ hours and received in addition to his basic pay and overtime a productivity bonus of £10.

His deductions for the week were:

Company pension fund 5 per cent of his gross wage.
National Insurance 10 per cent of his gross wage.
Income tax 30 per cent of all his earnings in excess of £40 per week.
Holiday and Welfare Fund £2.00 per week.

You are required to:

(a) Calculate his gross pay for the week ending 15 June 19–5.

(b) Show the amount of each deduction and calculate his take home pay for the same period.

(RSA 1)

26.06 Ace Garden Services employs John Brooke and Philip Daly to lay turves on new housing estates. Each is paid £5 for every 100 turves laid and if in any week a worker lays more than 2000 turves he receives a bonus of 50 per cent for laying the extra turves, in addition to the normal rate for all turves laid.

In the week ended 15 March 19–5 Brooke laid 2200 turves and Daly laid 2600 turves. Income tax of £18 is due from Brooke, and £32 from Daly.

5 per cent of the gross earnings of each must be deducted for Social Security contributions. Each makes a voluntary contribution of £2 weekly to the Lawn Layers' Union.

You are required to calculate the net pay of each employee and set out their payslips for the week ended 15 March 19–5.

(RSA 1)

NA 26.07 (a) Rule up a note-coin analysis for **26.03.**
(b) Calculate the number and denominations of notes and coins required to pay the four employees. (The owner will allow only one £50 note per pay packet.)

NA 26.08 Classify the following items relating to the business of a tent manufacturer as either capital or revenue expenditure.

A Wages of employees
B Extension of premises
C Canvas used in the making of tents
D Painting of premises
E New sewing machines

(PEI Elem)

NA 26.09 Which of the following does not appear in the Profit and Loss Account?

A Capital
B Wages
C Rent received
D Salesmen commission

(PEI Elem)

NA 26.10 Wages paid to men installing a machine are

A revenue expenditure
B credited to the Profit and Loss Account
C debited to the Trading Account
D capital expenditure

(PEI Elem)

27. Stock

Stock control

The need for stock control
Now that Joe's business has expanded he has introduced a stock control system to ensure that carpets are available when required and that a check is kept on stocks by having a stock recording system.

Asset of stock
You know that the value of stock at the year end has to be determined because as an asset it is shown in the final accounts. This figure has to be correct. A stock recording system can include a *Stock Ledger* which enables the value of stock at any one time to be easily determined. A stocktake (or stock check) at the year end will also verify the quantity of stock. If the value obtained from the physical counting and valuing doesn't agree with the Stock Ledger value then

1 an error has been made in the recording system; or
2 an error has been made in the stocktake; or
3 stock has been lost or stolen.

Joe is going to tell you how the system operates and the documents with which you need to familiarize yourself.

Orders received

Our business is to sell carpets and 99 per cent of these are fitted in the customer's premises. We need to keep stocks of the popular carpet sizes and patterns, as well as the fittings required such as gripper rods, door strips, nails, screws, etc. If a customer wishes to buy a carpet pattern which isn't in stock, then he will need to know when it will be delivered. So the salesman needs to know:

1 the carpets we can buy;
2 when they can be obtained;
3 what price to charge for both carpets and fitting;
4 when the fitters will be able to do the work if the carpet is in stock.

When the order is received and prices agreed with the customer, the salesman makes out a *Customer Order Form.*

The top copy is given to the customer and of the four copies, the salesman keeps one, one goes to the Accounts Department, two to the Carpet Fitting Department.

The Carpet Fitting Department will determine what fittings are required for the job and pass this list, together with the order forms to the storekeeper. If the order is for something to be delivered directly to the customer (with no fitting required) then two copies of the order form go straight to the storekeeper.

Stores Department

Issues and receipts—if materials are in stock

When the storekeeper receives a Customer Order Form, he collects together the carpet and fittings required and 'parcels' them together for delivery. At this point he enters the quantity issued on his stock card and reduces the stock balance. We use a *roll card* (for carpets) and a *bin card* (for mats, rugs, gripper rods, etc.). These stock cards are the storekeeper's own records of the items in stock (see example below).

The Customer Order Form acts as a *Stores Requisition* (in that someone is requesting materials) and it is the authorization for the storekeeper to issue materials and reduce the stock balance on his stock card.

	ROLL CARD		Stock no co/060/41 x		
Manufacturer Bolton		Pattern no 41 x		Location 2.1	
Minimum Stock: —		Unit of Issue Metre		Roll Size (metres) 6 x 18	
Maximum Stock: —			Re-order Level: —		
Date	Document Reference		Receipts	Issues	Balance
Oct 1	—		—	—	10
24	GRN 521		18	—	28
25	COF 96		—	18	10

ROLL CARD or BIN CARD

He marks one copy of the Customer's Order Form 'Ready for Dispatch' and sends it to

1   the Accounts Department, if no fitting is required; or
2   the Carpet Fitting Department if fitting is required.

In the case of (1) he receives back from the Accounts Department a *Dispatch/Delivery note*. This authorizes him to hand the carpets to the Transport Department, a representative of which takes the Dispatch/ Delivery note with him and gives it to the customer upon delivery.

In the case of (2) the carpet fitters collect the carpets and fittings and pass the Customer Order Form to the Accounts Department. See Diagram A.

Diagram A

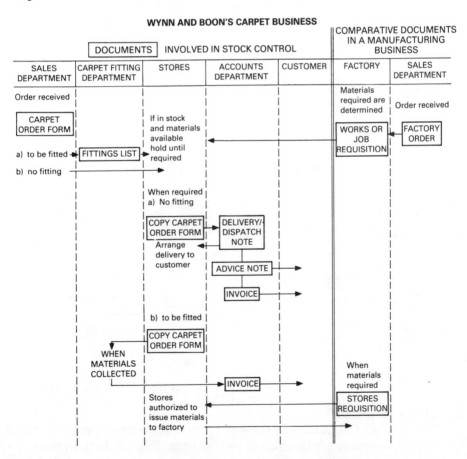

Issues and receipts—if materials are not in stock

The storekeeper will need to obtain the materials or carpets and he will make out a *Purchase Requisition* which he will send to the buyer.

He receives back from the buyer a copy of the Purchase Order placed by the buyer.

When the goods are received he will make out a Goods Received note and enter the quantity of goods received on his bin or roll card. He sends one copy of the Goods Received note to the buyer and one copy to the Accounts Department.

Having already received a Customer Order Form for these materials he will now proceed as at (1) above. See Diagram B below which illustrates this procedure.

Diagram B

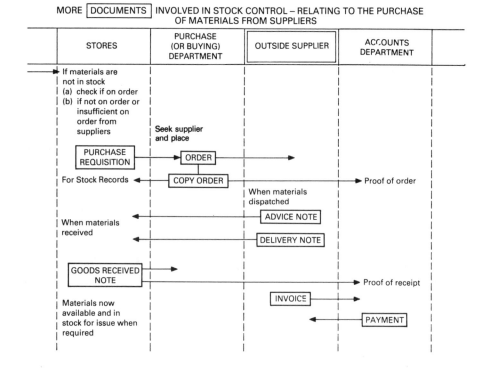

WYNN AND BOON'S CARPET BUSINESS

MORE | DOCUMENTS | INVOLVED IN STOCK CONTROL – RELATING TO THE PURCHASE OF MATERIALS FROM SUPPLIERS

Stock records

Bin cards (or roll cards) will show the quantities received, issued, and in stock. In order to see the overall picture regarding any item in stock it is also necessary to know the following:

1 How much of the item is required (for orders to be completed).
2 What quantities have been ordered from suppliers or manufacturers.
3 What deliveries have been made by suppliers to us and what quantities have still to be delivered to us.

The stores clerk has the job of keeping the stock record cards and the documents used to enter the card are:

1 Customer's Order Form to show the requirements to be met by the stores.
2 Purchase Order to show the quantity on order (and not delivered).
3 Goods Received note to show quantities received into stock—increasing the stock balance and reducing quantities on order and not delivered to us.
4 Customer's Order Form when marked 'Ready for Dispatch' to show quantities issued—reducing the stock balance and reducing the quantity required by customers.

An example of a stock record card is shown on page 316.

Accounts Department

Bookkeeping procedures
This department received a copy of the Customer Order Form which showed the agreed price for carpets sold and any fitting charges to be made.

When the stores copy is received showing goods ready for dispatch, the Dispatch/Delivery note, Advice note, and Invoice are all prepared.

The Dispatch/Delivery note is sent to the storekeeper authorizing dispatch (and it is delivered to the customer), the Advice note is sent by post to the customer to advise him that the goods have been sent and the Invoice is also posted to him to show the sum now owing to us.

The copy of the Invoice is used to enter the Sales Day Book.

If the goods are taken by the carpet fitters then only the Invoice is required.

Stock Ledger
Records of quantities in stock are kept by both the roll/bin cards and the stock record cards but these records do not give monetary values. To do this it is necessary to enter in the Stock Ledger the value of goods received (cost price plus carriage, etc.) and also the value of the goods issued.

STOCK RECORD CARD											Stock no co/o6o/41 x	
Description: Carpet Pattern: 41x Style: CO											Location 2.1	
											Unit of Issue Metre	
Manufacturer's Reference: 41x				Size 6x 18							Re-order level —	
Minimum Stock — Maximum Stock —											Re-order quantity 18	

Date	Document Reference	ORDERS			STOCK			ALLOCATED				FREE STOCK
		Placed	Rec'd	Bal	Rec'd	Issued	Bal	Job no	Allo-cated	Issued	Bal	
Oct 1	Bal	–	–	–	–	–	10	–	–	–	–	10
4	COF 96	–	–	–	–	–	10	AB/49	26	–	26	(16)
6	Po. 1101	36	–	36	–	–	10				26	20
24	GRN 521	–	18	18	18	–	28				26	20
25	COF 96	–	–	18	–	18	10	AB/49	–	18	8	20

STOCK RECORD CARD

Notes
1 Orders Balance + Stock Balance = Allocated Balance + Free Stock
2 Figures shown in brackets represent a minus quantity

Issues can mean either dispatches to customers or to the factory in the case of a manufacturing company.

Stock Ledger Sheet
For each item in stock a Stock Ledger Account is required. Such an account is referred to as a Stock Ledger Sheet since rather more details appear on the sheet than in a normal double entry account (see example on page 318).

Total stock value

If all the Stock Ledger Sheets are up to date and correct then totalling the sheets will give the stock value at that date.

Valuing or pricing stores issues

'Pricing' is the term used to mean 'putting a value on materials when taken out of stock'. This is not as simple as you may imagine. Surely, you will say, something is taken out at the same price it was put in? Yes, but;

Say, in week one 20 units are received costing £2 each.
In week two 20 units are received costing £2.20 each (the price has risen!)

When you issue 10 units in week 3 what 'price' do you value them at for the purposes of taking them out of the Stock Ledger? It could be either of the two receipt costs, or an average cost. The one chosen would depend upon the pricing system.

There are a number of cost price methods available for the pricing of stores issues. Three such methods are:

First in first out (FIFO)
Last in first out (LIFO)
Weighted average price

Remember   There is no direct relationship between the method of valuation and the order in which the stock is issued. Whichever method is adopted it *must* be used consistently.

Let us look at how these work.

1 *FIFO*   Materials are issued at the price of the earliest materials received still in stock.
2 *LIFO*   Materials are issued at the price of the latest materials received still in stock.
3 *Weighted average*   Whenever materials are received a new average price is calculated for all those items in stock and this price is then used for all issues until a new receipt alters the average price.

These different pricing systems are shown on the Stock Ledger Sheet. The illustration (page 318) should make the methods clear.

Assuming the following receipts and issues occur in one month, a Stock Ledger Sheet is shown illustrating the prices that would be used using each of the three cost price methods above.

STOCK LEDGER SHEET

DESCRIPTION	Rubber Mat	PATTERN	—	STYLE	Door	STOCK NO	MR 123
UNIT OF ISSUE	Each	SIZE	60 × 160 cms			LOCATION	1148

FIFO (1, 2)

DATE	REFERENCE AND DETAILS	RECEIPTS			ISSUES			BALANCE		
		Qty	Price	Value	Qty	Price	Value	Qty	Price	Value
Sept 1	GRN 123	20	£5	£100				20		£100
17	GRN 234	30	£5.20	£156				50		£256
18	SR 677				12	£5	£60	38		£196
26	SR 687				23	8 × £5 / 15 × £5.20	£118	15		£78
28	GRN 456	20	£5.33	£106.60				35		£184.60

LIFO (3, 4)

DATE	REFERENCE AND DETAILS	RECEIPTS			ISSUES			BALANCE		
		Qty	Price	Value	Qty	Price	Value	Qty	Price	Value
Sept 1	GRN 123	20	£5	£100				20		£100
17	GRN 234	30	£5.20	£156				50		£256
18	SR 677				12	£5.20	£62.40	38		£193.60
26	SR 687				23	18 × £5.20 / 5 × £5	£118.60	15		£75
28	GRN 456	20	£5.33	£106.60				35		£181.60

WEIGHTED AVERAGE (5, 6)

DATE	REFERENCE AND DETAILS	RECEIPTS			ISSUES			BALANCE		
		Qty	Price	Value	Qty	Price	Value	Qty	Price	Value
Sept 1	GRN 123	20	£5	£100				20	£5	£100
17	GRN 234	30	£5.20	£156				50	£5.12	£256
18	SR 677				12	£5.12	£61.44	38	£5.12	£194.56
26	SR 687				23	£5.12	£117.76	15	£5.12	£76.80
28	GRN 456	20	£5.33	£106.60				35	£5.24	£183.40

Notes 1 and 2

As the FIFO system is being used the price of issues is that of the material, still in stock, which was received earliest.

Therefore, of the issue of 23 items on 26 September, 8 still remain of the first batch received, so the rest of that issue must be at the price of the second batch received.

Notes 3 and 4

With the LIFO system the first issue will be at the latest priced stock still on hand. The second issue will firstly use up the latest received material, and, having done so, move to the price paid for that material, still in stock, of the next preceding batch received.

Notes 5 and 6

A new weighted average price is calculated at each receipt. (A simple average price = (£5 + £5.20) ÷ 2 = £5.10.) However, when weighted by quantity the price becomes £256 ÷ 50 = £5.12.

The weighted average price is used for issues made until a new receipt means a new weighted average price is calculated.

September	1	Received 20 units @ £5 each
	17	Received 30 units @ £5.20 each
	18	Issued 12 units
	26	Issued 23 units
	28	Received 20 units @ £5.33 each

Joe's Rule No 27

Stocks are assets. Stock quantities are recorded on stock cards, while the cost values are recorded in the Stock Ledger.

Stocktaking

Purpose

Stock is an asset and can often be of great value. The purpose of stock-taking is to verify the quantity held in stock. If this figure is compared with the quantities that should be in stock, any stock losses will be revealed.

Losses

Losses arise for many reasons:

Errors in physical location
Errors in counting
Errors in recording

Damaged goods discarded and not recorded
Theft
Errors on issuing, and so on

Writing off losses
Whatever is recorded as being in stock must be altered to agree with the actual physical quantity in stock. Such items 'lost' have to be valued and taken out of stock. The double entry for this will be:

Dr Stock Losses A/c: Cr Stock Ledger Sheet

Reason for losses
If losses do arise then efforts should be made to establish why this has happened.

1 If issues have been made to customers and not recorded—has the customer been charged?
2 If damages have occurred and not been recorded—Why? Who did the damage?
3 If stock has been stolen, what precautions need to be taken to avoid it happening again?
4 If documents have gone astray, why is the system not working?

Reconciling different stock totals
Before a loss is agreed, the actual quantity in stock may need to be 'reconciled' with the quantities shown on the various stock records. With a roll card, a stock record card, and a Stock Ledger Sheet in use it is possible for those three stock figures to differ—and for the physical stock counted to be different again! Usually these differences will be accounted for by various documents not having completed the full cycle of recording. A Goods Received note completed by the storekeeper may not have been entered by the stores ledger clerk. The stores ledger clerk may have entered issues on his stock record card but the document may not yet have reached the accounts ledger clerk.

A loss can only be established once the reconciliation has been made.

Frequent stocktakes
The more frequent the stocktakes the more quickly errors and losses are detected and the more quickly they can be rectified and avoided in the future.

27.01 (a) In October 19–8 Miss Mary Dean, who runs a leatherware wholesale shop, decided to stock a new line of umbrellas. These were red plastic umbrellas supplied by Fashion House Ltd. Their minimum re-order quantity is 50, minimum stock level 20, and cost is £2.00 each. Draw up a simple stock record card.

(b) On 15 October Mary ordered 500 umbrellas (Stock item no 1467) at £2.00 each on Purchase Order no 64R. They arrived on 1 November and Goods Received note no 192 was completed.

By 15 November she had sold 300 at £4.00 each.

On 29 November she purchased 750 more (on Purchase Order no 90B) at the same price.

By 30 November she had sold another 159 at £3.50 each. Enter the stock record card showing clearly the number of umbrellas in stock at the end of November.

27.02 Using Question **27.01**, calculate the answers to the following questions: (*Note*   (a), (b) and (c) are separate questions.)

(a) What would be the gross profit if the closing stock should have been valued at £40.00?

(b) What would be the gross profit if there had been an opening stock of umbrellas valued at £250 and the closing stock was valued at £282.

(c) What effect on the gross profit would be the result of destroying 10 umbrellas that had no saleable value.

27.03 The following information relates to component number PC 241. At 31 December 19–4 the opening stock was 210.

Jan	2	Received (invoice 6608)	20
	4	Issue V601	16
	7	Issue V628	41
	10	Issue V701	10
	21	Received (invoice 6601)	80
	21	Issue V780	27
	25	Issue V808	24
	28	Returns R14	6
	30	Issue V831	14

On 31 January it was discovered that there was a stock loss of five units.

Required:

(a) From the information given and using the pro-forma shown on page 322 write up the stock card for component number PC 241. Return the stock card with your answers.*

(b) How would you have discovered the stock loss on 31 January?

(RSA I)

*(*Author's note*   Copy the stock card on page 322.)

Item:		Stock card		Minimum Maximum Re-order level
Date	Reference	Receipts	Issues	Balance

27.04 Edward Greenwood is a sole trader whose year end is 31 January each year. Owing to pressure of business, he is unable to value his stock in trade at the close of business on 31 January 19-4 but he does so on 7 February 19-4 when the value, at cost price, is calculated at £2830.

For the period 1-7 February his purchases were £296, of which goods costing £54 were in transit at the time of stocktaking.

Sales for the period 1-7 February amounted to £460, all of which had left the warehouse at the time of stocktaking. Greenwood's gross profit is 20 per cent of sales. Also during the period 1-7 February, Greenwood took goods costing £38 for his personal use. Included in the valuation figure of £2830 given above were goods which cost £120, but which had a market price of £97 only at the date of the year end, i.e., 31 January 19-4.

Required:
Calculate the figure which should be shown as 'Stock at 31 January 19-4' in Greenwood's Trading Account for the year ended 31 January 19-4.

Note Calculations must be shown.

(LCCI Elem)

27.05 (a) Explain the meaning of the following terms, used in connection with stock valuation:
    (i) first in first out (FIFO);
    (ii) last in first out (LIFO).
(b) Use an example to show which of the two methods (FIFO or LIFO) will produce a higher figure of stock valuation in times of rising stock prices.
(c) Explain the effect on a firm's gross profit of overvaluing closing stock.

(RSA 1)

27.06 If the stock at start were undervalued the gross profit would be:

A overstated
B understated
C unaffected
D irrelevant

(PEI Elem)

27.07 If the stock-at-end were undervalued, the gross profit would be:

A overstated
B understated
C not affected
D stock cannot be undervalued

(PEI Elem)

NA 27.08 Mrs Margaret Price operated a small cash and carry warehouse and the Trading Account for her business for the year ended 30 November 19–8 was as follows:

Trading Account

		£
Sales		96 000
Opening stock 1 Dec 19–7	12 800	
Purchases	70 800	
	83 600	
Closing stock 30 Nov 19–8	11 600	
Cost of goods sold		72 000
Gross profit		24 000

During the night of 10 May 19–9 the warehouse was burgled and the entire stock was stolen.
    The following information is available from the books:

Sales   1 Dec 19–8 to 10 May 19–9 £33 120 (at selling price)
Purchases 1 Dec 19–8 to 10 May 19–9 £25 600 (at cost price)

You are required to calculate the value of the goods stolen.

27.09 The following details refer to door mats:

Re-order quantity	24
Minimum stock level	15*
Stock item number	6521

At 31 December 19–9 the stock on hand was 16 at a total value of £80.

* The item is to be re-ordered if stock falls below this minimum level.

During January the following occurred:

Jan   4   Customer Order Form 234 was received for 20 mats
      6   Purchase Order no 63B placed for 24 mats
   18   24 mats received (Goods Received note no 316 for Purchase Order 63B) at a total cost of £138
   25   20 mats were issued against Customer Order Form 234
   27   10 mats were issued against Customer Order Form 278
   30   Purchase Order no 81D was placed for 24 mats.

(a)   Draw up the Stock Record Card for the item above for the month of January showing clearly:

      (i)   the balance in stock
      (ii)   the balance on order
      (iii) the balance of stock allocated to customers
      (iv) free stock

(b)   Draw up the Stock Ledger Sheet for the item for the month of January, using the LIFO system of stores showing the value of the stock balance.

NA 27.10   (a)   From the following stock list calculate the value of J Brown's stock on 31 December 19-3

Item catalogue number	Quantity in stock	Cost price each £	Selling price each £
1	30	2.40	3.60
2	27	3.10	4.50
3	25	4.20	2.00
4	30	3.70	Nil

(b) A trading account shows the gross profit for three years ended 31 December to be as follows:

			£
19-1	..	..	16 000
19-2	..	..	15 000
19-3	..	..	17 000

It came to light that a quantity of stock, at cost price £400, purchased in 19-1 and sold during 19-3 had not been included in the stock valuation on 31 December 19-1 and 19-2.

Calculate the correct gross profit for the three years ended 31 December 19-1, 19-2 and 19-3.

(c) A firm started in business during 19-2. On 31 December 19-2 stocktaking showed the value of goods held to be £3700. On 31 December 19-3 the value of stock was £4200. Write up the stock account for the two years 19-2 and 19-3

(London 'O')

28. Computer-Based Bookkeeping

For many years large businesses have been using computers to help with their bookkeeping and accounting procedures. In recent years there have been dramatic changes in the types of computers available and their cost. Joe has decided that it is now worth while for him to buy a small computer to handle some of the bookkeeping.

Let Joe explain.

Advantages and disadvantages of a computer-based bookkeeping system

When I first thought about getting a computer I had to decide whether it was worth while for my business. I carried out a 'feasibility study' with a computer expert, to try and assess the benefits and problems associated with introducing a computer.

Advantages

Computers are particularly suited to some jobs and I judged that overall it would be an advantage for me because:

1 I have *large volumes of data* (data is the name given to all basic facts such as dates, amounts, and names). For example every month I need to process piles of invoices. Computers can handle large amounts of data.

2 It is essential that *accurate* records be kept (so that, for example, the trial balance does balance). Although the person using the computer may make an error, the computer itself should not.

3 There are many *repetitive* jobs to be done. Computers don't get bored repeating procedures time and time again (such as preparing and typing monthly statements to customers).

4 The computer should *save time* (and therefore money). Computers work at very fast speeds, for example, calculating wages should be quicker than at present.

5 Most of the data we record in one book is also written in another book. Such *common data* can be typed into the computer once, and then be automatically available for inclusion in other places. For example, an entry in the Sales Day Book can be used in the Sales Ledger and the Debtors' Control Account.

6 *Calculating* the weekly payroll involves some arithmetic. Such calculations are simple to a computer, which is able to perform very complex calculations.
7 The computer can be used as part of a word processor, saving a great deal of time when typing letters, preparing reports, etc.

Disadvantages

There are some disadvantages as well:

1 The *initial cost* of the computer and all the equipment is considerable.
2 There will be initial *changeover problems*. When the computer is first introduced it will cause some disruption:
    (a)   All the staff will need to become familiar with the computer and learn how to operate the new equipment while keeping the business going as usual.
    (b)   We can only find out through using the system if it really is suited to our needs.
3 The computer system is rather *inflexible* so that procedures cannot readily be altered. For example, if a new tax was introduced we could draw an extra column in the books, but it would not be so easy in a computerized system.
4 If the system *breaks down* it would be difficult to carry on as normal.

A computer-based system

Hardware

Hardware is the name given to the machinery of computer-based systems. This includes all the electronic and mechanical elements of a computer and all the devices used with it.

All sorts of hardware are available and what is used depends on the size and type of business.

I have decided to start with a relatively small system, which has the potential to be expanded should I need to do so in the future (see Figure 28.1).

The devices in my system are:

1 A keyboard which is used to type in—*input*—data and instructions to the computer.
2 The microcomputer itself, which is in the same casing as the keyboard. It accepts data, performs various operations on the data (as instructed), and then produces results.

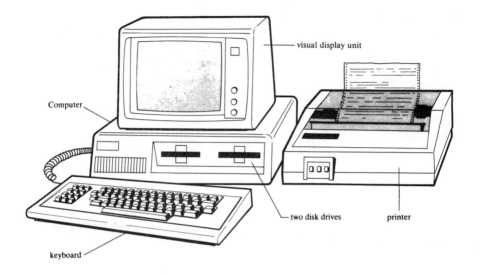

Figure 28.1   Joe Wynn's Computer System

3 A visual display unit (VDU)—this displays information (as required) at
   various stages of processing.
4 A dual disk drive, which can take two floppy disks at a time. Floppy
   disks look like single records (that have music on them), but they are
   made of a more flexible material. They usually contain either data or
   programs (but more about that later).
5 A printer to print out letters, invoices, trial balances, etc. This is
   called *output*.

There are many alternative devices:
Examples of input devices:

   Keyboard
   Disks
   Tapes

Examples of output devices:

   Printer
   VDU
   Disks
   Tapes

Examples of computer types:

Microcomputer
Minicomputer
Mainframe computer

Software
Software is a general term describing programs which can be used in computer systems.

Systems programs
These are programs which are built into a computer system. They control many of the functions a computer can perform, such as understanding a computer language.

Applications programs
The jobs that a user of a computer wants the computer to do are controlled by applications programs. I have several applications programs to help in my bookkeeping and accounting. They are:

Sales Day Book/Sales Ledger
Bought Day Book/Bought Ledger
Trial Balance/Final Accounts
Analysed Cash Book/Nominal Ledger
Wages
Stock Control

How the applications programs are organized
Traditional systems
Computers can be used in the same way as the traditional books for bookkeeping, so that each computer program is a separate entity. This approach does not use the computer to its potential.

An integrated system

I have chosen software to give me a system where there is coordination of activities. Several of the books are interlocked so that common data need not be typed in repeatedly. For example, when credit purchases data is typed into the computer, it will be used in the Bought Day Book and then automatically in the Bought Ledger.

Many businesses have a 'fully integrated' system, so that credit purchases data goes into the Bought Day Book, the Bought Ledger, the Purchases Account in the Nominal Ledger, and the Creditors' Control Account.

Database

Many companies use a database which allows *all* the data to be kept independently. For example, all the sales data is stored, together with various other data, the person using the computer then gives instructions to put the data together as required. The required data can be collected together to produce monthly statements to customers or to produce the Debtors' Control Account.

Practical use of the computerized system

Now I will show you four programs, so that you can see some of the practical problems you will need to understand.

Presentation and control

Let us look at the program I have for entering the Sales Day Book data. It demonstrates how data is typed into the computer and also shows some of the validation controls included in programs.

Screen 1

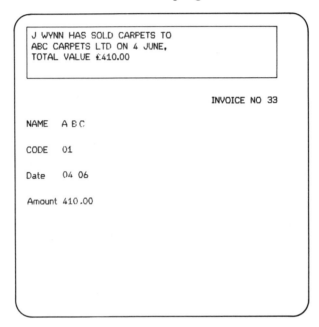

Entering data

Screen 1 shows the data which you would be asked to type into the computer from an invoice that is described in the box. The entries are as follows:

1   NAME   You type in the name as you would write it in the Sales Day Book.

     (*Control*   You will need to abbreviate the name if it is longer than 15 characters. (A character means a letter, space or figure.))

2   CODE   You type in the customer's code from a list (see Appendix A). If the code is listed as 09, you must type 09 and not 9 or 009 or 9.0. It is important for the code to be exact because the computer needs exact codes, but more about codes later.

     (*Control*   Codes would be checked to make sure they do exist.)

3   DATE   The date is usually typed in as figures. So 1 November will be typed in as 01 11, the first day of the eleventh month.

     (*Control*   Dates would be checked to make sure they exist—for example there is no 31 02.)

4 AMOUNT   The amount is typed in as figures, with no £ sign, for example £356.89 is typed as 356.89.
(*Control*   The amount would be checked to some upper limit such as £5000.00.)

Typical validation controls
These are controls which can be built into a program.

1 *Presence*   Making sure that all the items are typed in.
2 *Size*   There is a limit to the size of an entry.
3 *Character check*   This makes sure letters are typed where letters should be and numbers where numbers should be.
4 *Format*   In the Sales Day Book example we saw that the date had to fit a certain format.
5 *Reasonableness*   A check can be made to see if an entry is reasonable. Trade discount for example may be expected to be between 20 and 50 per cent.

User controls
Checking summaries   Having typed in the data a summary will appear which can be checked against the original invoice (see Screen 2). This check is important because, unlike written systems, you can't easily rub out an entry once it has been stored on a floppy disk.

Screen 2

```
 J WYNN HAS SOLD CORD AND UNDERLAY
 TO POPLAR TREADS LTD (CODE 09) ON 6 JUNE,
 TOTAL VALUE £52.50


                                    INVOICE NO 34
```

DATE	CUSTOMER	CODE	AMOUNT
6 JUNE	POPLAR T	09	52.50

```
 IS THIS RIGHT? Y OR N ......
```

Calculations and rearrangements

To demonstrate some other things a computer will do, I will show you the trial balance program. When all the ledger accounts have been totalled, we need to draw up a trial balance to test the arithmetical accuracy of the books. We enter the account name and the balance in that account on either the debit or credit side (see Screen 3).

Screen 3

```
J WYNN (CARPET SUPPLIERS)

TRIAL BALANCE AS AT 30 APRIL


ACCOUNT              DEBIT         CREDIT
ADVERTISING         21.32

BANK CHARGES         3.22

BANK INTEREST                      6.92

TOTALS              24.54          6.92
```

Calculation

The computer can then be instructed to add up the two sides and let us know the difference (if any). This is a very simple calculation for a computer to do.

Rearrangement

Once the trial balance is balanced, and all the end of year adjustments have been included we are ready to produce the Trading and Profit and Loss Accounts and the Balance Sheet.

It is a simple task for the computer (with an appropriate program) to use the data supplied and rearrange it to produce the Trading and Profit and Loss Accounts and the Balance Sheet and to print them out when required.

Files, records, and fields

Another important point is the facility for storing data on floppy disks.

The wages program demonstrates some of these features.

Two floppy disks are used for weekly wages calculations. Disk 1 contains a *file* of data. The file is made up of many *records*, one for each employee.

Each record has details of the employee's number, name, tax code, deductions, wages grade, and National Insurance number. It will also show cumulative gross pay and deductions.

Number	Name	Tax Code	Deductions 1 (Pension)	Deductions 2 (Union)	Wages Grade	Nat Ins No	Cum gross pay	Cum deductions	Next employee number
08	John Rodd	336	3.50	2.00	4	NP 01 23 45B	346.91	101.72	09

An employee record

Each of the items on the record is called a field. The computer recognizes each individual record using one *key field*. In this example it is the employee number which is the *key field*. Should we want to locate an employee's details we need to type in the employee number for the computer to locate that particular record.

28.01 When would the file be updated?

Disk 2 contains a program to calculate wages and deductions according to the number of hours worked that week. Once the hours each employee has worked are entered the computer calculates all the information required to produce the payroll. When instructed the payroll and individual payslips for the week can be printed out.

Screen 4 shows part of a simple wages calculation program in action. The top part of the screen uses data from Disk 1, but the calculation procedures are controlled by the program on Disk 2.

Codes and coding error

Codes

Codes are used to give unique identities to customers, stocks, and other items. The computer can use these codes more efficiently than long names. Our stock control program is probably the most useful program

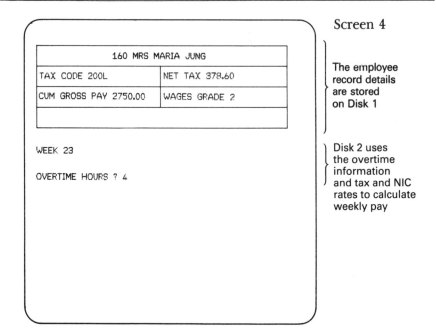

Screen 4

The employee
record details
are stored
on Disk 1

Disk 2 uses
the overtime
information
and tax and NIC
rates to calculate
weekly pay

to show this idea, and like the wages program, stock control uses two disks.

Disk 1 contains a file of stock records. Let us look at a part of a stock record.

Stock item number	Description code	Supplier	Balance in stock	Re-order quantity	Balance on order
0672	YE1/1/4/500	13 (Wearing Co)	200 (metres)	500	500

Part of a stock record

28.02   Which field would be used as the *key field*?

Each stock item has an individual number but this does not describe the carpet. I use a code for the description to give myself as much information as possible—I have so many carpets in the warehouse it is difficult to remember details of all of them.

I use an eight character code:

The first three characters give me an idea of the colour:

RED = red
GRE = green
BRO = brown, etc.

The fourth character tells me whether the carpet is patterned or plain:

0 for plain   1 for patterned

The fifth character indicates how hardwearing the carpet is:

1 = heavy duty
2 = very good quality
3 = good quality
4 = bedroom quality

The last three characters tell me the carpet width in centimetres:

350 = 3.5 metres wide
625 = 6.25 metres wide, etc.

28.03 Can you work out what the following carpets look like?

(a) GRE/0/2/500
(b) ORA/1/4/303
(c) BLA/0/1/275

Disk 2 has a program to manipulate stock data:

1 Creating new records for stock.
2 Deleting stock records which are not required.
3 Increasing stock balances when stock is ordered and received.
4 Decreasing stock balances when stock is sold or allocated to customers.
5 Altering records when cost or other details (e.g., supplier) change.

Also the stock control program can provide stock turnover information such as:

How quickly each carpet is selling.
How many customers buy a particular carpet.
What lengths of carpet are sold.

This information can be very useful in deciding which carpets to stock in future. Using conventional handwritten methods of stock control such information would normally be very time consuming to produce.

Coding errors

For its working purposes, a computer is only interested in the code numbers of stock. It is very important that code numbers are typed in correctly. There are many types of coding error, for example:

1 Omission,   typing   1123 for 11123
2 Addition,   typing   111223 for 11123
3 Transposition, typing   11213 for 11123

where two numbers are reversed

4 Transcription, typing   11125 for 11123

where a 3 has been mis-read as 5

5 Others, e.g.,   typing   11A23 for 11123
                or typing   15723 for 11123

The first two errors may be found by the type of validation techniques mentioned earlier (page 331). The other types of error may be impossible to detect, but might be found if the code typed does not exist.

We have looked at various topics demonstrated by one particular system of computer-based bookkeeping, but the best way for you to learn is to use a computer yourself.

Joe's Rule No 28

To operate a computer-based bookkeeping system, the same information needs to be typed into a computer as is written in the traditional books. But data often needs to be typed into the computer using special formats and codes.

28.04   A wages calculation program is:

    A   systems software
    B   systems hardware
    C   applications software
    D   applications hardware

28.05   Organizing data in a system which will allow it to be kept independently, but brought together as required is called:

    A   information retrieval
    B   systems analysis
    C   data control
    D   a database

NA 28.06 Reed Co runs a wholesale stationery business. The company has a microcomputer which is used for all of the bookkeeping (a fully integrated system). Three transactions are shown below.

(a) State which book should be used to enter data.
(b) List how the relevant data should be typed into the computer bearing in mind the following.
   (i) Details should be not more than 10 characters in length.
   (ii) Date is typed as numbers (e.g., 02 06 is 2 June)
   (iii) Computer codes for
       A Rudolph Co   016
       J Patt   008
       Quicksilver Print 910
   (iv) Amounts should be shown as £ and pence.

1 Ink was purchased on credit from Quicksilver Print on 1 May. Total cost £235.87.
2 J Patt returned 6 reams of paper (each £5.20) on 31 August.
3 On 30 November, Reed Co sold to A Rudolph Co stationery for £43.09.

28.07 A file on a floppy disk consists of 80 employee records. Each record contains details of one employee's name, address, number, date of birth, sex, wages grade, tax code, National Insurance number, and department.

(a) What is the computer term for each item on a record?
(b) How would you instruct the computer to find a particular employee record?
(c) Describe briefly how this file might be used for wage calculations.
(d) What other uses might the file have?

NA 28.08 Toolbox Ltd is run by a sole trader, the business makes 150 types of special size nuts and bolts. There are eight employees.
   The company is thinking of buying a computer to simplify the paper work.

(a) List three advantages and three disadvantages relevant to Toolbox.
(b) What applications programs would be particularly useful for this type of business?

NA 28.09 Gerald Joyce is using a computer for stock control. He sells bottles. These fall into various categories:

1 2 litre, 1 litre, and 0.5 litre
2 Clear and green
3 First and second quality

(a) Devise a 3 digit code which can distinguish any type of bottle. Show how the code works for a 2 litre green first quality bottle and a 0.5 litre clear second quality bottle.

(b) What errors might be made in entering the code into the computer?

(c) List six details which would normally be shown on a computer stock record for the above bottles.

28.10 Pennock and Williamson employs 12 monthly paid staff (employee numbers 01 to 12). The company uses a computer to calculate the monthly payroll. The employees are paid at a standard rate according to their wages grade, but any overtime will need to be added in each month.

Using the following information list the name, net pay, and deductions of each employee in September.

1 Employees 02 and 06 were upgraded to wages grade 4 from 1 September.

2 Employee 10 started contributing £2.25 each month to the savings fund from 1 September.

Hours of overtime worked in September:

Employees 01, 04 and 06—10 hours.

Employees 10, 11 and 12—4 hours.

Either answer this question using a suitable computer program *or* describe the procedures involved in using a computer program to calculate Pennock and Williamson's payroll for September.

28.11 Adam Conti employs six full-time staff, he has a computer program which will calculate wages and deductions and a printer to produce the payroll sheet and payslips.

At the end of Week 35 Robert Lee (018) left.
At the end of Week 36 Janet Lewis was employed.
The details on her P45 showed:

Tax code	220L
Cumulative gross pay	£1760
Tax paid to date	£120.00

She was employed at wages grade 6, and did not join the Savings Fund.
The employees worked the following hours of overtime

Code	Name	Overtime
142	Janet Lewis	0
011	Ralph Smith	10
101	June Brown	6
132	Nancy Evans	6
066	Richard Regan	4
021	Peter Driscoll	4

You are required to:
(a) Delete Robert Lee's record from the employee file.
(b) Create a new employee record for Janet Lewis.
(c) Use the wages program to calculate the pay and deductions for each employee. List the pay and deductions of all the employees for Week 36.

Either answer this question using a suitable computer program *or* describe the procedures involved in using a computer program to calculate Adam Conti's payroll for Week 36.

29. Some Different Bookkeeping Methods

Analysed books for small businesses

Single entry

The majority of small businesses (usually sole traders) do not keep a set of double entry bookkeeping records. It isn't necessary to do so since the number of assets are small and sales are all for cash. It is necessary to keep some records if only to enable the accountant to satisfy the Inspector of Taxes at the year end of the accuracy of the profit or loss that has been made. A registered VAT trader will also have to keep some records for Customs and Excise. Very many specially ruled and analysed books are available and these usually require a trader to record transactions daily (for sales) and weekly (for purchases and expenses).

An illustration of a weekly record for income and expenditure is shown opposite.

The weekly details are transferred to summary pages thus enabling the totals for the year to be calculated for purchases, sales, Drawings, expenses, and capital expenditure (see page 342).

For VAT registered traders suitably ruled books are shown on page 344.

Double entry

There are several different commercial systems available for the small businessman who wishes to keep a full set of double entry records while not fully understanding the principles of double entry. By following a set of instructions, transactions are recorded and posted, analysed and totalled. By using control accounts the monthly profit and loss accounts can be prepared. See pages 345–346 for an illustration of the type of records used in such a system.

The slip system

What is it?

Original documents are often used only for information to be copied from them into the books. They are then filed and forgotten unless a query arises at a later date.

Now, if for example, all the purchase invoices recorded on one page of the Bought Day Book were stapled together and totalled, this batch could replace the Bought Day Book page.

Example No. 2 — Bank Overdrawn | Week No. 14 | Commencing: 3RD APRIL 1981.

RECEIPTS

Day	Date	Gross Daily Takings (cash) Col 1	Gross Daily Takings (cheques) Col 2	Other Receipts Col 3	Particulars
Sunday	3/4	20 57			
Monday	4/4	37 53	10 00	5 60	RATE REFUND
Tuesday	5/4	42 67	15 47		
Wednesday	6/4	37 41			
Thursday	7/4	84 77	2 54		
Friday	8/4	141 42	9 53		
Saturday	9/4	117 15			
Totals		481 52	37 54	5 60	

PAID TO BANK

Cash Col 4	Cheques Col 5
	16 60
20 00	15 47
100 00	12 07
Totals 120 00	43 14

PAYMENTS FOR BUSINESS STOCK

Date or Chq. No.	To Whom Paid	Amount Paid By Cash Col 6	Amount Paid By Cheque Col 7
4/4	J. CONLAN & SONS	23 20	
"	J. BREWER & CO. LTD.		16 50
"	A. J. GOOD LTD.		17 50
"	J. BROWN & CO. LTD.	4 93	
"	PARKER CORTES LTD.	15 45	
"	A. NEWSOME		39 40
"	JOHN JACOBS LTD.		15 72
5/4	F. LIVESAY & CO.	16 27	
"	A. NEWCOMBE LTD.		23 72
"	W. SMITH LTD.		5 41
"	W. J. M. SMYTHE & CO.		16 47
"	J. JAMES LTD.		2 51
"	G. HEYWOOD & CO. LTD.		23 47
	Totals	59 85	160 70

PAYMENTS OTHER THAN FOR STOCK

Nature of Payment		Amount Paid By Cash Col 8	Amount Paid By Cheque Col 9
Rent		5 00	
Rates			
Light and Heat			10 27
Carriage		4 40	
Postages		1 20	
Paper			9 42
Motor Expenses	PETROL	3 03	
do	REPAIRS	25 00	
Travelling		4 72	
Cleaning		2 00	
Printing & Stationery			10 80
Repairs & Renewals			11 57
Insurance (Business)			
Advertising			
Telephone			
Wages (Wife)			
Wages (Employees)		55 75	
Sundries		1 05	
Private Pension Contributions			
Inland Revenue (PAYE - NI)			17 98
Drawings for Self (see Note. 10)		26 68	
—do—			
—do—			
Capital Items (see note 7)			
Totals		128 83	60 02

WEEKLY BANK REPORT

Opening Balance	brought forward	568	47
Add { Total Paid to Bank during week (Col 4 + Col 5)		163	14
	Total	405	33
Deduct { Cash drawn from bank		—	—
Stock Payments (Col 7)		160	70
Other Payments (Col 9)		60	02
Bank Standing Orders		—	—
Bank and Interest Charges		—	—
	Total	220	72
Closing Balance carried forward		626	05

WEEKLY CASH REPORT

Cash in Hand (as counted)	brought forward	6	46
Add { Gross Weekly Takings (Col 1 + Col 2)		519	06
Other Receipts (Col 3)		5	60
Cash Drawn from Bank		—	—
	Total	531	12
Deduct { Stock Payments (cash) (Col 6)		59	85
Other Payments (cash) (Col 8)		128	83
Amount paid to Bank		163	14
	Total	351	82
Cash Balance on books		179	30
Cash in hand (as counted)		179	30
Difference on books (+ or −)		—	—

© GEORGE VYNER LTD

COPYRIGHT RESERVED REPRODUCTION OF THIS BOOK IN WHOLE OR IN PART STRICTLY FORBIDDEN

A page from a Simplex D Cash Book

WEEKLY SUMMARY OF TAKINGS

WEEK No.	AMOUNT	WEEK No.	AMOUNT	WEEK No.	AMOUNT	WEEK No.	AMOUNT		
1	372 04	14	519 06	27		40			
2	473 95	15		28		41			
3	652 87	16		29		42			
4	530 06	17		30		43			
5	499 10	18		31		44			
6	600 23	19		32		45			
7	487 9i	20		33		46			
8	533 38	21		34		47			
9	476 55	22		35		48		Total Summary for Year	
10	549 89	23		36		49		1st Qtr.	6709 38
11	567 42	24		37		50		2nd Qtr.	
12	502 76	25		38		51		3rd Qtr.	
13	463 22	26		39		52		4th Qtr.	
						53		Trade Debtors	
Total 1st Qtr.	6709 38	Total 2nd Qtr.		Total 3rd Qtr.		Total 4th Qtr.		TOTAL	

WEEKLY SUMMARY OF GOODS TAKEN FOR OWN CONSUMPTION

WEEK No.	AMOUNT	WEEK No	AMOUNT	WEEK No	AMOUNT	WEEK No	AMOUNT		
1		14		27		40			
2		15		28		41			
3		16		29		42			
4		17		30		43			
5		18		31		44			
6		19		32		45			
7		20		33		46			
8		21		34		47			
9		22		35		48			
10		23		36		49		Total Summary for Year	
11		24		37		50		1st Qtr.	
12		25		38		51		2nd Qtr.	
13		26		39		52		3rd Qtr.	
						53		4th Qtr.	
Total 1st Qtr.		Total 2nd Qtr.		Total 3rd Qtr.		Total 4th Qtr.		TOTAL	

A summary page taken from a Simplex D Cash Book

This use of original documents is the basis of any 'slip system'. The documents themselves form both the 'book of original entry' and the Bought or Sales Ledger as required. The system usually embraces:

The Bought Day Book/Bought Ledger—using suppliers' invoices received
Returns outwards—using credit notes received.
Sales Day Book/Sales Ledger—using issued invoices.
Returns inwards—using issued credit notes.

Let us look at how the system works in detail.

Bought Day Book/Bought Ledger

Usually only one copy of the supplier's invoice is received. Many firms will record all invoices received in a daily register, and since all suppliers' invoices have different numbers, often with prefixes or suffixes, they are given a 'company' number which is printed on the supplier's invoice and in the daily register. If the slip system is being used then it will be useful to take a photocopy of the invoice. All the photocopies batched together and totalled at the end of each month become a part of the Bought Day Book. The total is used to debit the Purchases Account, and, if required, to credit the Bought Ledger Control Account (i.e., the summary account for creditors). The supplier's invoice is filed in his file or folder, in which all invoices, debit notes, credit notes, and statements from him are filed.

When a payment is made to a supplier the invoice is withdrawn from his 'live file' and put into his 'dead file'. The total payments made in the month are credited in the Cash Book. If a control account is used then the total payments will be debited. At any one moment the total of creditors will be those invoices in the supplier's 'live files'. This should balance with the Bought Ledger Control Account.

Sales Day Book/Sales Ledger

The top copy of an invoice is sent to the customer and the second copy is batched with all other invoice copies to form the Sales Day Book. The total is used for the credit entry in the Sales Account. A third copy of the invoice is put into the debtor's 'live file'. When payments are received the relevant invoice is taken out of the 'live file' and put into the debtor's 'dead file'. A control account can be kept and entered from 'totals' in the same way as explained above, i.e., debit the Sales Day Book 'batch' totals in the Sales Ledger Control Account and credit to this account total payments received from debtors.

Illustrative pages from a Simplex VAT record book

Company **CANTMISSEM POTTERS LTD.**   **CREDIT SALES   CS**

1 DATE 1994	2 CUSTOMER	3 INVOICE NUMBER	4 REF.	5 INVOICE TOTAL	6 V.A.T.	7 SALES	8 SUNDRIES
May 10	Brown Ltd	1	B1	115 00	15 00	100 00	
" 12	Jones Ltd	2	J1	23 00	3 00	20 00	
" 13	Smith Ltd	3	S1	57 50	7 50	50 00	
" 13	Jones Ltd	4	J1	230 00	30 00	200 00	
" 14	Brown Ltd	5	B1	46 00	6 00	40 00	
" 15	Green Ltd	6	G1	92 00	12 00	80 00	
" 18	Smith Ltd	7	S1	57 50	7 50	50 00	
" 22	Cash Sale	8	S2	11 50	1 50	10 00	
" 24	Brown Ltd	9	B1	92 00	12 00	80 00	
" 29	Smith Ltd	10	S1	138 00	18 00	120 00	
				862 50	112 50	750 00	
				SLC 4	VC 5	PLA 1(b)	

The Sales Day Book of the system. You can see from the half-size reproduction above that all invoices listed are analysed to show the VAT content and separate out goods sold outside the normal course of trading. The instructions make sure that the totals balance and entries are made correctly on the Sales Ledger Cards and in the appropriate Control Accounts. The handling of Credit Notes is also dealt with.

Company **CANTMISSEM POTTERS LTD.**   **CASH TAKINGS   CT**

1 DATE 1994	2 DETAIL	REF	3 STANDARD RATE TAKINGS	4 ZERO RATE TAKINGS	5 TOTAL TAKINGS	6 TRANSFERS TO PETTY CASH	7 CASH PAID INTO BANK	8 UNBANKED TAKINGS IN HAND
May 2	Till Roll		11 50		11 50			11 50
" 3	" "		23 00		23 00			34 50
" 4	" "		34 50		34 50			69 00
" 5	" "		23 00		23 00			92 00
" 6	" "		34 50		34 50			126 50
" 6	Petty Cash	RCB4				50 00		76 50
" 7	Till Roll		46 00		46 00			122 50
w/e May 14	" "		218 50		218 50			341 00
w/e May 21	" "		230 00		230 00			571 00
May 15	Petty Cash	RCB4				20 00		551 00
" 20	Cash to Bank	CB6					11 50	539 50
w/e May 28	Till Roll		241 50		241 50			781 00
" 27	Cash to Bank	CB6					88 00	693 00
" 31	" " "	CB6					115 00	578 00
			862 50		862 50	70 00	214 50	578 00

This section is for the business person whose sales consist mainly of cash transactions. You can see that takings are analysed for VAT and a record is kept of any cash used for petty cash or banked. A running total of cash in hand results. The instructions clearly show how to balance the book and post the totals to the cash book, petty cash book, and appropriate control accounts including the profit and loss account and working capital statement.

All illustrations half-size reproduction

Illustration of Credit Sales and Cash Takings record sheets used in the Guildhall 'Trio' System

Company **CANTMISSEM PUTTERS LTD.**   **WAGES BOOK   WB**

| NAME 1 | GROSS AMOUNT DUE 2 | STATUTORY SICK PAY 3 | TAXABLE SALARY DUE 4 | EMPLOYEES' DEDUCTIONS | | | | NET AMOUNT DUE 9 | EMPLOYERS NIC 10 |
				PAYE 5	NIC 6	OTHER DED 7	TOTAL DEDUCTIONS 8		
0 Month ending 31 May 1994									0
, H. Andicapp	460 00	– –	460 00	40 00	20 00	– –	60 00	400 00	40 00 ,

Both weekly and monthly paid staff are catered for in this section. The examples and instructions show how to make entries from calculations on the PAYE worksheet. A summary for each week during the month is shown, with the totals posted to the PAYE control account and profit and loss account. Statutory Sick Pay totals are entered in this system having been calculated in the Guildhall HA4SSP binder (not included).

SALES LEDGER CARD SL

REF No. .... B1 ....

Cantmissem Putters Ltd
21 St. Andrews Square, Scotland
Tel: 0743 325721 Telex 677293

STATEMENT

ANALYSIS OF OUTSTANDING BALANCE	
CURRENT	£ ....
30 DAYS	£ ....
60 DAYS	£ ....
90 DAYS	£ ....
120 DAYS	£ ....
TOTAL	£ ....

For the attention of   MR. H. OVIS ....
CUSTOMER   BROWN LTD. ....
ADDRESS   TENTSTER RD. ....
WELLING ....
KENT .... POST CODE DA16 1GQ.

TEL   01-304-6888 ....

1 DATE 1994	2 DETAILS	3 REF	4 SALES INVOICE TOTALS	5 CASH RECEIVED DISCOUNTS OR CREDIT NOTES	6 BALANCE
0 May 10	Goods	1	115 00		115 00 0
, " 14	"	5	46 00		161 00 ,

This section contains an alphabetical index and 25 ledger cards. The instructions and examples show how to keep a card for each customer and one for sundry accounts. Existing balances are entered and transactions from the credit sales section are shown in detail. A running balance of how much the customer owes is kept by deducting payment details from the cash book. Credit Notes and cash discounts are dealt with. The instructions show how to compare the monthly totals with the control account and to make sure that the balances agree.

The ledger card is designed so that the company name can be printed in the space provided. The card can be photocopied and used as a statement. The company name is in the correct position for insertion into the window of a DL size envelope.

All illustrations half-size reproduction

Illustration of Wages Book and Sales Ledger Card/statement used in the Guildhall 'Trio' System

Purchases Returns Book

Credit notes received from suppliers for goods we have returned will be photocopied. The photocopy will be batched to form the Purchases Returns Book and the note itself will be put into the supplier's 'live file' until such time as it is cleared. It will be cleared when used to reduce a subsequent payment to the supplier.

The 'batches' forming the Purchases Returns Book will be used to credit the Purchases Returns Account and debit the Bought Ledger Control Account if this is used.

Sales Returns Book

Using the second copy of our credit note to a customer to form a part of the Sales Returns Book and the third copy to form a part of the customer's 'live file', the procedure is the same as with the Purchases Returns Book above. The difference is that our credit notes are used to post to the debit of the Sales Returns Account (Returns Inwards Account) and, should it be in operation, to credit the Sales Ledger Control Account.

When should the slip system be used?

This system is operated by small firms that do not keep double entry bookkeeping records.

It is simple to operate and saves time by not requiring details to be copied into books and accounts. This in itself reduces the risk of errors being made in entering and posting to ledgers.

Once a business decides to operate a double entry bookkeeping system, the 'slip system' loses its reason for existing. The most important disadvantage of the slip system is the possible misfiling of a document. Documents can be easily taken out of a file—to deal with a query, when contacting the customer or supplier, when making repeat orders, and so on. If the document is not returned then the file is no longer accurate.

Simultaneous entry records

What are they?

In double entry bookkeeping the same transaction is always recorded at least twice (a debit and a credit). In some cases, such as Sales Ledger transactions, the same transaction may be recorded three times, i.e., Sales Day Book, Debtors' Account, monthly statement. How nice to be able to make the three entries all at the same time! It is possible by using special stationery and record cards, held together by means of a 'pegboard', to make entries simultaneously on two or three documents. Originally using carbon paper to achieve multiple entries, the systems now in operation use specially prepared no-carbon-required paper. In order to achieve the correct positioning of the documents involved they have holes punched along their left-hand edge or top. The pegboard (or clip board) has pegs located along one edge thus allowing the stationery being used to be located and held such that one set of details entered on the top document is simultaneously entered in the correct position on the other documents.

The most popular uses of such 'three-in-one' or multi-write systems, as they are sometimes called are:

1 Sales Day Book/Sales Ledger/Cash Receipts
2 Bought Day Book/Bought Ledger/Cheque Payments
3 Payroll Systems

Numerous other applications are available and can be tailor-made to suit individual business requirements. For example, computer input documentation linked to unit stock records, rent collection procedures, daily job records, customer records with enquiries/quotation/order register, requisitioning procedures, van load summaries, etc. 'Pegboards' come in a variety of styles. Where mobility or security is required they can be fitted with covers; Day Books or Journals can be held in a binder and the additional records held in place by a 'collator'. See page 349 for an illustration of a pegboard and documents.

Sales Day Book/Sales Ledger

1 The format of the Sales Ledger Account Sheet and the statement is similar to that of the three-column account; debit, credit, and balance. The first document placed on the pegboard is always the Day Book Record and this remains on the board until full. The Sales Ledger Sheet is placed over the Sales Day Book Record Sheet and the debtor's statement is placed over the Ledger Sheet. Positioning the Ledger Sheet and statement correctly is most important and needs to be lined up with the next available line on the Day Book Record Sheet.
2 By entering details of the transaction on the statement such details are entered simultaneously on the other two records.
3 Removing the statement and Ledger Sheet enables the next account sheet and statement to be placed on the Day Book Record Sheet— lined up as appropriate.
4 When required the Sales Day Book is totalled and posted to the Sales Account in the Nominal Ledger.

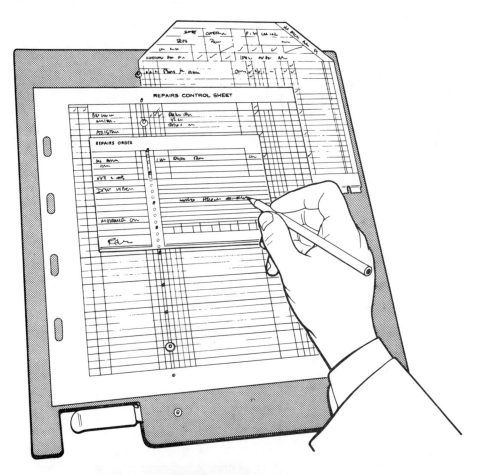

Illustration of a Kalamazoo-Gilberts Pegboard

5 Statements are posted to debtors at the end of the month and a new
   statement prepared with the Balance b/fwd entered.

Sales Ledger/Cash Receipts
Substituting a Debtors' Receipts Sheet (or Cash Received Sheet) for the
Sales Day Book Record Sheet, on the pegboard, enables receipts to be
recorded simultaneously on the debtor's statement, Ledger Sheet and
Cash Received Sheet. At the end of the day/week the Cash Received
Sheet is totalled and entered in the Cash Book.

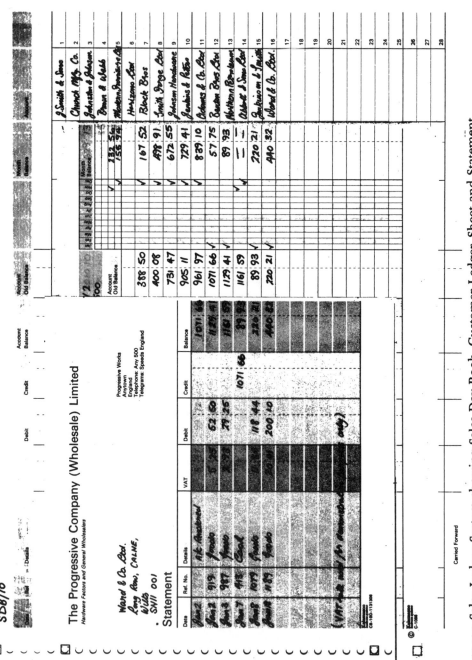

Kalamazoo Sales Ledger System showing Sales Day Book, Customer Ledger Sheet and Statement

Associated Sales Ledger documentation

1 *VAT summary*   You will see from the illustration of the Sales Ledger system (opposite) that a VAT column is provided on the documentation. VAT totals from each Sales Day Book page are transferred to a VAT Summary Sheet.

2 *Control Account*   A Ledger Control Account can be completed from the totals provided by the Sales Day Book.

Bought Day Book/Bought Ledger/cash payments to suppliers

Credit purchases from suppliers are recorded in the same way as the Sales Day Book/Sales Ledger, except that only two records are involved—the Bought Day Book Record Sheet and the Creditors' Ledger Sheet. When payments are made to suppliers the Day Book Sheet is replaced by a Creditors' Payment Record Sheet (or Cash Payments Sheet).

Returns

The methods used to record returns are as described above, the only change is that the Day Book Record Sheet is now either the Sales Returns Record Sheet or Purchases Returns Record Sheet. The debtors' records are entered from copies of credit notes issued and creditors' accounts being debited from credit notes received from them.

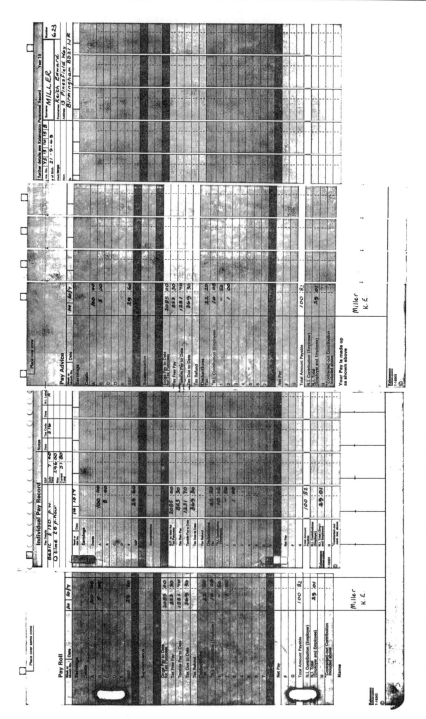

Illustration of the Kalamazoo Wages and Salaries System

Payroll systems

Three documents are involved in 'simultaneous entry':

1 *Payroll Record Sheet*   After completing the payroll calculations and entries, this sheet contains the complete details of the weekly/monthly payroll (see Wages, Chapter 26).
2 *Individual employee pay record*   This replaces the Deductions Working Sheet P11 (New) and contains all details of each employee's pay and deductions.
3 *Weekly/monthly payslip for employees*   Summarizing the Payroll Record Sheets enables the totals for gross pay, net pay, deductions due, etc., to be determined for posting to nominal accounts.

An illustration of the three documents involved is shown opposite.

Advantages and disadvantages of simultaneous entry

1 The main advantage of simultaneous entry systems is that of time saving. Unlike double entry bookkeeping these systems require only one entry. In the case of the Sales Ledger system the statement is prepared as the account is entered, thus saving its separate preparation at the month end.
2 One entry eliminates copying errors.
3 One entry reduces the possibility of misposting accounts.
4 By the use of extra 'balance' columns the numerical accuracy of the entries can be verified.
5 The major disadvantage of these systems is that the correct positioning of documents on the pegboard or with the collator is essential. This is time consuming but necessary to avoid the mistake of making two entries on the same line.
6 Figures have to be written carefully because they lose clarity on the underneath records.

Purposes of record keeping

Whatever method of bookkeeping is used or whatever system of record keeping is operated, the purposes are the same—to record the full details of transactions. Only in this way can we:

keep a record of debtors and creditors;
keep control of cash and bank;
record and control assets;
provide details of VAT transactions;
enable stock records to be kept;
provide details of wage payments;
enable final accounts to be prepared.

So long as the *full* details of all transactions are recorded the final accounts can be prepared even though a double entry system does not operate. Even if only one aspect of a transaction is recorded, e.g., cash received, the application of the double entry principle will tell us that the other aspect must have been either a cash sale or a payment made to us by a debtor, or a loan, or a cash sale of assets or scrap metal or whatever the details indicate. The details should give the reason for the receipt. In the same way a payment should indicate the reason why it has been made, e.g., for petrol, for an asset, to a creditor, for Drawings, etc. We also know that when a Balance Sheet is eventually prepared, *Assets = Liabilities + Capital*.

Joe's Rule No 29
Any method of bookkeeping must ultimately use the double entry principles when preparing the final accounts and Balance Sheet.

29.01   (a) Describe the 'slip' system of bookkeeping and how it operates.
         (b) Give *three* main advantages of using the 'slip' system.

(RSA I)

29.02   You have a friend who has opened a small shop selling stationery, maps, and artists' materials. He has no knowledge of double entry bookkeeping.
      Advise him on what financial records he should keep.

NA 29.03   You have just started as a junior clerk/bookkeeper with a small business selling electrical fittings and components and servicing domestic electrical machines.
      Draw up a chart of the main accounts you would expect to find in the double entry bookkeeping system, showing the documents from which entries are made.
         (Ignore the books of original entry. All sales and service charges are cash only.)

29.04   Explain the operation of a simultaneous entry recording system for the Sales Ledger.

NA 29.05 A large company will need several departments to deal with its 'accounts', while a small business may have only one clerk doing this work. Explain the work that the one clerk will be doing and how it compares with the work of the several departments in a large company.

30. Bookkeeping Terms and Rules

Today is the last lesson! I am going to remind you of some of the terms and ideas learnt so far. I shall also mention some of the alternative names used in bookkeeping terminology, in case you want to move one day to another company (which may seem to operate an entirely different system!).

Note my last important rule

Joe's Rule No 30
Always check even the simplest arithmetic—it may save hours later looking for errors.

Common terms

Try to remember what the words mean before I define them.

Assets Things owned by the business.
  Fixed assets Those assets that are kept and used by the business over a long period of time.
  Current assets Those assets whose values are constantly changing due to the daily transactions of the business.
Balance Sheet A statement or list that shows the assets and liabilities of a business at the year end.
Business Transaction An event between people involving the transfer of goods or services.
Capital The investment made by the owner in his business.
  Capital expenditure Money spent on buying fixed assets.
Cash Bank notes, coins, and our current Bank Account.
Costs See Expenses.
Debts Amounts owing to the business.
  Bad debt A debt which will not be paid.
  Doubtful debt A debt which is unlikely to be paid.
  Provision for bad debts An amount set aside out of profits for anticipated bad debts.
Depreciation The loss in value of an asset due to wear and tear, passage of time, depletion, obsolescence.
Discount A reduction in the price of goods.
  Cash discount A reduction given for prompt payment.

Trade discount A reduction from the list price of goods.

Quantity discount (or bulk discount) A reduction given for buying large quantities.

Drawings Money or assets taken out of the business for the owner's private use.

Double entry The name of the procedure whereby both aspects of a transaction (giving and receiving) are recorded.

Expenses The cost of goods and services.

Trading expenses Expenses related to the trading activities of the business.

Financial Transaction An event which involves the transfer of money.

Invoice A document sent to a customer showing details of the goods supplied, cost, additional charges, and terms of trade.

Liability Something owed by the business.

Payments The money paid out by the business.

Profit

Gross profit The amount by which sales exceed the cost of the goods sold.

Net profit The profit remaining after expenses have been deducted from the gross profit.

Purchases Goods that are bought for resale.

Receipts Money received by the business.

A receipt A document which serves as evidence of a payment.

Revenue Expenditure Expenses relating to the day-to-day running of the business.

Revenue Income Income arising from the daily sales and services of the business.

Routine Transaction An event which occurs regularly as a part of a planned programme.

Sales Income from goods or services supplied.

Trial Balance A list of balances on the accounts.

Banking terms

Bank charges (or service charges) Our bank will deduct amounts from our account for service charges and any interest on overdrafts.

Bank Reconciliation Statement A statement that enables a reconciliation of a bank statement balance with the balance in our Cash Book.

Commission The fee or percentage earned by an agent.

Credit Transfer One cheque sent to the bank enables the bank to transfer money to one or numerous specified bank accounts.

Current Account This is the bank account used routinely by the business to pay bills, and draw out money.

Deposit Account   This is a bank savings account and will be used by the business to save its surplus cash.

Direct Debit   Authorization to a bank to allow it to pay sums to a specified bank account at the request of the payee.

Loan   An amount lent by the bank for a specified time, which has a certain rate of interest.

Overdraft   The limit to which the bank manager will agree to pay cheques when we have a credit balance in our Bank Account in our books.

Payee   The person to whom payments are made.

Standing Order   The bank is authorized to pay a regular sum of money without making out a cheque. The payment is made direct to the Bank Account of the person to whom we are paying that sum.

Statement   A summary of all transactions on an account in a period.

Withdrawals   All payments made by cheque and the use of standing orders, etc., will cause a 'withdrawal' of money from the Bank Account.

Credit and debit

Debit and credit can be very confusing. Let us look at these terms from my (Joe's) point of view.

Credit Balance   A creditor has a credit balance in my books.

Credit Entries   These are shown on the right-hand side of the account.

Credit Note   If I need to make a refund to a customer, I will send a credit note to let him know the amount that I have credited to his account.

Credit Purchases   When I buy goods from a supplier who will later send me an invoice, the purchase is a credit purchase.

Credit Sales   When I sell goods to a customer who does not pay immediately, I will send him an invoice. This is a credit sale.

Credit Transfer   See Banking terms, page 357.

Creditor   A person to whom the business owes money.

Creditors' Ledger   See Bought Ledger in Ledgers, books, and accounts, page 361.

Debit Balance   A debtor has a debit balance in my books.

Debit Entries   These are shown on the left-hand side of the account.

Debit Note   If I undercharge a customer (by mistake) I may send a debit note which acts as an invoice.

Debtor   A debtor owes the business money.

Debtors' Ledger   See Sales Ledger in Ledgers, books, and accounts, page 362.

Direct Debit   See Banking Terms, above.

Sundry Creditors   Expenses underpaid are called amounts owing or accruals, they can be shown separately on the Balance Sheet, but usually they are shown together and called sundry creditors.

Partnership terms

Appropriation Account   An account showing the distribution of profit between partners.

Deed of Partnership   This is a formal agreement of partners outlining the terms of the partnership.

Fixed Capital Account   A capital account in which the partners' capital remains unaltered—showing only the agreed capital contributed to the business.

Fluctuating Capital Account   A capital account in which the share of profits is credited, and Drawings are debited.

Partner's Current Account   Where fixed capital accounts are used, each partner's position regarding the share of profits and Drawings is shown in this account.

Partnership   A legal term describing a business run by two or more partners.

Wages terms

Coin and Note Analysis   A sheet showing the coins and notes that need to be withdrawn from the bank to make up wage packets.

Credit Transfer   A method by which many employees are paid (see Banking terms, page 357).

Deductions Working Sheet   One is kept for each employee, showing all statutory deductions required to be made by the employer on behalf of the state.

Gross Pay   Pay before deductions.

Net Pay   Pay after deductions. Sometimes referred to as 'take home' pay.

P45   Leaving certificate.

P46   Starting certificate.

P60   Annual certificate of pay, tax deducted, and National Insurance Contributions.

Pay Advice Slip   See Payslip.

PAYE   Pay As You Earn, this is a system operated by an employer on behalf of the Inland Revenue to collect income tax from an employee when he is paid.

Payroll Sheet This is kept by the business and shows details of employees' pay and deductions.

Payslip (wage packet) Given to employee to show details of wages (as on payroll sheet).

Tax Tables These are provided by the Inland Revenue to calculate the tax to be paid by employees.

Time Card Card on which hours worked are recorded.

Stock terms

Bin Card A card which records issues and receipts of a stock item (stored in bins or racks) together with the stock balance.

Customer Order Form Document showing details of an order placed by a customer.

Delivery Note A document handed to the customer upon delivery of the goods indicating details of the goods.

Goods Received Note (GRN) A document completed by the storekeeper detailing goods received.

Net Realizable Value The income that will be received when stock is sold, *less* all the costs of bringing the stock to the point of sale.

Pricing Methods Methods of putting a value on materials issued.

   FIFO (First in First Out) Materials are issued at the price of the earliest materials received still in stock.

   LIFO (Last In First Out) Materials are issued at the price of the latest materials received still in stock.

   Weighted average Whenever materials are received a new average price is calculated for all those items in stock and this price is then used for all issues until a new receipt alters the average price.

Rate of Stock Turnover The number of times that the average stock held by a business is sold during the course of a year.

Roll Card A card that records issues and receipts of a stock item (stored on a roll) together with the stock balance.

Stock Ledger Contains Stock Ledger Sheets.

Stock Ledger Sheet (Also called Stock Ledger Account) This records the value of the stock balance of each item of stock.

Stock Record Card A card containing details of one stock item, it shows the stock balance, stock on order, stock allocated and free stock.

Stocktake A physical count of items in stock to establish the quantities held.

Stockturn See Rate of Stock Turnover.

Stores Requisition Document used to request materials from stores.

Total Stock Value Total value of all Stock Ledger Sheets.

Computer terms

Character A character is a number, letter or special sign or symbol (e.g., space, + or /) on the keyboard.

Common Data Data that may be used for several purposes.

Data All the basic facts such as dates, amounts, and names.

Database A system in which filed data is independent of applications programs, but the data can be used as required, with an appropriate program.

File A collection of individual related records (e.g., employee records, stock records).

Field One item of data within a record (e.g., name, date).

Floppy Disk A disk with a magnetic coated surface, which can be used for storing data.

Hardware All the electronic and mechanical elements of a computer and the devices used with it.

Input Entry of data, or a program or instructions into a computer.

Key Field The field which the computer uses to identify each record.

Output Anything given out by the computer (e.g., characters on a screen, a printout, stored data on a disk).

Record A record contains a number of related fields.

Software A general term describing the programs which can be used in computer systems.

Validation Controls Controls built into a program to prevent some errors in entering data.

VDU (Visual Display Unit) A computer terminal which has a screen for display.

Ledgers, books, and accounts

There are many ledgers and books. In my business I only use some of the books and ledgers listed below. Firms with other requirements will need to use different books.

Ledgers

Bought Ledger (or Creditors' Ledger or Purchases Ledger) Contains accounts of creditors.

Nominal Ledger (or General ledger) This contains all the income and expense accounts. A sole trader may also keep his private accounts here.

Personal Ledger A ledger containing accounts of debtors and/or creditors.

Private Ledger   Contains the Capital, Drawings, Trading and Profit and Loss, Loans and Wages Accounts.
Sales Ledger (or Debtors' Ledger)   Contains customers' accounts.
Stock Ledger   See Stock Terms, page 360.

Books

Bought Day Book (or Purchases Day Book or Purchases Journal)   A book recording day-to-day credit purchases.
Bank Cash Book   A book containing only the Bank Account.
Cash Book   A book containing the Cash and Bank Accounts.
Daily Cash Receipts Book   A book containing a detailed record of all cash receipts.
Journal   A book used to record all transactions which are not entered in the other books of original entry.
Petty Cash Book   A book containing the Petty Cash Account.
Purchases Returns Book (or Returns Outward)   A book for recording returns made to suppliers.
Sales Day Book (or Sales Book or Sales Journal)   A book recording day-to-day credit sales.
Sales Returns Book (or Sales Inwards or Returns Inwards)   A book recording returns made to us by customers.

Accounts

An *account* is a record of similar transactions.
Appropriation Account   See Partnership Terms, page 359.
Asset Account   The account of an asset.
Income and Expenditure Account   An account, which, by comparing the incomes and expenditure of a non-trading organization, shows the surplus or deficit for the year.
Nominal Account   An income or expenses account.
Partner's Current Account   See Partnership Terms, page 359.
Private Account   An account kept in the Private Ledger, above.
Profit and Loss Account   This account shows the net profit (or loss) for the year.
Receipts and Payments Account   A summary of receipts and payments recorded in the Cash Book.
Revenue Account   The Revenue Account is the Profit and Loss Account of a business which is providing (selling) services.
Suspense Account   An account used temporarily to place errors.

Trading Account   This account shows the gross profit (or loss) for the year.

Book of original entry (or first entry or prime entry or memorandum book)
A book that records the first record of any transaction, e.g.,

Bought Day Book
Cash Book
Journal
Petty Cash Book
Returns Book
Sales Day Book

Memorandum items
These may be accounts, books or just columns in a book, but they are *not part of the double entry system.*

Memorandum items may be stored until a 'total' is put into the double entry system such as:

Sales Day Book and Bought Day Book
Discount columns in the Cash Book

Any additional books used where there is a very large number of entries of a particular type, e.g., Daily Receipts Book where large numbers of receipts occur every day.

Memorandum accounts may be produced using information already in the double entry system such as Control Accounts.

Some rules, concepts, and conventions

Joe's Rules are intended to be a practical guide to help in carrying out the bookkeeping procedures.

The accountancy profession has developed certain rules which are designed to help bookkeepers and accountants in their work. Many of these rules have been formalized by the issue of guidelines explaining how accountants are expected to deal with various matters. These are called *Statements of Standard Accounting Practice.* Behind these formal rules are a series of established procedures (conventions) and ideas or thoughts (concepts) intended to guide us in making decisions.

Quite a few concepts have been considered in the earlier chapters although not explicitly referred to as such. The chapters where such concepts are relevant are as follows:

Concept		*Relevant chapter(s)*
Accrual (matching)	16	End of Year Adjustments
Business entity	8	Capital and Drawings
Conservatism (prudence)	16	End of Year Adjustment
	27	Stock
Consistency	17	Purchase of Fixed Assets
	27	Stock
Cost	15	Balance Sheet
	27	Stock
Dual aspect	6	Receipts from Debtors
	7	Nominal Ledger
Going concern	15	Balance Sheet
Materiality	17	Purchase of Fixed Assets
Realization	6	Receipts from Debtors

A brief explanation of these concepts will help you to understand what they mean.

Accrual or matching
The correct profit for a period can only be calculated if the expenses and incomes are 'matched' in that they relate to the same period of time and the same goods. At the end of a financial period amounts outstanding and prepayments need to be brought into the accounts.

Business entity
Although a sole trader works in his own business, the books are not recording his affairs, but the affairs of the business. The business is considered a separate entity or being. Of course, the owner puts money into his business and draws profits out—but these are 'transactions' with the business and recorded as such

Conservatism (prudence)
Accountants are careful people—financially that is. Profits should never be overstated and therefore all possible losses should be provided for.

Such losses include depreciation and provisions for bad debts. Prudence dictates that if the selling price of stock is less than its cost, such a loss is provided for by valuing stock at the lower figure.

Consistency

Having selected a method of depreciation, or stock valuation, it should be used every year. If not, a comparison between years is difficult. If it is necessary to make changes and the effect is materially to affect the profit (see Materiality below) then such an effect should be noted in the accounts.

Cost

This is an objective view of the value of an asset. Over time the value will vary; it may increase or decrease. Such increase or decrease may well be someone's personal opinion. To obtain a basis for comparison and measurement the cost price is at least unquestionable. Therefore it is usual to show fixed assets at cost price.

Dual aspect

This is fundamental to double entry bookkeeping. Every transaction has two financial effects on the business. Both effects are recorded—the giving and the receiving.

Going concern

A business normally expects to continue from year to year and the accounts should reflect this. The cost concept, for example, will apply to fixed assets. However, if it is known that the business is not going to continue, for example it is being closed down or sold to someone else, then the accounts may well need to reflect that position. A true and fair value can only be shown if the assets are shown at the value obtainable if sold.

Materiality

Does a financial event *significantly* affect the profit? If it does it must be recorded and shown separately from other events. If, however, it has no great effect on profit it can be dealt with in a way which simplifies the business procedures although technically it may appear incorrect. For example, half a dozen small pencil sharpeners, bought for the office, are obviously assets, but the cost will be treated as an expense of the period and charged entirely to the Profit and Loss Account. The decision as to what is *material* will depend upon the individual business. An item that is material to a small business may be quite immaterial to a larger firm.

Realization

When a credit sale is made, at what point is the sale considered to have taken place? When the order was received? When the goods were dispatched? When the goods were received? When the invoice was sent? When the customer makes the payment? Similarly, when do we incur the liability to pay for goods and services supplied to us? In our accounts credit sales are entered from copy invoices because we believe the customer has accepted the goods/services. We enter purchases from invoices 'passed for payment' when we have 'accepted' the goods. At the period end, although customers may not have paid, and we in turn owe sums to creditors, the transactions are nevertheless included in the accounts. Realization refers therefore to the acceptance of a financial event for recording and accounting purposes.

Joe's Rules

1   *Receipts are always on the left.*
    Payments are always on the right.
2   *The cash balance is the excess of the receipts over payments.*
3   *A credit balance on the Bank Account means that we have overdrawn and this amount represents a liability of our business. Therefore a debit balance must represent an asset, since this is money we have in the bank.*
4   *The first record of any transaction must be made in a book of original entry. For credit sales, the first record is made in the Sales Day Book.*
5   *Customers' accounts are debited with the value of credit sales made to them, by posting the entries from the Sales Day Book.*
6   *Receipts from debtors are entered in the Cash Account (or Bank Account) as a debit and in the debtor's personal account in the Sales Ledger as a credit.*
7   *For every debit entry there is a corresponding credit entry in another account.*
8   *The total of business assets always equals the total of business liabilities.*
9   *A trial balance can be prepared at any time in order to show that the books are correct, but it is always taken out before preparing the Trading and Profit and Loss Accounts.*
10 *The Cash Book is both a book of original entry and a record book, since it contains the Cash and Bank Accounts.*
11 *The Bought Day Book records only credit purchases of goods for resale and is not an account—it is a memorandum book.*
12 *Credit the supplier's account with the value of the goods we have purchased on credit, and debit the supplier's account with amounts paid to him.*

13 *If a record is made in a book of original entry, it must have a document as evidence of the transaction.*

14 *The owner of a business receives the profits, but also has to bear the losses. Therefore profits are credited to the owner's Capital Account and losses are debited to the owner's Capital Account.*

15 *All assets and all liabilities, together with capital must be shown in the Balance Sheet. It is called a Balance Sheet because assets of the business should balance with the capital plus liabilities.*

16 *When preparing the accounts for a trading period, the expenses and revenues to be included are those expenses that should be charged to the period and those revenues that should have been received in the period.*

17 *Assets bought for use in the business to earn income represent capital expenditure, while the expenditure incurred in the daily operating of the business is revenue expenditure.*

18 *The results of trading shown in the final accounts and Balance Sheet need to be understood and measured to find out how successful the business is.*

19 *Club members do not usually understand the accounts you present. Keep them as simple as possible.*

20 *Journalize all transactions that cannot be recorded in any other book of original entry.*

21 *In practice always 'correct' the Cash Book before preparing the Bank Reconciliation Statement.*

22 *By providing a summary of all the accounts in a ledger, the control accounts can give an 'instant' total (of debtors, creditors, stock, plant and machinery), and provide a check on the accuracy of the ledgers.*

23 *Analysis columns enable the posting to be made of the total of similar transactions (at a period end) thereby saving time and effort in posting the individual transactions.*

24 *Since a business must pay for the collection and payment of VAT, the records should be simple to understand and easy to operate.*

25 *Profits in a partnership are divided between partners in accordance with the Partnership Deed—which can be changed if the partners agree.*

26 *Of all the bookkeeping procedures, wages is the one where results have an immediate effect. Both employees and your employer expect wages to be calculated correctly, prepared for payment when due, and recorded accurately.*

27 *Stocks are assets. Stock quantities are recorded on stock cards, while the cost values are recorded in the Stock Ledger.*

28 *To operate a computer-based bookkeeping system, the same information needs to be typed into a computer as is written in the traditional books. But data often needs to be typed into the computer using special formats and codes.*

29 *Any method of bookkeeping must ultimately use the double entry principles when preparing the final accounts and Balance Sheet.*

30   *Always check even the simplest arithmetic, it may save hours later looking for errors.*

Miscellaneous terms

Accruals   Costs applicable to a period still owing at the end of that period.

Accumulated Fund   Those funds of a club owned by its members. In the Balance Sheet of a club, the accumulated fund is the equivalent of 'capital' in business accounts.

Auditor   A person appointed to examine the books, accounts, vouchers, and documents of a business and verify the accuracy, truth, and fairness of them.

E & OE   Errors and Omissions Excepted. Printed on documents (usually invoices) indicating that the supplier will not be bound by errors on the document—thus enabling him to issue corrected documents.

Float   The money provided by the cashier, and recorded in the Petty Cash Book, to pay miscellaneous and small expenses.

Imprest System   The system whereby payments made by the holder of the Petty Cash Account has his 'float' reimbursed. (Can also be applied to stock.)

Goodwill   The value of the reputation and trade derived from existing customers of an established business.

Profit Margin   That amount of sales income representing gross profit.

Simultaneous Entry (or multi-write or three in one)   This denotes the simultaneous entry of a transaction in two or more accounts by the use of a pegboard enabling documents to be held in alignment.

Slip System   A system in which original documents are bound together to form the book of original entry.

Turnover   Total sales.

Working Capital   The monetary resources of a business readily available to meet its daily needs. Usually measured as the difference between current assets and current liabilities.

Appendix A Customers' Codes

01	ABC Carpets Ltd
02	P P Berry
03	Boothroyd
04	Cannon-Taylor
05	Eagle Insurance
06	T T Edwards
07	Franks & Son
08	Harper & Co
09	Poplar Treads Ltd
10	Richards Flooring
11	Sounds Ltd
12	Star Hotel
13	S & R Supplies
14	Singer Ltd
15	G Tyler
16	Talyor Stores
17	Woodman & Son
18	Wilson Bros
19	XY Wearing
20	Zircon Stationery

Appendix B Suppliers' Codes

01	Allweather Covers Ltd
02	Ark Ltd
03	Barons
04	Blackmore Wholesale
05	BKW Carpets
06	Easi-File
07	Flooring Unlimited
08	Heavy Duty Carpets Ltd
09	Middlewich Looms
10	Office Supplies Ltd
11	Sampson Bros
12	Sevenways Garage
13	Wearing Co Ltd
14	Woodman Timber
15	Yates

Answers

'The University of London School Examinations Board accepts no responsibility whatsoever for the accuracy or method of working in the answers given.'

All answers given are entirely the responsibility of the authors. They have neither been provided nor approved by the Associated Examining Board, or any other examining board.

Chapter 1

1.01 Pieces of paper are easily lost, while a proper book will record receipts and payments over a long period of time.

1.02 My accountant: so it has got to be correct.

1.03 To help you add up the figures correctly.

1.04 You will not go home until I get a satisfactory answer, especially if the cash in the till is less than it should be.

1.05 £1761.75

1.06

	£	£
Total		1761.75
Less	54.68	
	12.35	
	+87.06	154.09
		£1607.66

This is the layout you should use for such calculations. It is quicker and neater than taking each amount away separately.

1.07

Row	Total	Column	Total
1	21.37	1	24.29
2	78.59	2	180.55
3	75.86		
4	29.02		

1.08

Total	=£204.84

1.09

Row	Total	Column	Total
1	175.45	1	208.94
2	246.43	2	194.36
3	235.63	3	443.19
4	188.98		
	846.49		846.49

Chapter 2

2.01   Small shops will put all takings into a till. The amount in the till at the end of the day will be the takings for the day plus any amount in the till to begin with. Large shops will have a till which automatically records the amount entered on the till register on a till roll within the machine. At the end of the day, this till roll is totalled and the total should be the same as the cash in the till.

2.02   (a) (b) (e).

2.03   (a) 12 (b) 29 (c) 42 (d) 39.51.

2.04   (a) £20.00 (b) £23.00 (c) £98.00 (d) £104.50 (e) £176.40 (f) £184.27.

2.05   Just the same as a cash payment. Simply write the details of the payment on the credit side of the Cash Account.

2.06   Debit balance.

Chapter 3

3.01   A loan made to our business.
Amounts owed to suppliers of goods.
Amounts owing for services—for example, British Telecom (telephone bill), the area electricity board.
A mortgage granted by a building society. (A mortgage = a loan.)
A bank loan.

3.02   (i)   Dr £318.00
(ii)   Cr £98.50

3.03

Cash Account

Mar	3	Bank	c	80	Mar	4	Office	
	6	Sales		72			Cleaner	15
	10	Sales		116	Mar	8	Stationery	14
						11	Purchases	100
						12	Bank	c 129
						12	Bal c/d	10
				268				**268**
Mar	12	Bal b/d 10						

Bank Account

Mar	1	A Smith 500			Mar	2	Rent	25
Mar	12	Cash c 129				3	Cash	c 80
						5	Purch.	385
						12	Drgs.	15
						12	Bal c/d	124
				629				**629**
Mar	12	Bal b/d 124						

3.04

Cash Account

Bal	b/d	75	Wages			48
Sales		16	Window cleaner			2
Bank	c	50	Wages			49
Sales		163	Groceries			3
Sales		192	Bank		c	179
			Drawings			25
			Bank		c	175
			Bal		c/d	15
		496				496
Bal	b/d	15				

Bank Account

Bal	b/d	455	J Walker			86
Cash	c	179	Cash		c	50
F Taylor		64	Drawings			20
Cash	c	175	Telephone			31
			Bal		c/d	686
		873				873
Bal	b/d	686				

Chapter 4

4.01

Star Hotel	172.50
ABC Carpets	410.00
Poplar Treads	52.50
Sounds Ltd	273.00

4.02

908.00

4.03 (a) £90;   £47.50; £71.50
      (b) £40;   £31.25; £18.25
      (c) £20;   £15.62½; £9.12½
      (d) £30;   £19.50; £12.75
      (e) £1.25; 50p; 5p;
      (f) £2.25; 60p; 12½p

4.04 (a) £1.10; £11.80
      (b) £11.00; £30; £24.60
      (c) £22.00; £24.00; £6.30
      (d) £31.50; £40.50; £58.50

4.06 Sales Day Book Total   £2830.64
      Cash Book   Dr £148.31
      Bank Book   Dr £1860.25

Chapter 5

5.01 Bank Book; Cash Book; and Sales Day Book

5.02 Cash Book and Bank Book

5.03 Sounds Ltd (Dr) £222
Hotel Swanlake £607 (Dr)

5.04 Bow Office Furnishers Ltd £505 (Dr)
Hotel Swanlake £133.60 (Dr)

5.05

Metro Shopfitters	Gross 1123.00		
Less Trade discount	224.60	Net goods	898.40
Containers			15.00
Invoice total			£913.40
Bow Office Furnishers Ltd			
	Gross 1232.00		
Less Trade discount	246.40	Net goods	985.60
Containers			12.50
			£998.10

Chapter 6

6.01 Sales Account

6.02 Cash Account balance £133.60 (Dr)
Bank Account balance £1334.00 (Dr)
Metro Shop Fitters A/c balance £913.40 (Dr)
Bow Office Furnishers Ltd balance £998.10 (Dr)

6.03

Sales Day Book total	£516.62
Cash Account	£92.50 (Dr)
Bank Account	£873.00 (Dr)
W Ing	£349.25 (Dr)
Garner	£16.85 (Dr)
Office furn	£317.68 (Cr)
Shop fittings	£404.80 (Cr)

6.04 Cash sales are recorded in the Cash Book; credit sales are recorded in the Sales Day Book; payments received are recorded in the Cash or Bank Book.

6.05 Cr Cash Account: Dr Sales Returns Account

6.06 £218.50 (Dr)

6.07 £116.00 (Dr)

Chapter 7

7.01 (a) Rent Account
      (b) Wages Account
      (c) Motor Running Expenses Account
      (d) Fixtures and Fittings Account
      (e) Sales Account
      (f) Insurance Account
      (g) Discounts Allowed Account
      (h) Rent Received Account

7.02 Credit the Bank Account

7.03   *Debited*   *Credited*
      (a) Motor van   Bank
      (b) Purchases   Cash
      (c) Rent   Bank
      (d) Cash   Sales
      (e) A Smith   Sales
      (f) P Taylor   Sales
      (g) Insurance   Bank
      (h) Wages   Cash
      (i) Drawings   Cash

7.04 (a) Sales—Nominal Ledger
      (b) Purchases—Nominal Ledger
      (c) A Smith—Sales Ledger
      (d) Machinery—Nominal Ledger
      (e) Wages—Nominal Ledger
      (f) Commissions received—Nominal Ledger
      (g) Losses on till takings—Nominal Ledger
      (h) Discounts—Nominal Ledger
      (i) D Jones—Bought Ledger

7.05(a) (b) Sales Day Book total   £192.80
             Cash Book balance   £236.20 (Dr).
             Bank Book balance   £35.00 (Cr).

      (c) List of balances

      Debits Cash £236.20; Wages £88.00; Printing expenses £15.50; Discount allowed
      75p; Drawings £10.00; Rent £48.00; Sales returns £8.00; Shaw £107.55; Miller
      £8.50; Shop fittings £18.90; Purchases £265.00.
      Credits Bank £35.00; Sales £771.40. Trial balance total £806.40.

7.06 Sales Day Book page 10.

7.07   *Dr*   *Cr*
      (a) Motor van   R A Garage Ltd
      (b) Shop fittings   Shop Fitters Ltd
      (c) Shop Fitters Ltd Bank
      (d) B Worth   Cash
      (e) Bank   Office equipment

7.08   Sales Day Book total £322.70.
Balances on accounts
Debits Cash £315.85; Bank charges £28.50; Office machine rental £18.70; Drawings £75; P White £56; Wages £231.45; Forklift truck (asset) £1950; S Bond £19.50.
Credits Bank £454.20; Sales £890.80; Forklifts Ltd £1700.

Chapter 8

8.01   (a)   Sales Day Book total £135.

       (b)   List of balances
           Debits Cash £277.45; P Rowler £93; Office equipt £425; Discount allowed £3; Motor running expenses £27; Drawings £35; Stock £500; Motor car £1450; Bank £3497; Rent £55; Purchase £611; Lease £3500; Stationery £4.25; Postage 85p; Packing material £12.45.
           Credits T Taylor £6950; Sales £616; Bank loan £2500; London Supply Co £425.

       (c)   Totals £10 491.

8.02

R Bell Capital Account

Aug 31 19-8	Drawings		2760	Sept 1 19-7	Bal	b/d	2845
	Bal	c/d	3235	Aug 31 19-8	Net profit		3150
			5995				5995
				Sept 1 19-8	Bal	b/d	3235

Drawings Account

Aug 31 19-8	Cash	1980	Aug 31 19-8	Capital A/c	2760
	Rates	200			
	Motor expenses	500			
	Heating	80			
		2760			2760

8.03   Capital = £7515.

8.04   List of balances
        Debits Cash £25; S Bade £48.75; Stock £285; Fixtures £290; Motor vehicles £800; Purchases £370; Telephone £46.75; Trade expenses £19.50; Drawings £103; T Tynn £98.42; Wages £128.20; M Mynn £57.60; F Fynn £147; P Pynn £107.65; Bank charges £5.50.
        Credits Bank £2.10; K Hick £43; S Hoe £33.45; Sales £883.97; Dividends £16.80; Capital—C Camp £1553.05.
        Trial balance total £2532.37.
        Note Owner's Drawings of stock (at cost price) are credited to Purchases Account.

Chapter 9

9.01   Trial balance total £55 690.

9.02   Trial balance total £45 949.

9.03   Trial balance total £5299.

9.04   (a)   Profit £705.
       (b)   Profit £2420.
       (c)   Loss £80.

9.05   D

9.06   B

9.07   Trial balance total £58 734.
       Owner's capital £26 686.

Chapter 10

10.01   Cash balance £368.50 (Dr). Bank balance £212.00 (Dr).

10.02   Cash balance £176.00 (Dr). Bank balance £380.50 (Dr).

10.03   Cash balance £193.10 (Dr). Bank balance £403.60 (Cr).

10.04   Cash balance £191.37 (Dr). Bank balance £222.00 (Dr).
        Discount Allowed total £26; Discount Received total £8.

10.05   D

10.06   Cash balance £48.00 (Dr). Bank balance £152.00 (Cr).
        Credit Discount Received A/c £9.00.
        Debit Discount Allowed A/c £13.00.

Chapter 11

11.01   *Credit* Cash £85.
        Debit Supplier's account £85.

11.02   Allweather Covers   Cr   £140.00
        Allday Protectors   Cr   112.50
        All purpose Sheeting   Cr   316.20

        Bought Day Book total   £568.70

11.03 List of balances
       Debits Bank £2053.20; Motor running expenses £55; Wages £166.85; Debtors:
       Tubular Poles £76, Wheeltappers £100; Purchases £1134.50; Rent £19.50;
       Discount allowed £4.90.
       Credits Capital £2648; Creditors: Round Wheels £256, Rollover £157, Square
       Way Dealers £73; Sales £475.95.
       Sales Day Book total £247.
       Bought Day Book total £486.

11.04 D

11.05 B

Chapter 12

12.01 Purchases Account

12.02 (a) Bought Day Book Total £860.07.
       (b) Balances: All Weather Covers £711.20 Cr; BKW Carpets £662.24 Cr; Easi-
            file £29.12 Cr; Yates £165.09.

12.03

Susan Cellar, The Cave Mountainside Wasteshire				*Statement*
To: Bill Byer				**Date**

Date	Details	Debit	Credit	Balance
Oct 5	Goods Inv SC/432	36.00		36.00
12	Credit–Cheque		34.20	
	Credit–Discount		1.80	Nil
18	Goods Inv SC/443	63.00		63.00
21	Debit Note–Containers	10.00		73.00

12.04 List of balances
       Debits Cash £40.50; Motor £800; Equipment £590; Wages and casual labour
       £158; Misc material £14; Stationery £7; Motor running expenses £89.50;
       Materials £321.50; Drawings £90; Debtors £937.
       Credits Bank £108; N Evans & Co £250; A Garage Ltd £39.50; Capital £1380; P &
       D Supplies £166; Allday Services £42; Sales £1062.
       Sales Day Book total £1025.
       Bought Day Book total £288.
       Trial balance total £3047.50.

12.08 (b) Bought Day Book total £1321.57
       (c) *Balances* Ark Ltd £10.03; Barons £66.23; Office Supplies Ltd £72.40;
            Middlewich Looms £834.60; Blackmore Wholesale £160.17; Sevenways
            Garage £45.81.

Chapter 13

13.01   Personal accounts balances:

Debits	T Jones	£30.00
	J Bright	£92.00
Credits	C Carter	£98.50
	F Hulse & Son	£65.00
	B Sharrock	£61.00

Cash Book balance £612.10

13.02 *Totals on 31 January* Sales Day Book £294.50; Bought Day Book £1011; Sales Returns Book £57; Purchases Returns Book £16.50.
Balances on 31 January Cash Book £30; Bank Book £780.25; Sales £1433.70; Sundry expenses £15.25; Discount allowed £1; Wages £187.50; Purchases £1261; Sales returns £57; Purchases returns £16.50.
Debtors R Rawson £219.50, P Sharp £4; A Cowley £49.50.
Creditors Allday Services £828.50; G Grove £166.
Stock £889; Premises £10 800; Fixtures £1500; Capital £13 428; Drawings £78.70. Trial balance total £15 872.20.

13.04 Opening, entering, and balancing the accounts will result in the following balances at 31 January;
Debits Purchases £2695; Returns Inwards £83; S Moran £105; K Wilson £255; Cash £650; General expenses £1155; Drawings £1340 = £6283.
Credits Sales £4035; Capital £2029; Returns Outwards £29; J Davis £130; H Worth £60 = £6283.

13.06   **T Pitt (Debtors' Ledger A/c)**

Jan 1 Balance b/d	£59.00	Jan 31 Bank	£29.00
		May 6 Bad debts	22.50
		Sept 30 Bank	7.50
	__59.00__		__59.00__

Bad Debts Account

| May 6 T Pitt | 22.50 | |

13.07 **Sales Ledger**

                         M Jones Account   L2

Jan 3 Sales SDB	60.00	Jan 20 Sales Returns	
10 Sales SDB	70.00	SRB	12.00
21 Sales SDB	70.00		

B Buston Account	L3
Jan 7 Sales SDB 180.00	

M White Account	L4
Jan 15 Sales SDB 162.00	

Sales Account (General Ledger)	
	Jan 31 Total SDB 542.00

Sales Returns Account (General Ledger)	
Jan 31 Total SRB 12.00	

13.11   £13.50 per hour

13.12
Materials £1600 + 5 per cent	=	£1680
Labour 60 hours × £13.50	=	810
		£2490

13.13   (a)   Completed units £1500; WIP c/d £500 (WIP of 200 units half completed = 100 fully completed (or effective) units. Therefore 300 transferred + 100 effective means that the input costs of £2000 were spent on completing 400 units at a unit cost of £5)

(b)   Completed units £3900; WIP c/d £600

(c)   Completed units £1425; WIP = £575

Material cost	= £1 per unit
Labour cost = £1200 for 400 effective units	= £3 per unit
Overheads = £300 per 400 effective units	= £0.75 per unit
Cost per effective unit	= £4.75

Chapter 14

14.01   *Trading Account for the year ended 31 December 19-0*

Purchases	3500	Sales	3000
Carriage inwards	145		
	3645		
Less Closing stock	1800		
Cost of goods sold	1845		
Gross profit c/d	1255		
	3000		3000
		Gross profit b/d	1255

14.02   At the end of the year the 'opening stock' no longer exists—it has been sold in the same way that purchases have been sold. Therefore the cost of the stock is added to the cost of the purchases.

14.03   Drawings is a personal account of the owner—showing how much he owes the business. It is offset against his profits by transfer to his capital account.

14.04   See Chapter 30, pages 356–357.

14.05

Trading and Profit and Loss Account for the year ended 31 May 19-8

Opening stock		1 240	Sales	16 840	
Purchases	10 260		Less Returns	190	16 650
Less Returns	210				
	10 050				
Plus					
Carriage inwards	156	10 206			
		11 446			
Less Closing stock		2 845			
Cost of goods sold		8 601			
Gross profit	c/d	8 049			
		16 650			16 650
Discount allowed		45	Gross profit	b/d	8 049
Wages and salaries		3 675	Commission received		82
General expenses		942	Rent received		364
Net profit		3 833			
		8 495			8 495

14.06   (a)   Quantity in stock: 1/9/–6

			£
Opening stock	500 × £5	=	2 500
Purchases	1000 × £5.25	=	5 250
Purchases	2500 × £4.55	=	11 375
	4000		19 125
Sold	3000 × *		14 575
	1000 × £4.55		4 550
Returns in	50 × £4.55		227.5
(b) Value in stock	1050	=	4 777.5

```
*   500 × £5        2 500
  1000 × £5.25      5 250
  1500 × £4.55      6 825
                   14 575
```

Trading Account

Opening stock	2 500	Sales	3000 × £6.25	18 750
Purchases	16 625	*Less* Returns	50 × £6.25	312.5
	19 125			18 437.5
Less Closing stock	4 777.5			
	14 347.5			
Gross profit	4 090.0			
	18 437.5			18 437.5

14.07   Gross profit £1783; Net loss £1219. Trial balance total £11 125.

Chapter 15

15.01   *Balance Sheet items*
Liabilities side   Capital 31 Dec 19-5 £6647; Mortgage £5000; Current liabilities £1860; Total £13 507.
Assets side   Fixed assets £8080; Current assets £5427; Total £13 507.

15.02   (a)   Capital £6255.
(b)   Balance Sheet totals £6975.

15.03   Gross profit = £8352; Net loss = £1479.
Balance Sheet totals = £14 065.
Assets   Fixed £7100; Curent £6965.
Liabilities   Capital £8871; Current £5194.

15.04   (a)   Corrected net profit £680.
(b)   Balance Sheet totals £3440.
Assets side   Fixed assets £560; Current assets £2880.
Liabilities side   Capital £1780; Current liabilities £1660.

15.05   Balance Sheet totals £31 244.
Assets side   Fixed assets £19 460; Current assets £11 784.
Liabilities side   Capital £24 364; Current liabilities £6880.

15.06   (i)   *Capital as at 31.10.19-3*

Total assets	=	5050
External liabilities	=	1630
	=	£3420

Capital as at 31.10.19-4

Total assets	=	6860
External liabilities	=	1030
Capital	=	£5830

(ii)   *Net profit for year ended 31.10.19–4*
       (Opening Capital + Profit − Drawings = Closing Capital)

∴ £3420 + Profit − 1540   = £5830
∴ Profit   =   5830 − 3420 + 1540
                                  =   3950

Or

Opening capital		3420
Add Profit	3950	
Less Drawings	1540	2410
Closing capital		5830

15.07   (a)   **Balance Sheet of J Seymour as at 31 Dec 19–4**

			£
Assets			
Fixed assets:			
Freehold land and buildings			22 000
Motor vehicles			3 000
Fixtures and fittings			2 000
			27 000
Current assets:			
Stock		3 600	
Trade debtors		1 750	
Cash and bank		850	
Sundry debtors		125	
		6 325	
Less Current liabilities:			
Trade creditors	3 000		
Sundry creditors	125	3 125	3 200
			£30 200
Financed by:			
Capital A/c 1 Jan 19–4			29 000
Add Profit		5 200	
Less Drawings		6 000	(800)
			28 200
Bank loan			2 000
			£30 200

Chapter 16

16.01   Insurance Account: Dr balance b/d £39 (amount transferred to Profit and Loss Account £102).
Commission Receivable Account: Dr balance b/d £25 (amount transferred to Profit and Loss Account £100).

Telephone Account: Cr balance b/d £76 (amount transferred to Profit and Loss Account £369).

Carriage Expenses Account: Cr balance b/d £15 (amount transferred to Profit and Loss Account £92).

16.02   *Wages Account*

Dec 31 19-9	Bal	b/d	9174.62	Jan 1 19-9	Bal	b/d	87.55
	Bal	c/d	110.76	Dec 31	P & L A/c		9197.83
			9285.38				9285.38

16.04   Profit Adjustment Statement

		Net profit			£8975
(a)	Rates unpaid	−200			
(b)	Sales not recorded		+28		
(c)	Closing stock overvalued	− 48			
(d)	Depreciation	−200			
(e)	Rent receivable–due		+50		
(f)	Sales returns	− 22			
(g)	Rent prepaid		+10		
(h)	Provision required	− 20			
		−490	+88	=	−402

Adjusted net profit   =   £8573

16.05   *Rent Received Account*

31 Oct 19-4	Profit and Loss A/c	175	31 Oct 19-4	Balance	155
			31 Oct 19-4	Balance c/d	20
		175			175
1 Nov 19-5	Balance b/d	20			

Stationery Account

31 Oct 19-4	Balance	240	31 Oct 19-4	Stationery Stock A/c	55
			31 Oct 19-4	Profit and Loss A/c	185
		240			240

General Expenses

31 Oct 19-4	Balance	125	31 Oct 19-4	Profit and Loss A/c	150
31 Oct 19-4	Balance c/d	25			
		150			150
			31 Oct 19-4	Balance b/d	25

Profit and Loss Account for...

Stationery	185	Rent Received	175
General Expenses	150		

16.08 (a)

Sales A/c

19-4			19-4		
Dec 31	Trading A/c	£13 850	Dec 31	Total	£13 850

Purchases A/c

19-4			19-4		
Dec 31	Total	£10 820	Dec 31	Trading A/c	£10 820

Stock A/c

19-4			19-4		
Jan 1	Balance b/d	£1360	Dec 31	Trading A/c	£1360
Dec 31	Trading A/c	1884	Dec 31	Balance c/d	1884
		3244			3244
19-5					
Jan 1	Balance b/d	1884			

Wages and Salaries A/c

19-4			19-4		
Dec 31	Total	£2190	Jan 1	Balance b/d	90
Dec 31	Balance c/d	50	Dec 31	Profit & Loss A/c	2150
		2240			2240
			Jan 1 19-5	Balance b/d	50

Rates A/c

19-4				19-4			
Jan 1	Balance b/d	£40		Dec 31	Profit & Loss		£375
Dec 31	Total	260					
Dec 31	Balance c/d	75					
		375					375
				Jan 1	19-5 Balance	b/d	75

(b)

P Shaw
*Trading and Profit and Loss Account
for the year ended ...*

		£
Sales		13 850
Less Cost of sales*		
Opening stock	1360	
Purchases	10820	
	12180	
Closing stock	1884	10 296
Gross profit		3 554
Less Wages and salaries	2150	
Rates	375	2 525
Net profit		£1 029

*Usually referred to as 'cost of goods sold'.

16.09   Gross Profit = Net Sales − Cost of Goods Sold
                = £83 350 − £50 750 = £32 600
        Net Profit   = £21 340

Chapter 17

17.01   (a)   Office equipment; motor lorries; land and buildings; and machinery.
        (b)   Wages; rent; insurance; and petrol.

17.02   (a)   Real = assets. Nominal = incomes and expenses. Personal = of a person.
        (b)   Profit would be £400 too little. No effect on Balance Sheet except that assets would be understated (offset by a lower profit).
        (c)   Asset account.

17.03 (a)   £1600, (b) £1450, (c) £140, (d) £500.

17.04 (a)   Year 1 = £300, Year 2 = £255, (b) Year 1 = £1600, Year 2 = £1280.
       (c)   Year 1 = £60, Year 2 = £54, (d) Year 1 = £40, Year 2 = £37 (to the
              nearest £).

17.05 (a)   £35, (b) £40, (c) £3500.

17.06 (a)   Simple method

Fixed assets	£	£
Office machinery		324
Office machinery at cost	400	
Depreciation provision	76	324

Usual method

17.07 (a)   WDV end Year 1 = £450, Year 2 = £400, Year 3 = £350.
       (b)   WDV end Year 1 = £450, Year 2 = £405, Year 3 = £364.

17.09 (a)   Capital—new asset
       (b)   Revenue—motor running cost
       (c)   Revenue—motor maintenance
       (d)   Revenue—motor running cost
       (e)   Capital—increase in asset worth

17.11 (a)

Machinery A/c

Jan 1	City Traders	6000	Dec 31	Yr 1	Depreciation	600
				Yr 2	"	540
				Yr 3	"	486

       (b)   Profits would be lower by (60 + 114) £174

17.12 *Fixed assets* Machinery £2830; Vans £2000
       Current assets Stock £1100; Debtors £1300; Bank £25; Cash £825
       Capital £3000; Net profit £1030; Drawings £450
       Creditors £2500 Loan £2000
       (Balance sheet totals = £8080)

Chapter 18

18.01 (i)   19-7 = 2.5 per cent   19-8 = 3.3 per cent
       (ii)   19-7 = 5 per cent   19-8 = 3.3 per cent

18.02 (i)   Yes—much better
       (ii)   Because of the risk involved in running a business

18.03   *Cash Flow Statement*

	£	£
Bank and cash balance 1 Jan 19-9		1840
Add Net profit	4500	4500
		6340
Less Increase in fixed assets	600	
Increase in stock	150	
Increase in debtors	110	
Decrease in creditors	450	
Drawings	5000	6310
Balance 31 December 19-9		30

18.04   (a)

Trading Account for year ended 31 May 19-6

Stock 1 June 19-5	8 500	Sales	37 000
Purchases	29 000		
	37 500		
Less Stock 31 May	7 900		
	29 600		
Gross profit	7 400		
	37 000		37 000

(b)   Debtors at 31 May 19-6 = 3 400 + 37 000 − 36 000 = £4 400

18.05   (a)

Cost of goods sold	=	£48 000
Gross profit	=	£24 000
Net profit	=	£14 400
Expenses	=	£9 600

(b)   Average stock held = £4800 (Divide turnover at cost price
by rate of stock turnover = £48 000 ÷ 10 = £4800)

18.06   (a)   Net Profit ÷ Average Capital × 100
Measures his 'return'; for comparison between years and with returns to
be earned if capital is invested outside the business.

(b)   Net Profit ÷ Sales × 100
To enable comparisons to be made, from year to year, on the level of profit
within sales.

    (c)   Current Assets *less* Current Liabilities
           What the owner has available to meet the daily cash requirement of his business.

    (d)   Cost of Goods Sold ÷ Average Stock
           How quickly is the stock being sold? (If the rate of stock turnover = 4 then it takes three months to sell the average stock held.)

18.07 (a)   £225
       (b)   (i) 66.7 per cent (ii) 40 per cent

Chapter 19

19.01   Amount transferred to Income and Expenditure Account £450
        Credit balance b/d on Subscription A/c £15

19.02   Amount transferred to Income and Expenditure Account £480
        Debit balance b/d on Subscription A/c £30 ⎱ *Note* Two balances
        Credit balance b/d on Subscription A/c £15 ⎰

19.03   Amount transferred to Income and Expenditure Account £460
        Credit balance b/d on Subscription A/c £15

19.04   Transferred to Income and Expenditure Account

        31 Dec 19–6   £600
        31 Dec 19–7   £600
        31 Dec 19–8   £600

        Credit balance b/d on Entrance Fees Account 1 January 19–9, £1200.

19.05   Receipts and Payments Account:
        Debits   Balance b/d £15.12; Subscriptions £30.00
        Credits Expenses £31.23; Balance c/d £13.89

        Income and Expenditure Account
        Debits   Expenses £34.50
        Credits Subscriptions £32.00; Excess expenditure £2.50

19.06   Income and Expenditure Account
        Debits   Loss on disco £300; Loss on raffle £40; Rent £75; Rates £640; Secretary's expenses £20; Depreciation on furniture £53; Surplus of income £1517.
        Credits Profit on bar £250; Subscriptions £2395.

Chapter 20

20.01

			£	£
(a)	Office Equipment Account Dr		75.00	
	B Kirkland and Co			75.00
	Credit purchases per invoice			
	no . . . dated . . .			
(b)	Safeway Insurance Co Dr		750.00	
	Motor Vehicle Disposal Account			750.00
	Loss claim agreed per letter			
	ref . . . dated . . .			
(c)	Bank Deposit Account Dr		23.00	
	Interest Received Account			23.00
	Per statement no . . . dated . . .			
(d)	P Carter Dr		4.50	
	Discount Allowed Account			4.50
	Discount now disallowed upon return			
	of cheque no . . . marked R/D			
(e)	B Waltham—Drawings Account Dr		18.50	
	Purchases Account			18.50
	Value of stocks withdrawn by owner			

20.02   (a)   C
        (b)   B

20.03   19-4   *Opening Balances at 1 June 19-4*

			£	£
June 1	Freehold premises Dr		25 000	
	Motor vehicle		2 700	
	Fixtures and fittings		2 000	
	Debtors		1 580	
	Stock		2 750	
	Rates in advance		120	
	Insurance paid in advance		40	
	Mortgage			12 500
	Amount owing on motor			1 400
	Bank overdraft			920
	Electricity owing			72
	Capital—T Jones			19 298
			34 190	34 190

20.04

(a)	C Shell—Drawings Account Dr
	    Wages Account
	    Materials Account
	Private expenditure transferred
			800	560
				240

(b)	A H Clark Dr H Clarkson Correction of the misposting of cheque payable to A H Clark		84	84
(c)	Office Equipment Account Dr Purchases Account Transfer of asset purchases, wrongly debited to Purchases Account		300	300

20.06

			£	£
(1)	Fixtures and fittings Dr Wages Transfer of capital expenses		128	128

(2)	Fixtures and fittings Dr
	    Jackson Bros Ltd
	    Thomas Franks Ltd
	Purchase and installation of safe
			638	545
				93

(3)	Bank Dr Profit and Loss Account Sum recovered from debt w/o		39	39

(4)	(i) Delivery van A/c Disposals A/c Bank Purchase of van with part exchange value		1650	490 1160
	(ii) Disposals A/c Delivery van A/c Book value of old van transferred	Dr	530	530
	(iii) Profit and Loss A/c Disposals A/c Loss on disposal of old van	Dr	40	40
	(iv) Motor Expenses A/c (Insurance) Motor Expenses A/c (Road Tax) Bank Motor expenses paid by cheque	Dr Dr	176 70	 246

Chapter 21

21.01 Balance per Cash Book 1 May   £511.25
        Less Debits in Cash Book not on statement   54.62   54.62

                                                   456.63

        Add Credits in Cash Book not presented to
            bank for payment Rent   30.00
                        Y   64.10
                        Z   24.10   118.20
Balance per bank statement   £574.83

21.02 (a) Cash Book balance = £413 (£390 + 48 − 25).

      (b) *Bank Reconciliation Statement April 30 19-6*   £
           Balance per statement   414
               Less Unpresented cheques (21 + 42)   63

                                  351
           Add Item not credited   62
                                  413

21.04 (a) Cash Book balance = £55 (overdrawn) (£40 + £15).

(b) *Bank Reconciliation Statement June 30 19–6* £

Balance per statement 75 OD

Add Unpresented cheques (35 + 25) 60

  135 OD

Less Item not credited 80

  55 OD

(c) To prove the accuracy of the figures both in the Cash Book and on the statement.

21.06

J Williams—Cash Book

29 Feb	Balance	634		Feb	Rent	65
	Interest	27	29 Feb		Balance c/d	596
		661				661
1 March	Balance b/d	596				

BRS

Balance per Cash Book		£596
Add Cheques not yet presented	38	
	42	
	17	97
		693
Less Credit not on statement		74
Balance per statement		£619

21.08 Corrected Cash Book total = £1363.25.

Bank Reconciliation Statement	£
Bal per statement	1134.00
Add Items not credited	473.75
	1607.75
Less Unpresented cheques	244.50
	1363.25

Chapter 22

22.01 (a) Sales Day Book; (b) and (c) Cash Book

22.02 Memorandum records—Day Books; Discount columns in the Cash Book; Control Accounts; and other records or accounts containing entries which do not represent one of the two 'double entries'. The role is that of a 'collector', i.e., collecting details of transactions in order to provide (a) totals for posting to an account within the double entry system, thereby eliminating individual postings, or (b) summaries.

22.03 D

22.04 D

22.07 (2) (i) The agreed closing balance carried down, i.e., agreed with the list of balances abstracted from the Purchases Ledger.
      (ii)   Purchases Day Book.
      (iii)   Purchases Returns Book.
      (iv) Memorandum column in the Cash Book.
      (v)   Memorandum column in the Cash Book.

Chapter 23

23.01 Bank Cash Book Balance £633.94

23.02 Cheque to restore imprest on 7 March, £16.25
Postage and telemessages = £3.70 Travel expenses = £3.15
Stationery = £6.10 Misc = £3.40

23.03 (ii)   Balance c/d on 31 December = £2.90
      (iii)   Amount to restore float on 1.1.19-4 = £37.10
Total of Analysis columns; Postage, £10.25; Stationery, £7.85; Wages, £13.40; Ledger, £5.60.

23.04 Total bank receipts = £3278.50
Total cash receipts = £555.80
Analysis columns; Debtors, £1606.20; Rent, £250. 00;
Services, £210.65; Sales, £1767.45

23.05 Total bank payments = £1660.98
Total cash payments = £71.37
Analysis columns; Creditors, £1203.96; Motor expenses £112.27;
Drawings, £150.00; Wages, £128.00; Stationery, £17.50;
Misc, £120.62

23.06   (a)   Petty Cash reimbursed— 1 Sept £13.80
                                          15 Sept £16.21.
               Postage column £5.30; Travelling £7.65; Stationery £1.91; Miscellaneous £1.35.
      (b)   The analysis columns are totalled as in (a) and debited to the nominal accounts in the ledger.

23.07   Total purchases = £812.40   (Credited to individual suppliers)
      Analysis   Repairs—£103.00   (Debit Repairs Account)
                  Petrol, oils—£433.60   (Debit Petrol, Oils Account)
                  Spares—£275.80   (Debit Spares Account)

23.08   Total purchases = £3016

23.12   (a)   Invoices received for goods, services, assets.
      (b)   Vouchers signed by persons using the cash.
      (c)   Receipts: (i)   Cash till rolls; salesman's receipts—for cash sales.
                         (ii)   Bank paying-in book for *contras* and cheques received.
                         (iii)   Cash Received Book—if used.
               Payments: Cheque counterfoils; bank statements; petty cash vouchers.
      (d)   As (c) (i) and (ii) above.
      (e)   Copy credit note sent to customer.

Chapter 24

24.01   Amount of VAT   Payable by
      (a)   £700 less 5 per cent = £665
               VAT at 15 per cent of £665   = £99.75   Sue Woodpecker

      (b)   VAT at 15 per cent of £300   = £45   Sue Woodpecker

               (If the £45 has actually been paid to Customs and Excise then the VAT on the amount lost can be reclaimed, i.e., 15 per cent of £240 = £36.)

      (c)   VAT at 15 per cent of £60   = £9   Disco, if a registered VAT business

      (d)   £16.10 $\times \frac{15}{115}$ = £2.10   Garage

      (e)   VAT at 15 per cent of £30   = £4.50   Solicitor

24.02 (a)   SALES INVOICE

A Bembridge & Son Maldon Way Swansea		Invoice no . . . Date 1 March 19–8		
VAT Registration No . . .				

To James Foster
   26 Broad Street
   Newtown 4				

Order No 162 Delivery Note . . .		Tax Point 1 March 19–8		
	Terms:			
Quant.	Description & Price	Cost	Total	VAT Rate
10 000 12 000 20 000	Coils sealing tape @ £4.46 per 1000 Sheets Bank A4 @ £4.20 per 1000 Sheets Bank A5 @ £4.50 per 1000	44.60 50.40 90.00		
	Total goods Total VAT		185.00 27.75	15%
	SALE TOTAL		212.75	

(b)   PERSONAL LEDGERS
(In A Bembridge & Son's books)

James Foster

19–8 Mar 1	Sales (Inv No)	212.75		

(In James Foster's books)

A Bembridge & Son

		19–8 Mar 1	Purchases (Inv No)	212.75

24.06   (a)   *Purchases Ledger P Ellison Account*   *Debits*: Returns + VAT £44; Bank £85.80; Discount received £2.20. *Credits*: Purchases + VAT £132; Purchases + VAT £165.
Balance £165 (Cr).
Sales Ledger G Brandon Account   *Debits*: Sales + VAT £330; *Credits*: Returns + VAT £44; Bank £616; Balance nil.
R Strong   Debit balance £440 (2 × Sales + VAT of £220).

      (b)   *VAT Account*   *Debits*: Ellison £12; Returns Brandon £4; Ellison £15.
Credits: Brandon £30; Strong £20; Returns Ellison £4; Strong £20; Brandon £30.
Balance £73 (Cr).

24.07   Accounts to be posted are:

Feb   4   Ace Tyres—credit £935

     14   Fast Exhausts Ltd—credit £528

     25   Ace Tyres—credit £990

     28   Debit to Tyre Purchases Account £1750
           Debit to Exhaust Purchases Account £480
           Deibt to VAT Account £223

Chapter 25

25.01

		£	£
Goodwill	Dr	69 050	
Premises		290 000	
Fittings and equipment		11 000	
Motors		3 250	
Debtors		24 000	
Stock		106 000	
Bank and cash		4 000	
Creditors			28 000
VAT			4 200
Inland Revenue			5 100
Capital Account—Wynn			250 000
—Boon			220 000
		507 300	507 300
Opening entries of new partnership on 1.9.19-8			

25.02   Current Account George Boon:
Debits   Total Drawings £15 000; Interest on Drawings £750. Balance c/d £15 075
(Total £30 825)
Credits   Interest on capital £13 200; Salary £10 000; Share of profit £7625 (Total
£30 825) Balance b/d £15 075

Current Account Joe Wynn:
Debits   Total Drawings £34 000; Interest on Drawings £1700; (Total £35 700)
Balance b/d £1075
Credits   Interest on capital £15 000; Salary £12 000; Share of profit £7625;
Balance c/d £1075.

25.03   *Boyd and Girled Balance Sheet as at 1.1.19–8*

Assets		£
Goodwill (2600 + 600)		3 200
Net tangible assets		36 300
		£39 500
Capital—Boyd	20 000	
—Girled	19 500	£39 500

25.04   Current Account G   1 Oct 19–7   Balance b/d £2440 (Cr)
                  H   "   "   £ 470 (Cr)
                  I   "   "   £2080 (Dr)

25.06   *F Moore and C Potter*

*Trading, Profit and Loss and Appropriation Accounts for the year
ended 31 May 19–4*

Opening stock		1 480	Sales		19 860
Purchases		11 620	*Less* Sales returns		540
		13 100			19 320
Less Stock 31.5.19–4		1 380			
		11 720			
Gross profit	c/d	7 600			
		19 320			19 320
Bad debts	w/o	190	Gross profit	b/d	7 600
Rent and rates					
(600 – 40)		560	Discounts received		290
Wages and salaries					
(2170 + 70)		2 240			
Discounts allowed		570			
Sundry expenses		180			
Depreciation—Fittings		50			
—Van		100			
Net profit	c/d	4 000			
		7 890			7 890
Interest on capital:			Net profit	b/d	4 000
Moore	£200				
Potter	150	350			
Salary—Potter		650			
Share of profit:					
Moore	1 500				
Potter	1 500	3 000			
		4 000			4 000

F Moore and C Potter

Balance Sheet as at 31 May 19-4

			£
Fixed assets			
Fixtures and fittings (WDV)			800
Delivery van (WDV)			1100
			1900
Current assets			
Stock		1380	
Debtors		2110	
Bank and cash		4270	
Prepaid expenses		40	
		7800	
Less Current liabilities			
Creditors	1040		
Accruals	70	1110	
			6690
			£8590

Financed by	*F Moore*	*C Potter*	
Capital	4000	3000	7000
Current A/cs:			
Interest on capital	200	150	
Salary	–	650	
Share of profit	1500	1500	
	1700	2300	
Less Current A/c balance 31.5.19-4	1270	1140	
	430	1160	1590
			£8590

Chapter 26

26.01   Note/coins required

£20	×	10	=	£200
£10	×	3	=	30
£5	×	3	=	15
£1	×	14	=	14
50p	×	3	=	1.50
10p	×	12	=	1.20
5p	×	2	=	0.10
2p	×	1	=	0.02
2p	×	1	=	0.01
				261.83

26.02   (a)   Income tax; National Insurance Contributions. (Additional deductions can be required under a Court Order.)

(b)   Savings; sports club subscription; trade union subscription.

(c)   Determines the employee's 'free pay'.

26.03   (b)   Payroll sheet totals will be
(i)   Gross wages £889.50
(ii)   Deductions (a) Tax £180.15 (b) NIC £75.71
(c) Others £3.90 (d) Total deductions £259.76
(iii)   Net pay £629.74
(iv)   Employer's NIC £88.95

26.06   J Brooke   Gross pay   £115.00   Net pay   £ 89.25
P Daly   £145.00   £103.75

Chapter 27

27.01   (a)   Stock record card will show:

Qty Purchased	−	Qty Sold	=	Closing Stock	+	On Order
1250	−	459	=	41	+	750

(b)   Trading Account: *Debits*   Purchases £1000 (*Less* Closing Stock of £82 =
Cost of sales of £918)
Gross profit £838.50
Credits   Sales £1756.50

27.02   (a)   Gross profit   =   £796.50
(b)   Gross profit   =   £788.50
(c)   Gross profit   =   £818.50

27.03   (a)   Closing balance = 179 units
(b)   On January 31 the stock card showed a balance of 184 units. A physical stock check would reveal 179 in stock

27.04   Stock value on 7 February   =   £2830
         Deduct Purchases received 1–7 Feb = £296 − £54   =   242
                                                                           ————
                                                                            2588

         Add Sales (at cost price) = £460 less 20 per cent   =   368
                                                                           ————
                                                                            2956
         Add Drawings (of stock at cost)   =   38
                                                                           ————
                                                                            2994
         Deduct Reduction in stock value of goods costing £120   =   23
                                                                           ————
                        Value of stock at 31 January   £2771
                                                                           ════

27.05   (a)   See text
         (b)   Say (i)   20 received at £1 each   = £20
                    (ii) 20 received at £1.50 each = £30
                    (iii) 20 then issued
                Using FIFO the issue price is £1 each—leaving in stock £30
                Using LIFO the issue price is £1.50 each—leaving in stock £20
                Therefore, in times of rising prices FIFO gives a higher valuation.
         (c)   Overvaluing stock gives a higher (and overstated) gross profit.

27.06   A

27.07   B

27.09   (a)   At the end of January (i) 10   (iii) Nil
                                      (ii) 24   (iv) 34
         (b)   During January   Receipt of 24, total cost £138.00
                                 Issue of 20, total cost £115.00
                                 Issue of 10, total cost £53.00
                Stock balance at end is 10 at a cost of £50.00

Chapter 28

28.01   (i)   When an employee leaves, starts, changes wages grade, tax code, or
                other details.
         (ii)   Each week when cumulative totals are altered.

28.02   Stock Item Number.

28.03   (a)   Green, plain, very good quality, 5 metres wide.
         (b)   Orange, patterned, bedroom quality, 3.03 metres wide.
         (c)   Black, plain, heavy duty, 2.75 metres wide.

28.04   C

28.05   D

28.07   (a)   Field.
        (b)   Using an appropriate applications program, by typing in the employee number. This is the *key field*, and should locate the corresponding record.
        (c)   If the file is used with a wages program, weekly or monthly wages can be calculated, together with deductions.
              All the details could be used to produce the payroll sheet and payslips.
        (d)   The file might be used for keeping employee details by the personnel department, for circulation lists (e.g., sending out letters about meetings, social events, etc.) or for employee surveys (e.g., age distribution in the company).

28.10

Code	Name	Net pay	Tax	NIC	Savings Fund
01	R Arran	552.05	145.80	69.30	2.85
02	B Green	429.50	80.10	50.40	–
03	C Contas	443.65	136.50	57.60	2.25
04	R Khan	405.10	68.10	46.80	–
05	G Henry	294.70	64.80	36.00	4.50
06	A Singh	415.40	121.50	53.10	–
07	F Levi	422.00	87.60	50.40	–
08	Y Bird	475.90	106.50	57.60	–
09	O Beer	348.00	88.80	43.20	–
10	D Clarke	262.71	43.80	23.24	2.25
11	J Cap	308.26	69.30	37.44	–
12	S Suliman	264.96	43.80	23.24	–

28.11

Code	Name	Gross pay	Net pay	Tax	NIC	Savings Fund
142	J Lewis	75.00	98.23	(28.50)*	5.27	–
011	R Smith	151.25	108.24	26.40	13.61	3.00
101	J Brown	110.25	79.93	20.40	9.92	–
132	N Evans	153.12	101.03	33.30	13.79	5.00
006	R Regan	126.50	92.99	20.10	11.41	2.00
021	P Driscoll	126.50	96.49	18.60	11.41	–

*Refund of tax.

Chapter 29

29.01   See text.

29.02   (a)   (i)   Unlikely to need a full double entry set of books.
              (ii)   If VAT registered use a VAT record book similar to that shown on page 344 and a Cash Book similar to that shown on page 341.
              (iii) In the unlikely even of not being registered for VAT use only the Cash Book at (ii) above.

(b) Because he is not keeping double entry records he should keep a separate record of assets purchased; wages paid, if any, and deductions made; sales on credit (if any); stock in the shop at the year end.

(c) Invoices received should be put into an 'Awaiting Payment' file and when paid, recorded as such in the book and the invoice moved to a 'Paid' file.

(d) Ensure that personal money paid into/taken out of the business is recorded.

29.04 See text. Answer should refer to both credit sales and receipts from debtors.

Index